The Liṅgarāja Temple of Bhubaneswar

Art and Cultural Legacy

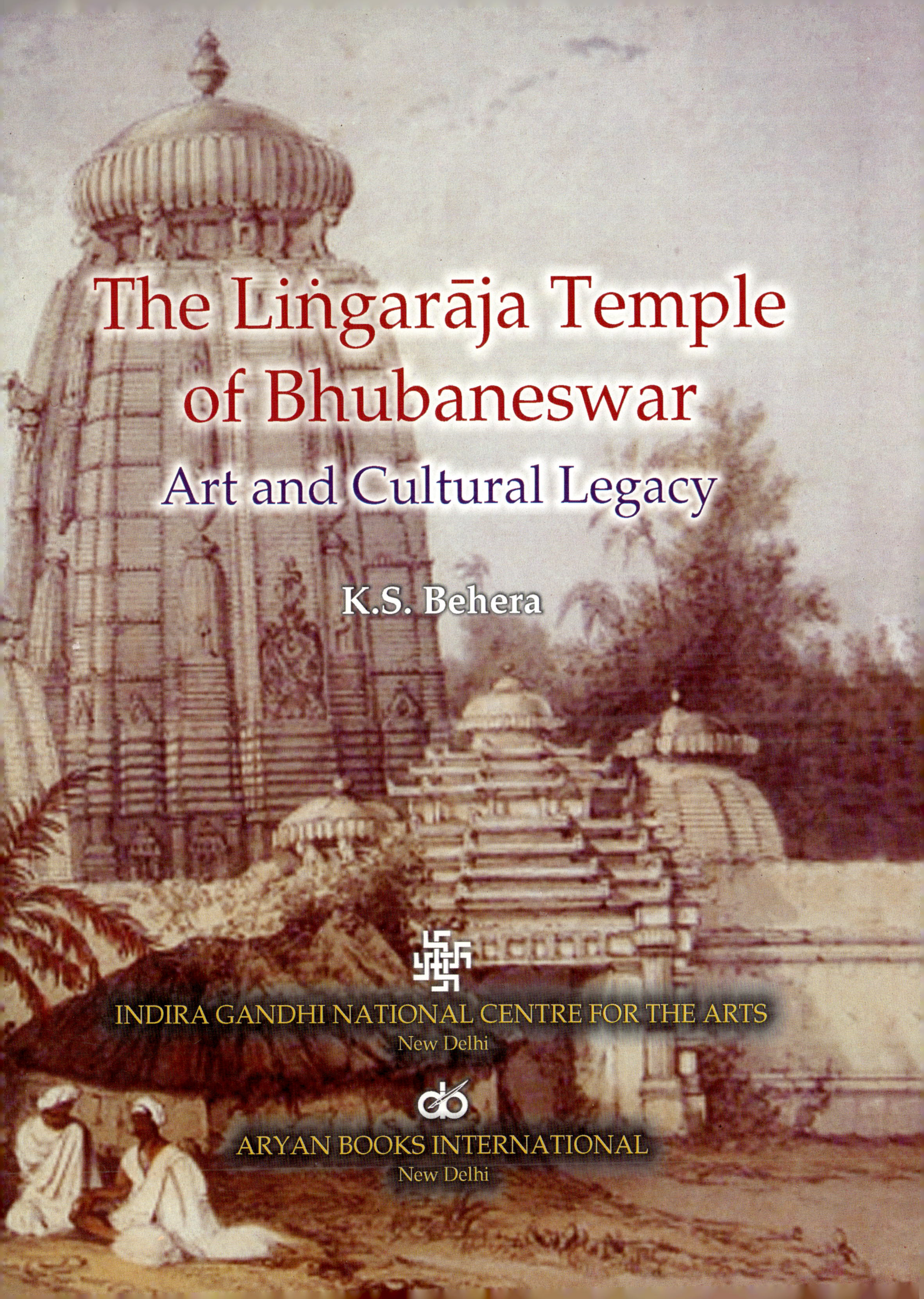

The Liṅgarāja Temple of Bhubaneswar

Art and Cultural Legacy

K.S. Behera

INDIRA GANDHI NATIONAL CENTRE FOR THE ARTS
New Delhi

ARYAN BOOKS INTERNATIONAL
New Delhi

THE LIṄGARĀJA TEMPLE OF BHUBANESWAR
Art and Cultural Legacy

ISBN-10: 81-7305-340-5
ISBN-13: 978-81-7305-340-5

First Published in **2008** by

INDIRA GANDHI NATIONAL CENTRE FOR THE ARTS
Central Vista Mess, Janpath, New Delhi - 110 001 (India)

and

ARYAN BOOKS INTERNATIONAL
Pooja Apartments, 4B, Ansari Road
Darya Ganj, New Delhi - 110 002 (India)
Tel.: 23287589, 23255799; Fax: 91-11-23270385
E-mail: aryanbooks@vsnl.com

Computer Typeset and Printed in India at
ABI Prints & Publishing Co., New Delhi

यानि ब्रह्मन् पद्मयोने त्वयैतत्, ज्योतिर्लिङ्गान्यर्चितानि पृथिव्याम्।
अन्ये तस्याप्यंशभूतानि विद्धि, तत् कन्दं त्रिभुवनेशं च लिङ्गम्।।
लिङ्गानां वै ज्योतिषां द्वादशानां, राजत्येतत् संस्थितं लिङ्गराजम्।।

(एकाम्रचन्द्रिका – २.५-६)

(Vedavyāsa reveals to Brahmā)

O' Lotus-born Brahman (the Creator), know ye that all the Jyotirliṅgas on the Earth venerated by thee are but partial manifestations of Śrī Tribhuvaneśa, the Supreme. Lord Liṅgarāja situated majestically here (in this *kṣetra*), is verily the overlord of all the twelve *Jyotirliṅgas*.

(*Ekāmra Candrikā* - II.5-6)

Foreword

The IGNCA feels very happy in presenting to its readers this excellent all round study of one of the wonders of Indian Art which has been marvelled by Indian and foreign visitors alike since centuries. The temple complex of Lingarāja-Tribhuvaneśvara is a unique contribution of the Śilpins of Orissa to their motherland and represents the best of the North Indian *Rekhā* style of the temple architecture. It is a unique achievement in stone, a most fortunate blend of delicate beauty with a well balanced proportion and style. It is poetry in stone and a monumental memorial to that unknown patron who commissioned it and to the artistic skill of those unknown, unnamed and unsung artisans of this great land.

The temple of Lingarāja is a class apart and everyone who happens to stand before it beholding it with abated breath, soon gets lost forgetting himself in its splendid grandeaur. Not even an inch of this great edifice is without an input of artistic skill leading one to wonder whether those artisans were lapidaries or goldsmiths!

It is for the first time that such a detailed and comprehensive study of this unique treasure of Art is being presented to the scholars covering not only the aspect of art, but also shedding light on its history, rituals, festivals and organisation. The inscriptions engraved on its walls have also been assigned their rightful place and with its around 150 plates which leave out no important sculpture or decorative motif, it has virtually become a picture album of the Lingarāja temple. The study has thus become a model for further such attempts of the scholars.

The charter of the Indira Gandhi National Centre for the Arts sets out as its objective a holistic approach to the study of art; it says that it would study each form of art not in an isolated manner but always in relation to other forms of art and to those aspects which contribute towards its emergence and to the formation of its specific character. There cannot be a better example of such a study than the present one which, though centring around the aspect of art, does full justice to other appurtenant factors as well, hence it is unique in its field and is miles ahead of once the only available work on Bhubaneswar temples by K.C. Panigrahi titled: *Archaeological Remains at Bhubaneswar* published in the mid-sixties of the previous century.

The present work is a very significant outcome of the Indira Gandhi Memorial Fellowship of IGNCA awarded to Prof. K.S. Behera in the years 1999-2001. There could not have been a more suitable scholar to carry out this study than he who has adorned the office of the Professor and Head of the Deptt. of History at the Utkal University for long years and that of the Vice-Chancellor of the F.M. University of Balasore. Not only is he keenly interested in interpreting the art and culture of Orissa, but also has a deep knowledge of Orissan history. His many valuable publications are a testimony to this. It is a matter of personal satisfaction to me that this work of my old friend and well wisher is now being published under my supervision with whom I have had the occasion to interact since many years.

New Delhi
25 February 2008

G.C. Tripathi
Professor and Head
of the Kalākośa Division
IGNCA, New Delhi

Preface

The objective of this monograph is to make a comprehensive study of the temple of Liṅgarāja at Bhubaneswar, which is one of the finest temples in India. The temple was built in the 11th century. From the first quarter of the 19th century, a number of scholars, both Indian and Western, such as R.L. Mitra, M.M. Ganguly, R.D. Banerjee, K.C. Panigrahi, T.E. Donaldson and others, described the Liṅgarāja temple, with emphasis on the archaeological and architectural aspects. Thus, in spite of many valuable studies on the art history of Orissa, there was no independent monograph on the temple of Liṅgarāja. While there are detailed monographs on the temples of the Khajuraho, Madhya Pradesh, the Brihadesvara temple, Tamilnadu, etc. no endeavour has been made to conduct an in-depth study of the Liṅgarāja temple. In the present monograph, an attempt has been made to study the temple in all its aspects, such as its history, architecture, sculpture, religious context, festivals, conservation measures, inscriptions, etc. in a systematic manner. The purpose is to understand the temple in its totality. The temple has not been viewed merely as an archaeological monument, but as a living centre of great religious significance. The architecture of the temple has been studied in the light of the *Śilpa śāstra* texts and the architectural lore of Orissa. The study of sacred texts, such as *Ekāmra Purāṇa, Ekāmra Candrikā* and *Svarṇādri Mahodaya* have thrown light on the system of worship, daily rituals and periodic festivals indicating changes and continuity. Thus, an integrated and multidimensional study of the temple is expected to provide new insights for the understanding of this great temple and its varied aspects.

My interest in the temples of Bhubaneswar began in 1962, when I joined the Post-Graduate Department of History, Utkal University, Bhubaneswar. I am grateful to my respected Professor Dr. M.N. Das for instructing me to conduct research on the art and archaeology of Orissa. At first, I concentrated my research on the famous Sun temple of Konarak. All along, however, Liṅgarāja had a special fascination for me as I lived in Bhubaneswar. I am grateful to the Indira Gandhi National Centre for the Arts for granting the award of fellowship in November 1999 to conduct research on the Liṅgarāja temple. The fellowship enabled me to conduct field work and to understand this great temple from a comparative perspective. After working for about eight months, I accepted an assignment to head the newly established Fakir Mohan University, Balasore as its Vice-Chancellor.

During my research, I have received valuable help from a number of scholars and institutions. I wish to record my gratitude to Dr. Kapila Vatsyayan, Shri M.N. Despande, Shri M.C. Joshi and Prof. M.A. Dhaky for their interest in my research.

I am grateful to the authorities of IGNCA for undertaking the publication of my work. I thank Dr. K.K. Chakravarty, Member Secretary, IGNCA and Shri A.N. Jha, Joint Secretary, IGNCA for making the publication of this volume possible. My good friend Prof. G.C. Tripathi, an eminent Sanskrit scholar and a specialist on Orissan Studies was kind enough to go through the text and provided valuable inputs. He also graciously accepted my request to write a foreword to the book. I also thank Dr. (Mrs.) Advaitavadini Kaul for her meticulous care in seeing this publication through the press.

I thank the authorities of the American Institute of Indian Studies, New Delhi and the Archaeological Survey of India, New Delhi for supplying me photographs from their collections. I am grateful to Dr. Sanjaya Acharya, Department of Ancient Indian History, Culture and Archaeology, Utkal University for his kind help to photograph the Liṅgarāja temple and other temples of Bhubaneswar. Shri Soumya Darshan Behera, my son, helped me in photographic documentation. I also thank Shri Pradosh Patnaik for his help in taking some photographs of the temple. I am grateful to Prof. Santosh Mishra, Orissa University of Agriculture and Technology, Bhubaneswar for permitting me to use the photographs and architectural drawings in his collection. I am grateful to Shri Rakesh Kumar, Archaeological Survey of India, Bhubaneswar for preparing plans and drawings of the temple.

I am grateful to Dr. Snigdha Tripathy, Epigraphist, Government of Orissa for giving me the benefit of her readings and compilation of the inscriptions of the Liṅgarāja temple. I am grateful to Prof. A.N. Parida, Department of Ancient Indian History, Culture and Archaeology, Utkal University; Dr. B.K. Rath, Superintendent, Orissa State Archaeology; Dr. Jeeban Kumar Patnaik, Archaeological Survey of India, Bhubaneswar; and Shri Ramakanta Mishra (O.A.S.), Administrator, Liṅgarāja temple for their kind help and co-operation.

I am indebted to Late Dr. U.N. Dhal for familiarising me with the Sanskrit sources on Bhubaneswar. I am thankful to the priests of Liṅgarāja temple for giving me insights into the rituals, festivals and religious traditions of Bhubaneswar.

I wish to record my thanks to Shri Pradeep Kumar Gan for providing me Secretarial Assistance throughout this project.

I am grateful to my family members, particularly to my daughter Prajna Paramita and my son-in-law Shri Bijaya Kumar Kalta for helping me in various ways.

I cannot adequately express my thanks to Smt. Shantipriya Behera, my wife, for her support and encouragement to carry out this project.

And finally I am thankful to Mr. Vikas Arya of Aryan Books International for his keen interest in co-publishing this work and taking special care of all the aspects of its production.

Sivaratri (16 February 2007) **K.S. Behera**
Bhubaneswar

CONTENTS

List of Illustrations

27. Liṅgarāja: *deula, alasa-kanyā*, upper *jaṅghā*, details.
28. Liṅgarāja: *deula, gaṇḍi*, details.
29. Liṅgarāja: *deula*, decorative programme of *gaṇḍi*.
30. Liṅgarāja: *deula, kanyā*, upper *jaṅghā* recess, west.
31. Liṅgarāja: facial expressions of female figures.
32. Liṅgarāja: facial expressions of female figures.
33. Liṅgarāja: facial expressions of female figures.
34. Liṅgarāja: facial expressions of female figures.
35. Liṅgarāja: *deula, kanyā* removing anklet, upper *jaṅghā*, north.
36. Liṅgarāja: *deula*, female figure, *ḍākinī*, upper *jaṅghā* recess, south.
37. Liṅgarāja: *deula*, Śiva as *yogī pīḍha-muṇḍi*, west.
38. Liṅgarāja: *deula*, female figure with *triśūḷa* and *kapāla*.
39. Liṅgarāja: *deula, pāṇigrahaṇa, khākarā-muṇḍi*, west.
40. Liṅgarāja: *deula*, Ācārya, *khākarā-muṇḍi*, north.
41. Liṅgarāja: *deula*, Gaṇeśa as Pārśvadevatā, south.
42. Liṅgarāja: *deula*, Kārttikeya as Pārśvadevatā, west.
43. Liṅgarāja: *deula*, Pārvatī as Pārśvadevtā, north.
44. Liṅgarāja: *deula*, Pārvatī, details.
45. Liṅgarāja: *deula, dikpāla* Agni.
46. Liṅgarāja: *deula, dikpāla* Niruthi.
47. Liṅgarāja: *deula, dikpāla* Varuṇa.
48. Liṅgarāja: *deula, dikpāla* Īśāna.
49. Liṅgarāja: *deula*, a couple, pilaster left side of Pārvatī, north.
50. Liṅgarāja: *deula*, churning of curd, *bāḍa*, south-east corner.
51. Liṅgarāja: *deula*, domestic scene, *bāḍa*, south-east.
52. Liṅgarāja: *deula*, Jagannātha, cell below Pārśvadevatā shrine, west.
53. Liṅgarāja: *deula*, Lakulīśa, Rāhā, east.
54. Liṅgarāja: *deula*, Andhakāsura-vadha-mūrtti, Rāhā, south.
55. Liṅgarāja: *deula*, Naṭarāja Rāhā, west.
56. Liṅgarāja: *deula*, Dancing Cāmuṇḍā, Rāhā, north.
57. Liṅgarāja: *deula, gaṇḍi, vajra-mastaka* south.
58. Liṅgarāja: *deula, gaṇḍi, vajra-mastaka* west.
59. Liṅgarāja: *deula, gaṇḍi, vajra-mastaka* north.
60. Liṅgarāja: *deula*, Overlapping of *deula* and *jagamohana*.
61. Liṅgarāja: *jagamohana*, south.
62. Liṅgarāja: *jagamohana*, south, 1868 (R.L. Mitra).
63. Liṅgarāja: *jagamohana*, arrangement of *pīḍhas*.
64. Liṅgarāja: *jagamohana*, details of *pīḍhas*, south.
65. Liṅgarāja: *jagamohana, vajra-mastaka, gaṇḍi*, north.
66. Liṅgarāja: *jagamohana, bandhanā* and upper *jaṅghā*, north.
67. Liṅgarāja: *jagamohana, alasa-kanyā*, upper *jaṅghā* recess.
68. Liṅgarāja: *jagamohana, staṁbha jāli gavākṣa*, north.
69. Liṅgarāja: *jagamohana gavākṣa*, south.
70. Liṅgarāja: *jaṅghā* miniature temple with flanking *kanyās*, south.
71. Liṅgarāja: Miniature temple with dancing Gaṇeśa and Naṭarāja.
72. Liṅgarāja: Pārvatī Pariṇaya scene, *gavākṣa*, south.
73. Liṅgarāja: *jagamohana Rāhu*, upper *jaṅghā*, north.
74. Liṅgarāja: *jagamohana, gajavyāḷa*, south.
75. Liṅgarāja: *jagamohana, kanyā* with attendants, south-west.
76. Liṅgarāja: *jagamohana*, lady looking at the mirror, north-west corner.
77. Liṅgarāja: *jagamohana, mithuna*, upper *jaṅghā*, south.
78. Liṅgarāja: *jagamohana, mithuna*, upper *jaṅghā* recess, north.
79. Liṅgarāja: *jagamohana*, man with sword, upper *jaṅghā*, south.
80. Liṅgarāja: *jagamohana*, seated female figure with attendants, north.
81. Liṅgarāja: *jagamohana, dvārasakhā*, north flank.
82. Liṅgarāja: *jagamohana*, Pārvatī worshipp-ed as Rāja Rājeśvarī.

83. Liṅgarāja: *nāṭa-mandira*, seated Ardhanāriśvara.
84. Liṅgarāja: *jagamohana*, Mahiṣamardinī.
85. Liṅgarāja: Compound, Mahiṣamardinī in a minor shrine.
86. Liṅgarāja: *nāṭa-mandira*: (a) *pīṭha* (b) miniature temple design in the *bāḍa*, south.
87. *Nāṭa-mandira, vaiṣṇava dvārapālas.*
88. Liṅgarāja: *bhoga-maṇḍapas* with *vāhana staṁbha* in the foreground, east.
89. Liṅgarāja: *bhoga-maṇḍapa*, Lakṣmī-Nārāyaṇa.
90. Gaṇeśa, Viśvakarmā Temple.
91. Gaṇeśa, Caṇḍeśvara Temple.
92. Gaṇeśa, Gaṇeśa Temple as Pārśvadevatā.
93. Gaṇeśa, Kārttikeya Temple, detached image.
94. *Nṛtta* Gaṇeśa, Ekāmbareśvara Temple.
95. Kārttikeya in a minor shrine.
96. Kārttikeya, Viśvakarmā Temple.
97. Kārttikeya, *nāṭa-mandira*.
98. Pārvatī, minor shrine.
99. Dancing Bhairava, Liṅgarāja Temple.
100. Ekapāda Bhairava, Bhairaveśvara Temple.
101. Sūrya, Vṛṣabha Temple.
102. Sūrya, Kalpataru *maṇḍapa*.
103. Sūrya *pūjā*, Liṅgarāja compound.
104. Varāha, Lakṣmī Nṛsiṁha Temple.
105. Nṛsiṁha, Viṣṇu temple, Malayagiri sea.
106. Vāsudeva trinity, Ananteśvara temple.
107. Hari-Hara, detached image, Liṅgarāja compound.
108. Lakulīśa, in a minor shrine.
109. Mātṛkā, Indrāṇī image recovered from *Bhajana maṇḍapa*.
110. Mātṛkā Cāmuṇḍā from *Bhajana maṇḍapa*.
111. Standing goddess, Liṅgarāja Temple.
112. Caturdhāmūrtti of Jagannātha fixed on the outer compound wall, east.
113. View of the minor shrines in Liṅgarāja compound, north.
114. Gaṇeśa Temple: *gaṇḍi* design, north-west.
115. Two ruined Śiva Temples to the South-east of Gaṇeśa Temple.
116. Viṣṇu Temple, Malayagiri area.
117. Lakṣmī Nṛsiṁha Temple.
118. Kitchen Block, Liṅgarāja Temple.
119. Śīva Temple near the kitchen block.
120. Vajra-mastaka: Śīva Temple near the kitchen block, western *rāhā*.
121. Sāvitrī Temple.
122. Rāmaliṅgeśvara Temple, east.
123. Rāmaliṅgeśvara Temple, north.
124. Rāmaliṅgeśvara compound, *Rāmāyaṇa* scene.
125. Lavaneśvara and Laḍukeśvara Temples.
126. Viṣṇu Temple: southern side.
127. Vaiṣṇava Temple: north of No. 126.
128. *Makara maṇḍapa*.
129. Pārvatī Temple, north.
130. Pārvatī Temple, south.
131. Pārvatī Temple: *pīṭha* and *pābhāga*, west.
132. Pārvatī Temple: *pābhāga*.
133. Pārvatī Temple: *bāḍa*.
134. Pārvatī Temple: Elongated *khākarā-muṇḍi*, north.
135. Pārvatī Temple: *gaṇḍi* of the *deula*.
136. Pārvatī Temple: *vajra-mastaka*.
137. Pārvatī Temple: Pārśvadevatā, southern *rāhā* of the *deula*.
138. Pārvatī Temple: *bāḍa* of the *jagamohana*.
139. Pārvatī Temple: *bāḍa* of the *jagamohana*, north.
140. Pārvatī Temple: *jagamohana, staṁbha, jāli, gavākṣa*, north.
141. Pārvatī Temple: *jagamohana*, door-frame.
142. Ugreśvara Temple.
143. Bhubaneśvarī Temple.
144. Ekāmbareśvara Temple.
145. Nandī in the Vṛṣabha Temple.
146. Eastern entrance porch of the Liṅgarāja Temple, west.
147. Brahmā in the entrance porch, used as *sārathi* in the Car Festival.
148. Liṅgarāja Temple, in 1868 (R.L. Mitra).

ACKNOWLEDGEMENTS

Courtesy: American Institute of Indian Studies

Plates 2, 6-7, 10-25, 39, 41, 45, 47, 48, 57-60, 63-66, 68-69, 72-74, 80-81, 84, 88, 90-91, 96, 114-15, 117-23, 125-27, 129-44, 146.

Courtesy: Archaeological Survey of India

Plates 1, 3, 5, 8-9, 26-28, 30-34, 36, 38, 40, 42-44, 46, 49-54, 61, 67, 70-71, 75-79, 82-83, 85-86, 89, 95, 99, 107, 111, 113, 145.

I

BHUBANESWAR IN HISTORICAL PERSPECTIVE

EARLY HISTORY

Bhubaneswar (latitude 20° 15′ North; longitude 85° East) was chosen as the new capital of Orissa in 1946.[1] It is, however, better known for its magnificent temples. The name Bhubaneswar is derived from the city's presiding god, Lord Śiva, called 'Tribhuvaneśvara', which means "the Lord of the Three Worlds". In the popular abbreviated form, the deity is called 'Bhubaneśvar' and after the deity, the place is called Bhubaneswar. As an important religious centre, the temple town was famous as Ekāmra Kṣetra. Legends trace the sanctity of the place, when there was a single mango tree with Śivaliṅga below it. The religious centre initially developed around it, and with the construction of the famous Liṅgarāja temple in the 11th century, the Ekāmra Kṣetra rose into splendour and was treated as a major religious centre of Śaivism. Despite changes over the centuries, Bhubaneswar continues as a living centre of pilgrimage in Orissa.

The Ekāmra Kṣetra or Ekāmra Kānana was much more extensive than the present temple town. According to the orthodox texts, such as *Svarṇādri Mahodaya*[2] and *Ekāmra Candrikā*,[3] it extended from Khaṇḍācala (Khaṇḍagiri) on the west to Kuṇḍaleśvara on the east; from Valahadevī on the north to Bahiraṅgeśvara at the top of the Dhauligiri on the south. The area is believed to be circular in shape.

The early history of Bhubaneswar, prior to the emergence of Ekāmra Kṣetra, is known from the available archaeological remains. The Edicts of Aśoka at Dhauli about 8 km south of Bhubaneswar, suggest that the area was a part of the empire of the famous Mauryan emperor Aśoka. The rock-cut elephant carved at Dhauli dates back to the time of Aśoka. It is known from his 13th Rock Edict, which is not engraved at Dhauli, that Aśoka had conquered a place called Kaliṅga, eight years after his coronation, i.e., about 261 BC. After conquest, Toṣali became the headquarters of the newly conquered province. This seems to be identical either with Dhauli or the fortified city of Śiśupālagarh. Excavations at Śiśupālagarh[4] have provided evidence that the area was in occupation from the 3rd century BC to the middle of the 4th century AD. Śiśupālagarh, as an early historical city, was distinguished by its systematic layout with rampart, gateways, residential buildings and watch towers. The antiquities recovered from the site indicate the level of the city life and its trade contacts. The discovery of roulated ware, roman bullae, imitation Kuṣaṇa coins and an inscribed gold medallion, throw light on its unique character as a city. Some scholars think that possibly this fortified town was the capital of the ancient Kaliṅga during the Maurya and the Mahāmeghavāhana era.

The Hāthigumphā Inscription,[5] on the Udayagiri hill, about 8 km from the Liṅgarāja temple, contains the details about the activities of Khāravela, the Chedi ruler of the Mahāmeghavāhana family who is believed to have ruled during the 1st century BC. It appears that after the decline of Maurya dynasty, the Chedi kings ruled over Kaliṅga and established the independent kingdom of Kaliṅga. During Khāravela, military campaigns were launched against different parts of India. The Kaliṅgan army marched towards west without caring for King Śātakarnī of the Sātavāhana dynasty. Even the Rāṣṭrika and Bhojaka chieftains were defeated in the west. In the south the Tamil confederacy was defeated. In the north, the Kaliṅgan army stormed Gorathagiri and caused panic to the people of Rājagriha. The army marched as far as the Uttarāpatha (north-west) and on the way back to Kaliṅga defeated Bahasatimitra, the ruler of Aṅga and Magadha. Khāravela was a follower of Jainism and during his time Khaṇḍagiri and Udayagiri hills became important centres of Jainism with the excavation of caves for the Jaina ascetics. It is believed by scholars that Kaliṅganagara, the capital of Khāravela, probably represented the fortified town of Śiśupālagarh.

The post-Khāravela period, on the basis of numismatic evidence is referred to as a probable period of Andhra and Murunda supremacy in the early centuries of the Christian era,[6] but as coins change hands during commercial transactions, one has to be cautious in using coins for reconstructing political history. After Khāravela, the history of Bhubaneswar is quite obscure. The colossal figures of Nāga[7] and Yakṣa[8] indicate the popularity of these folk cults in Bhubaneswar. The discovery of large bell capital[9] near the Aśoka Jhara tank and a lion sculpture[10] near Bhāskareśvara temple, led scholars to believe that, there was an Aśokan pillar at Bhubaneswar of which the pillar inside the Bhāskareśvara temple formed a part. The difference of style and the quality of stone used, seem to suggest that the pillar may have belonged to a period later than Aśoka's. Similarly, the discovery of a lion capital near the Bibhīṣanesvara temple seems to suggest the existence of more than one pillar imitating Aśokan pillar. The discovery of a number of railing pieces in the Baḍagaḍ Bhāskareśvara temple area indicate the existence of a stūpa enclosed by railings[11]; but its religious association with Buddhism or Jainism cannot be precisely determined. On ground of style, however, these may be assigned to the early centuries of the Christian era.

It is not known precisely the nature of Gupta political influence over Orissa, but it seems that in the post-Gupta period the art traditions of the Guptas lingered in Bhubaneswar. This is suggested by several sculptures, such as Pārvatī, Kārttikeya found in the premises of the Liṅgarāja temple and a *catur-mukha liṅga* recovered from the sacred tank of Bindusāgara. It appears that Śaivism had already become popular much earlier than the 6th-7th centuries AD, when temple building activities had already started at Bhubaneswar in honour of Śiva. Epigraphical records found from village Paṭiākillā[12] on the suburbs of Bhubaneswar indicate that it was a part of the territorial division of Dakṣina Toṣali during the rule of Mahārājā Śaṁbhu-Yasas of the Mana dynasty, who was a worshipper of Maheśvara.

Bhubaneswar in the 7th century witnessed the growing influence of Śaivism. The early Śaiva temples of Bhubaneswar carry representations of Lakulīśa. This seems to suggest that temple building activities at Bhubaneswar in the 7th century were connected with the Lakulīśa Pāśupata sect of Śaivism. The sculptural representations of Lakulīśa at Bhubaneswar are known from the temples, such as Bharateśvara (early 7th century AD), Śatrughneśvara (early 7th century AD), Paraśurāmeśvara (7th century AD), Vaitāl (mid-8th century AD), Śiśireśvara (8th century AD), Tāleśvara (8th century AD), Mukteśvara (10th century AD), Rājarānī (early 11th century AD), Liṅgarāja (mid 11th century AD), and Megheśvara (12th century AD). In earlier centuries Bhubaneswar came under the influence of Buddhism, Jainism, Yakṣa and Nāga worship, but from about 6th century AD, Śaivism came to be the dominant religion of the place, although the earlier religions continued in the area and existed side by side with Śaivism.

EMERGENCE OF EKĀMRA KṢETRA AS A RELIGIOUS CENTRE

In early medieval period, Bhubaneswar emerged as the major centre for Śaivism and was known through various names, such as Ekāmra, Ekāmra Kānana, Ekāmra Kṣetra, Svamakuta, Svamachala, etc. The earliest epigraphical evidence about Ekāmra is to be found in the Gupta year 280 (AD 600).[13] The inscription belonging to the Vigraha dynasty mentions a *maṭha* of Maninägeśvara-bhaṭṭāraka of Ekāmbaka, which evidently represents Ekāmraka or Ekāmra. This seems to suggest that Ekāmra, as the ancient name of Bhubaneswar, was already known by that name during the 6th and 7th centuries AD. Bhubaneswar also came to attract attention as a centre of pilgrimage. A ruler named Śāntikaradeva, presumably a feudatory of Bhaumakara, came to Ekāmra on pilgrimage and at the bank of Bindusāgara donated land to a Brāhmaṇa in his own territory of Yamagartta Maṇḍala[14] (Angul-Talcher region of Orissa). The inscription also mentions Vīrajā Kṣetra (modern Jajpur in Jajpur district), which is another centre of pilgrimage. On grounds of palaeography, the inscription has been assigned to the 9th or early 10th century AD. This would suggest that the tank of Bindusāgara in Ekāmra had already become an important *tīrtha* of Bhubaneswar.

The temple inscription of Brahameśvara at Bhubaneswar belonging to 11th century mentions the erection of Brahmeśvara temple at Ekāmra-Siddhatīrtha.[15] In the 13th century Ekāmra was the well known name of the temple town. A commemorative inscription of Ananta Vāsudeva temple records that the said temple was built by Candrikādevī, sister of Narasiṁha I of the Eastern Gaṅga dynasty in the Śaka year 1200 (AD 1278).[16] According to the inscription, the temple was built on the bank of Bindusāgara at Ekāmra. The inscription mentions that in earlier times the place was famous for a single mango tree (Ekāmra), but later on hundreds of mango groves came up. There stood a temple of god Śiva surrounded by many temples. The presiding deity of the Kṣetra was called Kṛttivāsa and the temple is said to have been located near the Gandhasindhu, which represents a varient of Gandhavatī, identical with the small river called Gaṅguā. In early medieval inscriptions, the presiding deity of the Ekāmra Kṣetra is called Kṛttivāsa or Kīrttivāsa. Hence, the place was also called Kīrttivāsa Kaṭaka, as mentioned in the inscription of Sūryavaṁśī Gajapati king Puruṣottamadeva.[17] It is not known clearly, when the name Bhubaneswar was given to this holy city. An inscription of Liṅgarāja temple of the time of Vīrocoḍa (12th century AD) mentions the presiding deity as Tribhuvanādhiśvara.[18] It appears that subsequently the name Bhubaneswar became more popular than Kīrttivāsa. In the Oriya inscription of the time of Puruṣottamadeva, the presiding deity is mentioned as Bhubaneśvaradeva or Bhubaneśvara or Bhubaneśvara Liṅga.[19] Sāraḷā Dās (15th century AD), the composer of Oriya *Mahābhārata*, mentions Bhubaneswar *tīrtha* in the *Vana Parva* in context of killing of the two demons Kīrtti and Vāsa at Ekāmbaravana (Ekāmravana).[20] It seems that in course of centuries the city, named after deity Bhubaneśvara, came to be known as Bhubaneswar. Bhubaneswar as the name of the sacred city had already become popular by the 17th century. This is suggested by a 17th century Sanskrit text, called *Śatpañcāśaddeśavibhāga*,[21] which forms a part of the *Śaktisaṅgama Tantra*. The work, among others, mentions the name of Bhubaneśa as a territory adjoining Aṅga and Gauḍa. Bhubaneswar, thus had become popular although Ekāmra Kṣetra as the name of the temple town was not al-together replaced. Bhubaneswar, at least the temple town, evokes the glory of the Ekāmra Kṣetra, which was not completely to be rediscovered, but remains a living heritage displayed through its temples and other antiquarian remains.

The Sanskrit texts provide evidence about the sanctity of the Ekāmra Kṣetra. The *Matsya Purāṇa*[22] refers to Ekāmra and its chief goddess Kīrtimati. She could be goddess Pārvatī, who is described in the *Ekāmra Purāṇa* as Kīrttirūpā.[23] The *Brahma Purāṇa*,[24] however, provides interesting details about its territorial extent, temples, gardens, houses, streets and beautiful women. The area of Ekāmra Kṣetra comprises of two-and-a-half *yojanas*. The Kṣetra is said to have evolved from a single mango tree. Its presiding deity is mentioned as Kīrttivāsa. The *Purāṇa* mentions the sacred tank Bindusara, Kapila *tīrtha*, and the Śivaliṅga called Bhāskareśvara. This excellent Kṣetra, containing one crore Śivaliṅgas, is considered sacred as Vārānasī. The devotee, who sees the presiding Śivaliṅga of the Kṣetra, Devī Pārvatī, Gaṇacaṇḍa, Kārttikeya, Gaṇeśa, Vṛṣabha and Kalpadruma, attains *Śivaloka*.

The *Śiva Purāṇa*,[25] which refers to numerous Śivaliṅgas of India, mentions Kīrttivāseśvara, Kedāreśa and Bhubaneśa. Kirttivāseśvara, evidently, belongs to Vārānasī, but Bhubaneśa is no other than the presiding Śivaliṅga of the Ekāmra Kṣetra. The *Śiva Purāṇa*[26] specifically mentions Bhubaneśa in the land of Puruṣottama as the bestower of *siddhi*. The *Śiva Purāṇa*[27] (*Uttara Khaṇḍa*), which consists of forty-five chapters, devotes nearly five chapters to describe the greatness of Ekāmra Kṣetra and the Lingarāja-Tribhubaneśvara. The text, however, seems to have been composed in Orissa during the medieval period, sometime in the 15th or 16th century AD.

In course of time the Ekāmra Kṣetra became a major centre of Śaivism and attracted many pilgrims. Several *Sthala Māhātmyas* were written to describe its sanctity. Among such works *Ekāmra Purāṇa*,[28] *Ekāmra Candrikā*[29] and *Svarṇādri Mahodaya*[30] deserve special mention. These texts describe in detail the important temples, the legends around them, sacred tanks and the notable festivals taking place in Bhubaneswar. These orthodox texts mention several shrines inside the Liṅgarāja compound. These texts cannot be precisely dated, but they contain good deal of traditional accounts of much earlier dated than the date of their composition. The textual analysis of these above-mentioned three texts, suggests that *Ekāmra Purāṇa* is possibly the earliest and it was followed by *Svarṇādri Mahodaya* and *Ekāmra Candrikā*. The *Ekāmra Candrikā* is apparently later than the *Śiva Purāṇa (Uttara Khaṇḍa)*. R.C. Hazra[31] believed that the *Ekāmra Purāṇa* was composed between AD 950 and AD 1150. But K.C. Panigrahi[32] on the basis of a reference to the Ananta Vāsudeva temple (AD 1278) places the text in the 13th century AD.

The *Ekāmra Purāṇa*[33] mentions the *Māhātmya* of Kapileśvara, the construction of which is attributed to Sūryavaṁśī king Kapilendradeva (AD 1435-1467). This would suggest that the *Ekāmra Purāṇa*, or at least the chapter on *Kapileśvara Māhātmya*, belonged to the 15th century. The text refers to *Kapila Saṁhitā* suggesting further a later date than accepted by R.C. Hazra and K.C. Panigrahi. The *Svarṇādri Mahodaya* quotes identical verses from the *Ekāmra Purāṇa*, while there are identical verses in the *Svarṇādri Mahodaya* and *Ekāmra Candrikā*. These *Sthala Māhātmya*s collectively throw a good deal of light on the religious and the cultural milieu of the Ekāmra Kṣetra and its numerous temples. These works may be dated between the 13th and 15th century.

The *Kapila Saṁhitā*[34] is another important Sanskrit text, which describes the four important religious centres of Orissa dedicated to Kṛṣṇa, Arka, Pārvatī, and Hara. These centres are Puri, for the worship of Kṛṣṇa-Jagannātha; Konarak for the worship of Sūrya; Vīrajā (Jajpur) for the worship of Devī and Ekāmra (Bhubaneswar) for the worship of Śiva. The section devoted to Ekāmra Kṣetra throws light on the notable temples and festivals of Bhubaneswar. The text provides evidence that in the 15th-16th centuries, Bhubaneswar was a vibrant centre of pilgrimage. The *Tīrtha Cintāmani*[35] of Vācaspati Miśra (15th century AD) includes Ekāmra Kṣetra as an important centre of pilgrimage and quotes verses from the *Brahma Purāṇa* to prove its sanctity. The Oriya *Mahābhārata*[36] of Sāraḷā Dās (15th century AD) refers to the legends about Kīrtti and Vāsa and mentions several temples, such as Ekāmbaranātha, Kedāreśvara, Mukteśvara, Sūkhmeśvara, Yameśvara and others. Sāraḷā Dās mentions that Ekāmravana had fifty-two crores of Śivaliṅgas and the most excellent of them was the Liṅgarāja.

Apart from being an important Śaiva centre, Bhubaneswar was also a notable *Śākta Pīṭha*.[37] Several tantric texts, such as *Jñānārṇava Tantra, Bṛhannīla Tantra, Tantrasāra*, etc. mention that Ekāmra was a leading *Śākta Pīṭha*.[38] The chief goddess of Ekāmra is called Kīrtimatī according to the *Prāṇatoṣanī Tantra*,[39] the *Matsya Purāṇa*[40] and the *Devī Bhāgavata Purāṇa*,[41] while *Tantrasāra* mentions Bhāgavahā as the chief goddess of Ekāmra. The *Śiva Purāṇa*[42] (*Uttara Khaṇḍa*) mentions four *pīṭhas* in the Kṣetra, such as *Bhava Pīṭha*, dedicated to Kedāra and Gauri; *Mahāśmaśāna Pīṭha* with Uttareśvara and Uttareśvarī; *Sva Pīṭha* inside the Liṅgarāja temple, before Gopālinī and under the Kalpavṛkṣa; and *Bṛhat Pīṭha* where Vaidyanātha is present.

The orthodox texts on the Ekāmra Kṣetra, such as *Ekāmra Purāṇa, Ekāmra Candrikā* and *Svarṇādri Mahodaya* help us to understand Bhubaneswar from the point of view of the tradition. The sacred geography of the Kṣetra along with its temples are very clear on the basis of these texts. Ekāmra Kṣetra is considered to be circular[43] (*Maṇḍalākāra*) and one *kośa* in area. Another concept associated with the Kṣetra is its division into eight *āyatanas*,[44] possibly following the *aṣṭamūrtti* or the eight forms of Śiva-Tribhuvaneśvara.[45] The term *āyatana* denotes a place, abode, a sanctuary, etc.[46] In describing the *āyatanas*, the Śivaliṅgas are mentioned along with their distance from each other and their direction. The concept of *āyatanas* is found in all the above mentioned three texts. In some temples, as in the *Svarṇādri Mahodaya,* there is apparent confusion and overlapping of the names of the *liṅgas*. In the narration of the eight *āyatanas*, the *Ekāmra Candrikā* has been followed as it is later than *Svarṇādri Mahodaya.*

The first *āyatana* of Ekāmra Kṣetra includes Bindusara, Ananta Vāsudeva, Devīpādaharā, Tīrtheśvara and Tribhuvaneśvara.[47]

The second *āyatana* contains Maitreśvara, Varuṇeśvara, Īśāneśvara, Yameśvara and *tīrthas*, such as Pāpanāśana Kuṇḍa.[48]

The third *āyatana* includes Gaṅgā-Yamunā *tīrtha* and the Śivaliṅga called Gaṅgeśvara.[49]

The fourth *āyatana* contains several Śivaliṅgas, such as Koṭīśvara, Svarṇajaleśvara, Suparṇajāleśvara, Sureśvara, Siddheśvara, Mukteśvara, Kedāreśvara, Rudraliṅga, Maruteśvara, Daityeśvara and Indreśvara. The *tīrthas* associated with the Śivaliṅgas are Koṭitīrtha, Siddhakuṇḍa and Gaurīkuṇḍa.[50]

The fifth *āyatana* contains the shrines of Brahmeśvara, Gokarṇeśvara, Utpaleśvara, Amṛtakeśvara, Madhyameśvara and Jaṭileśvara, besides the Brahma kuṇḍa.[51]

The sixth *āyatana* contains *liṅgas*, such as Megheśvara along with Meghakuṇḍa, Bhāskareśvara and its associated *kuṇḍas* and Kapālamocana Śiva.[52]

The seventh *āyatana* has Śivaliṅgas, such as Alābukeśvara with Alābu tīrtha, Uttareśvara and Bhimeśvara.[53]

The eighth *āyatana* of the Ekāmra Kṣetra contains Rāmeśvara along with Rāma kuṇḍa, Sīteśvara, Hanumadīśvara, Lavaṇeśvara, Bharateśvara, Lakṣmaṇeśvara, Śatrughneśvara, Gosahasreśvara and Paradareśvara.[54]

In the Ekāmra Kṣetra, there are eight *tīrthas.*[55] These are Bindu tīrtha, Pāpanasinī kuṇḍa, Gaṅgā-Yamunā tīrtha, Koṭi tīrtha, Brahma kuṇḍa, Megha tīrtha and Rāma kuṇḍa. Of these eight *tīrthas,* Bindusara is the most excellent. Taking bath in the Bindu tīrtha, a devotee should visit Puruṣottama *(Ananta Vāsudeva),* Devīpādaharā and Tribhuvaneśvara. The orthodox texts elaborately mention the legends and the sanctity of Bindu tīrtha. Taking bath in the Pāpanāśinī kuṇḍa, the devotees visit Mitreśvara and Varuṇeśvara. The twin *tīrthas* of Gaṅgā and Yamunā are associated with Gaṅgeśvara. The Koṭi tīrtha is associated with Koṭiśvara; Brahma kuṇḍa with Brahmeśvara; Megha tīrtha with Megheśvara; and Rāma kuṇḍa (now called Aśokajhara) with Rāmeśvara. The *Śiva Purāṇa (Uttara Khaṇḍa)* while mentioning the eight *tīrthas* actually names seven *tīrthas* and omits Alābu tīrhta,[56] which is mentioned in the *Ekāmra Candrikā.* The Alābu tīrtha is in the vicinity of Alābukeśvara.

The orthodox texts locate eight *Caṇḍīs* in the Kṣetra. The *Svarṇādri Mahodaya*[57] and the *Ekāmra Candrikā*[58] refer to these eight *Caṇḍīs;* they are Rāmāyaṇī, Kāpālinī, Mohinī, Vindhyagā or Vindhyavāsinī, Ambikā, Dvāravāsinī, Uttareśvarī, and Gaurī. These *Caṇḍikās* are placed on the four sides of the Bindusāgara. On the western side Ambikā, in the east Dvāravāsinī; on the southern bank are Mohinī and Vindhyagā; while on the northern side Uttareśvarī and Gaurī.

The textual evidence about the sanctity of Ekāmra Kṣetra and its numerous temples are amply corroborated by archaeological evidence at Bhubaneswar. Dr. K.C. Panigrahi first made an exhaustive

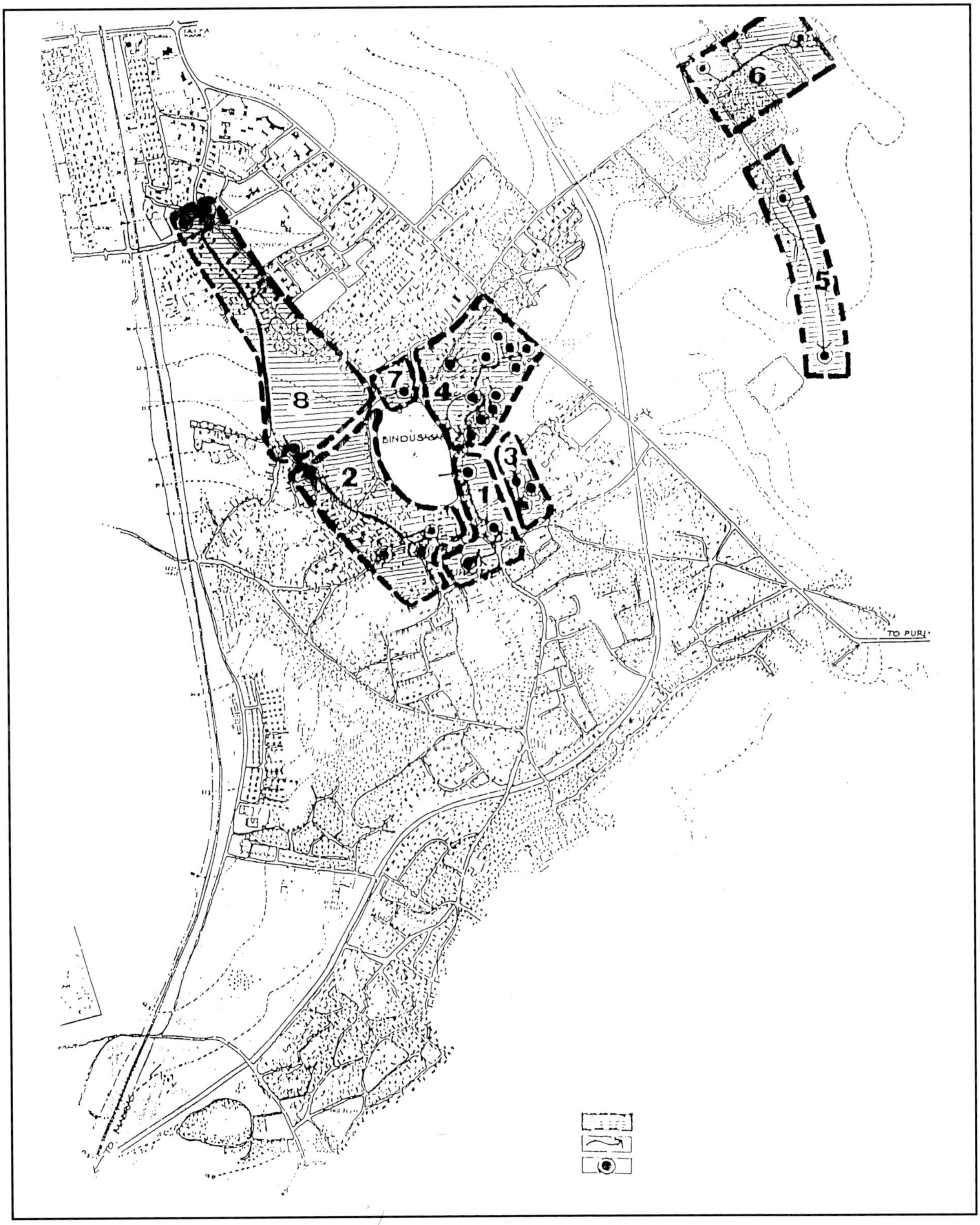

Fig. 1. Aṣṭāyatana Plan of Ekāmra Kṣetra.

study of the archaeological remains at Bhubaneswar.[59] His study was based on the available sources, such as the extant temples, detached sculptures, architectural fragments, inscriptions, Sanskrit texts on Bhubaneswar and the *Mādalā Pāñji.*[60] He, on the basis of epigraphical records and typological study of the temples, assigned the temples of Bhubaneswar to different periods. The dynastic division of temples in the context of political history of Orissa, though convenient, is not always conclusive. The temples, on the basis of the development of their architectural and decorative programme, may be assigned approximately to two different centuries. Starting with Śatrughneśvara in the 6th century, the temple building tradition reached its climax with the construction of the Liṅgarāja temple in the 11th century and it continued as late as the 15th century, when the Kapileśvara temple was built. Many of the temples still retain the traditional names mentioned in the Sanskrit texts, such as *Ekāmra Purāṇa, Ekāmra Candrikā,* etc. which were in the nature of pilgrims guides. For the followers of Śaivism, Ekāmra Kṣetra is not a mere piece of land studded with numerous Śivaliṅgas, but a city of homage to Śiva.

The tradition of religious tolerance is attested by vestiges of diverse sects at Bhubaneswar. As early as 1st century BC Khāravela, a devout Jaina, in the Hāṭigumphā Inscription has specially mentioned that he honoured all religious sects and repaired the shrines of all the deities.[61] Jainism flourished at Bhubaneswar in the Khaṇḍagiri and Udayagiri areas. On the basis of the Hāṭigumphā Inscription, it is claimed that Mahāvīra preached his religion in this centre. The caves at Khaṇḍagiri and Udayagiri belong to 2nd-1st centuries BC, while the images of Tīrthaṅkaras were carved there in the 11th century AD, when Bhubaneswar had already become a major centre of Śaivism. In the Mukteśvara temple (10th century AD), small figures of Tīrthaṅkaras are found on its low enclosure wall. The continuance of Jainism at Khaṇḍagiri during the later period is proved by Tīrthaṅkara images, stylistically datable to the 15th century.

Buddhist influence reached Bhubaneswar after the conquest of Kaliṅga by Aśoka in 261 BC. The rock-cut elephant at Dhauli seems to be associated with Buddhism as this noble animal is symbolic of the birth of the Buddha. Several detached railings, probably associated with Buddhism, have been discovered from Baḍgaḍa-Bhāskareśvara area, Kapilaprasād, Kurkimuṇḍiā and Aragarh.[62] Evidence about the continuance of Buddhism at Bhubaneswar is provided by images of Tārā, Lokanātha, Halāhala Lokeśvara, etc. which may be assigned to the 11th-12th centuries AD.[63]

Even though Bhubaneswar was a centre of Śaivism, evidence about the existence of Vaiṣṇavism is known from detached sculptures of Ananta Vāsudeva (7th century AD) fixed on the eastern side of the Bindusara, the representation of Varāha in the Paraśurāmeśvara temple (7th century AD) and *avatāra* sculptures in the Manibhadreśvara temple (10th century AD). The only major Viṣṇu temple in the Ekāmra Kṣetra is the Ananta Vāsudeva temple. In course of time, Liṅgarāja came to represent Hari-Hara and even the *Kapila Saṁhitā* refers to Ekāmra as *Hariharātmaka Kṣetra.*[64] Thus, over the centuries, Bhubaneswar gives the impression of a city with diverse religious sects and traditions.

BHUBANESWAR FROM 7th TO 18th CENTURIES AD

During the 6th-7th centuries AD, Bhubaneswar seems to have formed a part of the Śailodbhava territory which comprised the areas of present Khurda, Puri and Ganjam districts.[65] It was probably during this period that several early temples were constructed at Bhubaneswar. The Bhaumakaras ruled over coastal Orissa extending from Midnapur to Ganjam district in the 8th-9th centuries.[66] Their association with Bhubaneswar is suggested by the Dhauli cave inscription and the Gaṇeśa gumphā inscription at Udayagiri.[67] The Bhaumakara capital Guhaśiva Pāṭaka was located in the vicinity of Vīrajā, identical with Jajpur in Jajpur district.[68] Vīrajā and Ekāmra as centres of pilgrimage, are mentioned in the copper-plate grant of Śāntikaradeva, who seems to have been a feudatory king of the Bhaumakara dynasty.[69]

The Somavaṁśīs, who started their rule in Orissa with Suvarṇapura (Sonepur) as their capital, under Janmejaya I Mahāśivagupta (AD 880-920), gradually extended their sway and controlled coastal Orissa including Bhubaneswar during the time of Yayāti I Mahāśivagupta by uniting Kośala and Utkala.[70] A commemorative inscription in the Brahmeśvara temple indicates that it was built by Kolāvatī devī, the mother of Uddyota Kesarī (Uddyota Kesarī IV Mahābhavagupta, AD 1040-1065).[71] In the popular traditions, the Somavaṁśīs are known as the Kesarī kings. The *Mādalā Pāñji*[72] attributes the construction of the Liṅgarāja temple to Lalātendu Kesarī or Lalāta Kesarī. Epigraphical records engraved in a cave at Khaṇḍagiri hill mention that a Jaina teacher, Ācārya Subhacandra, a disciple of Kulacandra, visited Jaina centre of Khaṇḍagiri during the time of King Uddoyata Kesarī. The age of the Somavaṁśīs at Bhubaneswar witnessed the construction of several beautiful temples, such as Mukteśvara, Rājarānī, Brahmeśvara, and the Liṅgarāja.

Bhubaneswar came under the control of the Eastern Gaṅgas of Kaliṅga about the beginning of the 12th century AD. The Liṅgarāja temple bears an inscription of Anantavarman Coḍagaṅgadeva[73] (AD 1078-1147). The inscriptions of the Gaṅga rulers are to be found at Bhubaneswar in several temples, such as the *jagamohana* of the Lingarāja, Kedāreśvara, Megheśvara and Ananta Vāsudeva. The Gaṅga rule was followed by the rule of the Sūryavaṁśī Gajapati kings. According to traditions of the *Mādalā Pañji*, Kapilendradeva (AD 1435-1467) had his coronation at Kṛttivāsa Kataka, i.e., Bhubaneswar.[74] Inscriptions of Kapilendradeva[75] and his successor Puruṣottamadeva[76] (AD 1467-1497) are found on the *jagamohana* of the Liṅgarāja temple. The Oriya inscription of Puruṣottamadeva refers to Kṛttivāsa-Kaṭaka,[77] which probably suggests the existence of a royal camp or residence at Bhubaneswar. According to local tradition, a mound on the south-west of the Liṅgarāja temple represents the remains of a royal palace. Bhubaneswar seems to have continued as an important religious and cultural centre during the Sūryavaṁśī rule. During the reign of Pratāparudradeva (AD 1497-1540), Śrī Caitanya came to Puri. He spent nearly eighteen years of his life and also died at Puri. On his way to Puri he is said to have worshipped Liṅgarāja after taking bath in the Bindusāgara as he believed in the Hari-Hara cult.[78] The major biographies of Śrī Caitanya, such as *Caitanya Caritāmṛta*, refer to his visit to the Liṅgarāja temple, but later works believe that he also possibly visited the Ananta Vāsudeva temple.

Orissa lost its independence in AD 1568 and passed into the hands of the Afghan rulers of Bengal. Subsequently, Mansingh annexed Orissa to the Mughal Empire in AD 1592. In AD 1751 the Marathas controlled coastal Orissa and ruled it till AD 1803.

BHUBANESWAR AFTER 1803

On October 14, 1803, the British conquered Orissa by defeating the Marathas. By the treaty of Deogaon, concluded on December 17, 1803, Raghuji Bhonslā ceded to the East India Company in perpetual sovereignty, the province of Cuttack, including the port and the district of Balasore.

In 1815, the artist of Colin Mackenzie prepared several drawings of the images at Bhubanswar. Andrew Stirling, a British Officer, who was in Orissa till 1822, visited Bhubaneswar and described it as a "ruined city, consisting entirely of deserted and dismantled towers and temples sacred to the worship of Mahadeo, under the innumerable titles, which absurd legends or the fancy of his votaries have assigned to that deity. From amidst the whole, the great Pagoda of the Liṅgarāja, or Lord of the Liṅgaṁ, lifts its singular form, eminently conspicuous both for size, loftiness and the superior style of its architecture".[79] No effort, however, was made by the British to repair the temples of Bhubaneswar. This is evident from the accounts of Andrew Stirling and the drawing published by him in the *Asiatic Researches*[80] (1825). He has mentioned that, "Standing near the chief Pagoda, one cannot turn the eye, in any direction, without taking into the view upwards of forty or fifty of these stone towers."[81]

In 1837 James Fergusson visited Bhubaneswar and the great temple of Liṅgarāja exercised a profound impression on him. He observed, "There are many in India more elegant in their details, and more elaborately ornamented – perhaps, therefore, more beautiful – but no one that I know of is more imposing in effect, or conveys more clearly the idea of solid and lasting grandeur than this; and as it stands surrounded by an immense number of smaller and more modern temples, it forms the worthy centre of an architectural panorama unequalled, at least in Hindostan; for there are more ancient temples in this single deserted city Bobeneswar than in all the cities of Northern India put together."[82]

Around the middle of the 19th century, as known from the notes of F.B. Lourie, Bhubaneswar was an interesting place for the inquisitive travellers. The ancient city presented a veritable 'World of temples'. According to Rev. Lourie, "The most picturesque view of the great Pagoda of Bhobaneser is to be obtained by proceeding two or three miles westward on the road to Khandagiri, when, from its vastly superior height, it becomes the only temple observable; then it certainly does present a most majestic appearance, towering to the skies like an apotheosis of science, asserting the undisputed right of India to claim a high rank among the scientific nations of antiquity".[83] He further mentioned that, "A few hundreds of pilgrims annually visit the place on their way to the Puri festivals; and a Car-festival in April brings considerable numbers of people of the district to the spot; but it is not difficult to observe that Bhobaneser has fallen – Jagannath is now the centre of attraction. Bhobaneser enjoys no support from government in any way; and we question very much whether it now receives any from the Rajah of Khurdah although it did formerly the present Rajah's ancestors having granted some of the lands and endowments attached to it."[84] Bhubaneswar seemed to him as a "poverty-stricken place."

In 1868 Rajendra Lala Mitra visited Bhubaneswar. At that time the boundary of Bhubaneswar extended from "the temple of Rāmeśvara to a little to the west of that of Bhuvanesvara on the west; from the latter to the temple of Kapileśvara on the south; from the last to the temple of Bhāskareśvara on the east; and from the last to Rāmeśvara on the north".[85] The entire area measured around two miles and a half. According to him, "the greater part of this area covered by arid plains of laterite, waste lands interspersed with patches of paddy-fields, ruins of old buildings, and deserted temples".[86] Of the total area one-third constituted the waste land. Of the balance land 1196 acres belong to Bhubaneswar and the rest of the *Devottra* land belongs to deities, such as Kapileśvara, Ananta Vāsudeva, Paradareśvara, Uttareśvara and Gopālinī. Rajendra Lala Mitra

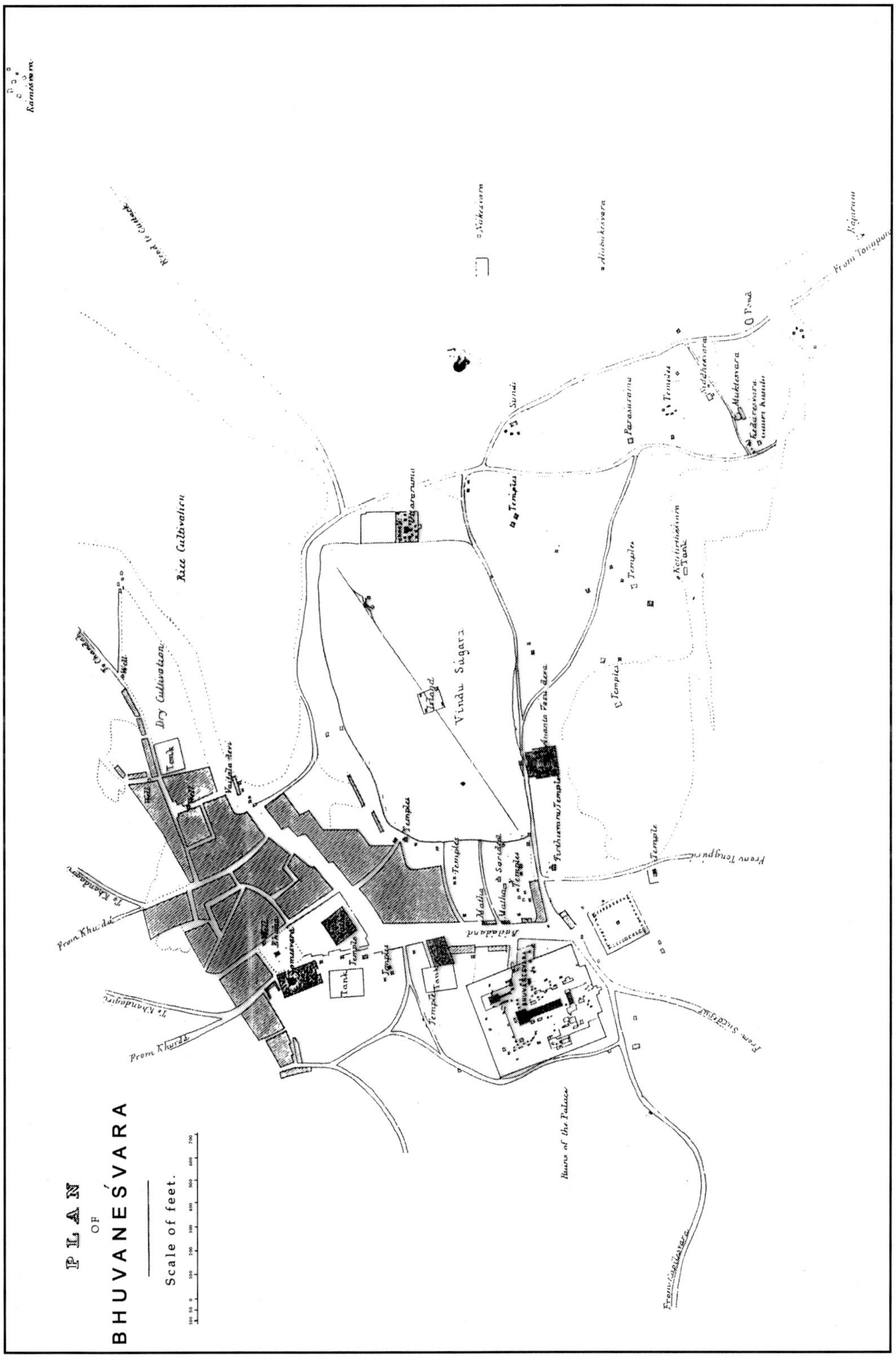

Fig. 2. Plan of Bhubaneswar (R.L. Mitra, 1868).

gives an interesting account of the houses of the Bhubaneswar. He observed, "For so large an area, the number of houses is small, being only 716, of which 249 belong to Kapileśvara. The bulk of these houses is thatched. The masonry houses, which include five monasteries, the Zamindar's office, and a very few dwellings are partly of brick and partly of rubble stones laid in mortar, and plastered."[87]

According to the census of 1872, the population of Bhubaneswar was only 3,926. The bulk of population consisted of Brāhmaṇa-priests. There were nearly 862 professional priests and non-professional Brāhmaṇas.[88] The town was inhabited by various caste groups. The Muslims, however, did not live in the city, but could be found in the suburbs. The Kapileśvara area was comparatively in a flourishing condition than the main township. On the whole, according to R.L. Mitra, Bhubaneswar was "insignificant, uninviting place with no wealth, no commerce and no manufactory, peopled by hungry priests, and desolate in every respect".[89] Nevertheless, R.L. Mitra agreed that, "it was a most interesting field for the antiquarian, abounding as it does in architectural remains of the highest value and connected as it is with historical associations of rare importance."[90]

The main line of the Bengal-Nagpur Railway from Calcutta passed through Bhubaneswar in 1900. From Khurda road station a branch line connected it to Puri town. The railway line marked the western boundary of Bhubaneswar and facilitated the visit of the pilgrims.

The Puri District Gazetteers by L.S.S. O'Malley, published in 1908, describes Bhubaneswar as a village in the Khurda sub-division, which included the village of Kapilaprasād and a part of Bargad.[91] Its boundary, "extended from Rāmeśwar temple on the north to the Kapileśwar temple on the south, and from the District Board bungalow on the west to the Brahmeśwar temple on the east".[92] According to the census of 1901, its population was 3,053, mostly dominated by the Brāhmaṇas and priests. Traditionally, however, Bhubaneswar covered a wide area from Khaṅḍācala (Khandagiri) on the west to Kuṅḍaleśvara temple near Taṇkapāni village on the east, and from Valahādevī's temple near Miyapalli Village (Nayapally) on the north to the Vahiraṅgeśvara temple at the Dhauli hills on the south. In the first decade of the 20th century, however, this wider circle was not used by the pilgrims for their circumambulation of the Kṣetra.

In 1908, the area of Bhubaneswar was 3½ square miles with length of 2 miles and a breadth of 1¾ miles.[93] It had a dispensary, Middle English School, Police Outpost, Post Office, Kanungo's Office and two bungalows one each of the District Board and the Public Works Department. As usual, the pilgrims visited Bhubaneswar on their way back from Puri, but more frequently they also chose it as their exclusive destination. The Liṅgarāja temple had an office near the temple. There were also a few lodging houses in Bhubaneswar.

BHUBANESWAR: THE NEW CAPITAL OF ORISSA

On April 1, 1936 Orissa became a separate province. Its capital was Cuttack. From 1936 to 1946 attempt was made to select a suitable site for the provincial capital. In 1946, H.K. Mahtab, the then premier of Orissa decided that, "the best place for the capital from all points of view should be Bhubaneswar."[94] On September 30, 1946 a motion was moved in the Assembly that, "the capital of the province be located at Bhubaneswar and steps be taken to construct the building at the capital as early as possible".[95] Mahtab explained the factors, which guided the decision of the

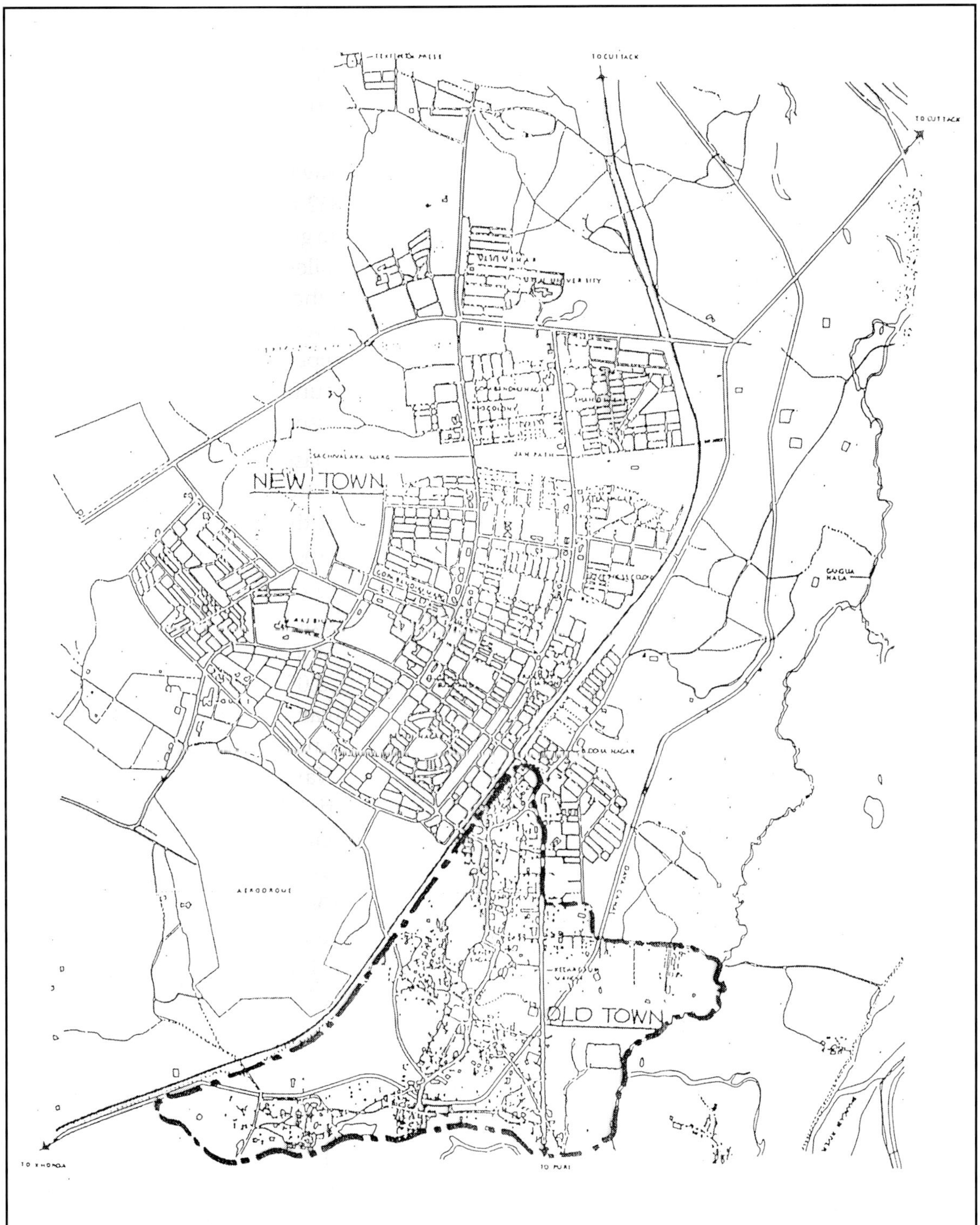

Fig. 3. Bhubaneswar: Old Town and the New Capital.

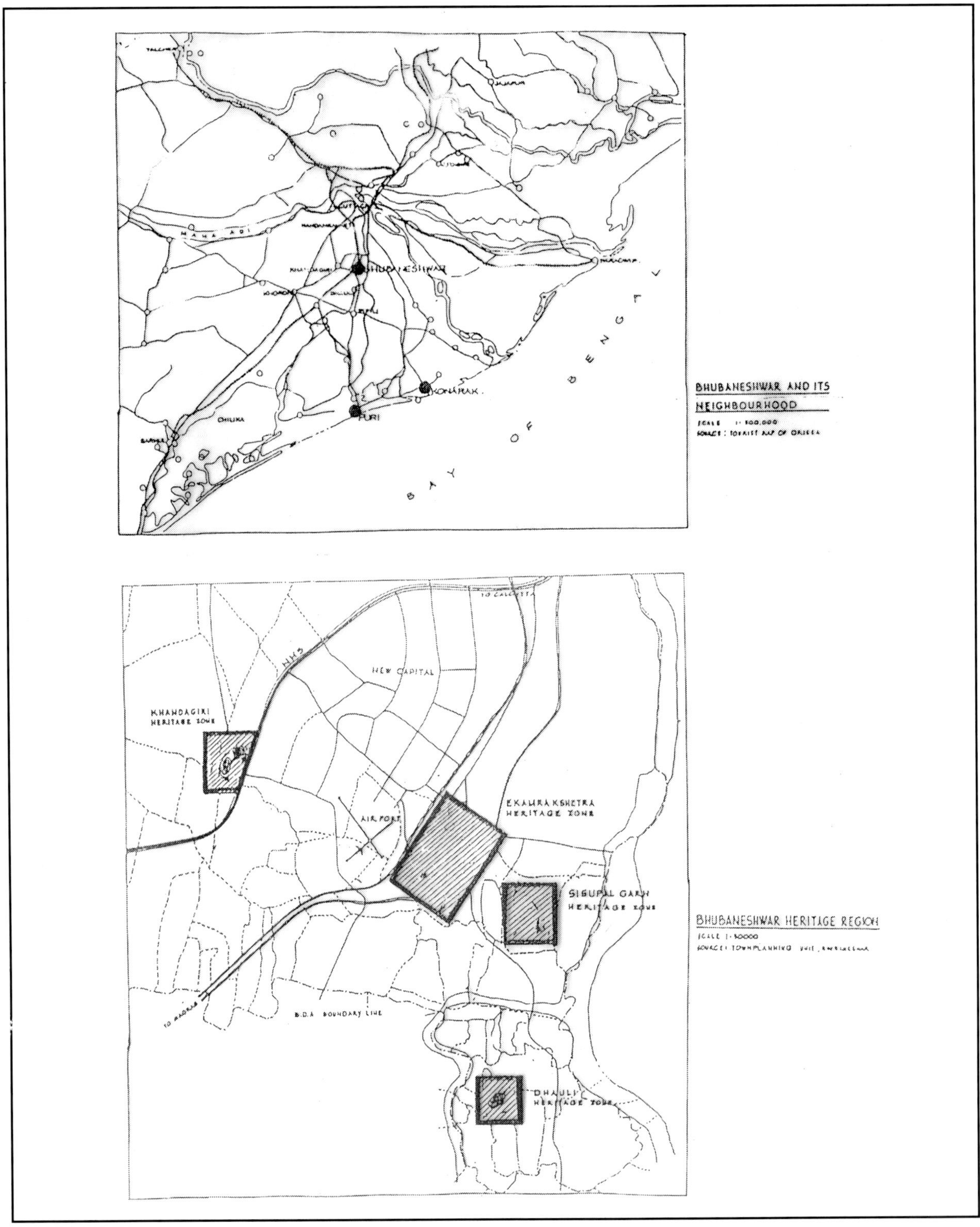

Fig. 4. Bhubaneswar: Heritage Zone.

government. Among others, the reasons for the decision were availability of plenty of wasteland and uncultivated land, buildings constructed during the Second World War, construction of highway and bridges linking Bhubaneswar, availability of building materials at a very cheap rate, the good climate of Bhubaneswar throughout the year, and above all the historical importance of the place and the monuments, which were expected to inspire the people to build a new and prosperous Orissa.[96] The resolution was passed unanimously. Mahtab moved the Central Government for funding the construction of the new capital at Bhubaneswar.

In April 13, 1948 the foundation stone for the capital city was laid by Jawaharlal Nehru. Nehru declared that the new capital "would not be a city of big buildings for officers and rich men without relation to common masses. It would accord with our idea of reducing differences between the rich and the poor". He believed that "the new city would be a place of beauty."[97]

The plan for the new capital city had been prepared by Otto H. Koenigsberger in the form of neighbourhood units combining the basic amenities of urban life and rural life with units placed in short distance to give access to the amenities. With the construction of the capital to the west of the temple town, the vacant lands became the scene of building activities. The capital site, during construction work at places yielded ancient remains. In July 1949, H.K. Mahtab wrote to Prime Minister Jawaharlal Nehru, "It is now definite that there was another capital underneath the site where the new capital is being built."[98]

In course of time the capital city came to possess official buildings and houses for the officers. The rise of a new urbanised and a secular city near a traditional temple town, led to mutual influence on each other. In the process, the old Bhubaneswar slowly lost its identity and came to possess an urban character. With the construction of big buildings, its old landscape changed and ancient monuments came to be sandwiched between modern buildings. Nevertheless, it attracted people from the new city to seek spiritual solace. On festive occasions, the temple town is filled with spiritual fervour. The growth of Bhubaneswar represents a fine balance between tradition and modernity and a fine synthesis between the old and the new. The new Bhubaneswar with its new buildings and urban character could not replace the temple town and both exist side by side, the temple symbolic of the quest for the divine and the new city symbolic of transformation into an era of science and technology.

Over the years, the capital city has grown in a haphazard manner into an amorphous city and it is not my intention here to analyse the trends and tendencies of its development. I would like to confine to a few observations as to the impact, the modern town has exerted on the old temple town. As one who has lived in Bhubaneswar for the last forty years and loved its beautiful monuments, it is disturbing to note its environmental degradation and decay of several monuments. Several temples in Bhubaneswar are neither protected by the Archaeological Survey of India nor by the State Government. Several tanks including Bindusāgara remain uncared for. The old monasteries also are in a bad shape. The civic amenities are also not on par with the modern capital city. As early as 1950 Koenigsberger, who planned the new capital, recommended that, "Old Bhubaneswar must become a self-contained town with standards of living comparable to those in the capital and that construction may take place only where it is desirable in the interest of the planned development of the capital as a whole."[99] He pleaded for uniform standards of living and amenities for the whole of Bhubaneswar, both old and new. He emphasized that the area between the Bindusāgara and the Railway Station should be properly planned, so that the temple could be linked with the development of the whole capital area.

The Ford Foundation Group, which assessed the development of Bhubaneswar in 1958, recommended, among others, that a physical separation should be maintained between the old and new Bhubaneswar. In 1989 the INTACH made a noble attempt to prepare a comprehensive report on the preservation of the Heritage of the Ekāmra Kṣetra. The study recommended that the temple town should be declared as a "Heritage Zone". The Liṅgarāja temple in the old town should constitute the core of the Zone, but the Dhauli hill, Śiśupālagarh and Khaṇḍagiri-Udayagiri hills should also be included as important landmarks of the Heritage zone.

The Ekāmra Kṣetra Heritage Project suggested, among others, the preservation of the neglected temples and prevention of expansion towards the areas of archaeological importance. It recommended the redevelopment of the environs of the Liṅgarāja and the Bindusāgara. This core Zone is to be free from vehicular traffic, while permitting access to various parts of the temple town. The basic facilities, such as adequate water supply, lighting arrangements, parking places, effective sewage disposal system, etc. should be provided for the benefit of the people. Bhubaneswar should be developed as a tourist centre with emphasis on "Heritage Tourism" with adequate facilities for the tourists.

The valuable suggestions of the report have not yet been implemented. Hence, there is need for an imaginative master plan and architectural design of the old town. This requires vision and deep respect for this historic city. The old Bhubaneswar should retain an identity of its own. Any plan on Bhubaneswar should have the Liṅgarāja temple as its focus and it should continue to dominate the skyline of the city as the proud symbol of Orissa's glorious past.

NOTES AND REFERENCES

1. *Orissa Legislative Assembly Proceedings*, Vol. II, 1946, p. 963.
2. *Svarṇādri Mahodaya*, Chapter-I, 28-29.
3. *Ekāmra Candrikā*, Chapter-I, 19-20:

   एकाम्रकवनं श्रीमत् क्षेत्राणां उत्तमं वरं।
   खण्ड़ाचलं समासाद्य यत्रास्ते कुण्डलेश्वर:।।

   आसाद्य वलाहां देवीं बहिर्ङ्गेश्वरावधि।
   क्षेत्रं एतत् समादिष्टम् चक्राकारं मुने।।
4. *Ancient India*, Bulletin of the Archaeological Survey of India, No. 5, 1949, pp. 62-105.
5. B.M. Barua, *Old Brahmi Inscriptions*, pp. 7-30.
6. K.C. Panigrahi, *History of Orissa*, pp. 39-42.
7. K.C. Panigrahi, *Archaeological Remains at Bhubaneswar*, Fig. 2.
8. *Ibid.*, Fig. 4.
9. *Ibid.*, Fig. 7.
10. *Ibid.*, Fig. 1.
11. *Ibid.*, Fig. 3.
12. *Epigraphia Indica*, Vol. IX, pp. 285ff.
13. *Ibid.*, Vol. XXVIII, pp. 331ff.
14. *OHRJ*, Vol. XIII, pp. 1-14.

15. *JASB,* Vol. VII, pp. 557-562.
16. *Epigraphia Indica,* Vol. XIII, pp. 150ff.
17. *JASB,* Vol. LXII, 1893.
18. S.N. Rajaguru, *Inscriptions of Orissa,* Vol. III, Part-I, p. 67.
19. S. Tripathy, "Ekāmra-Bhubansvara", *OHRJ,* Vol. XXXIII, 1987, p. 149.
20. A.B. Mohanty (ed.), *Sāraḷā Mahābhārata* (Oriya), *Vanaparva,* Part-II, pp. 80-97.
21. D.C. Sircar, *Studies in the Geography of Ancient and Medieval India,* pp. 75ff.
22. *Matsya Purāṇa,* Chapter-13, 26-53.
23. *Ekāmra Purāṇa,* Chapter-36, 46.
24. *Brahma Purāṇa,* See Appendix-A.
25. *Śiva Purāṇa, Umā Saṁhitā,* Chapter-44, 60-73.
26. *Śiva Purāṇa, Koṭirudra Saṁhitā,* Chapter-17.
27. *Śiva Purāṇa (Uttara Khaṇḍa),* Chapter-III, XXVI, XXVII, XXVIII and XXX.
28. *Ekāmra Purāṇa,* by U.N. Dhal, Delhi, 1986.
29. *Ekāmra Candrikā* (Oriya), Kedarnath Gaveshana Pratisthan, Bhubaneswar, 1995.
30. *Svarṇādri Mahodaya,* by Ratnakara Gargabatu, Calcutta, 1912.
31. R.C. Hazra, "The Ekāmra Purāṇa – A Work of Orissa", *Poona Orientalist,* Vol. XVI, Nos. 1-4, pp. 70-76.
32. K.C. Panigrahi, *Archaeological Remains at Bhubaneswar,* Cuttack, 1981, pp. 22-23.
33. *Ekāmra Purāṇa,* Chapter-42.
34. *Kapila Saṁhitā,* Chapters-10-19; also see *Kapila Purānam,* Chapter-10-19.
35. *Tīrthacintāmaṇi* of Vācaspati Miśra, ed. by K. Smrititirtha, *Bibliotheca Indica,* No. 1256, Calcutta, 1912.
36. *Sāralā Mahābhārata* (Oriya), *Vanaparva,* ed. by A.B. Mohanty, Part-II, pp. 80-97.
37. K.S. Behera, "The Evolution of Śakti Cult at Jajpur, Bhubaneswar and Puri", in *The Sakti Cult and Tara,* ed. by D.C. Sircar, Calcutta, 1967, pp. 74-86.
38. T.E. Donaldson, "Bhubaneswar (Ekāmra Kṣetra): Temple Town and Cultural Centre", *Marg,* Vol. 52, No. 3, Mumbai, 2001, pp. 12-27.
39. *Ibid.,* p. 14.
40. *Matsya Purāṇa,* Chapter-13, 26-53.
41. *Devī Bhāgavata Purāṇa,* Chapter-7, 30, 53-102.
42. *Śiva Purāṇa (Uttara Khaṇḍa),* Chapter-30, 24-31.
43. *Ekāmra Purāṇa,* Chapter-24, 7; also see *Ekāmra Candrikā,* Chapter-1, 21.
44. *Ibid.,* Chapter-54; also see *Śiva Purāṇa,* Chapter-30; *Ekāmra Candrikā,* Chapters-5-8; *Svarṇādri Mahodaya,* Chapters-8-16.
45. *Ibid.,* Chapter-5, 6.
46. J. Gonda, *The Meaning of Sanskrit Term Āyatana,* pp. 1-79.
47. *Ekāmra Candrikā,* Chapter-5, 4-5.
48. *Ibid.,* Chapter-5, 6-33. The *Svarṇādri Mahodaya* mentions Kapila Kuṇḍa in the second *āyatana, Svarṇādri Mahodaya,* Chapter-9, 6.
49. *Ibid.,* Chapter-6, 1-27.
50. *Ibid.,* Chapter-6, 28-95; 7, 1-47.
51. *Ibid.,* Chapter-8, 1-25.
52. *Ibid.,* Chapter-8, 26-56.

53. *Ibid.*, Chapter-8, 57-93.
54. *Ibid.*, Chapter-8, 94-132.
55. *Śiva Purāṇa (Uttara Khaṇḍa)*, Chapter-30, 32-53.
56. *Ekāmra Candrikā*, Chapter-13, 69.
57. *Svarṇādri Mahodaya*, Chapter-17, 23-27.
58. *Ekāmra Candrikā*, Chapter-9, 23-28.
59. K.C. Panigrahi, *Archaeological Remains at Bhubaneswar*, Cuttack, 1981.
60. *Mādalā Pāñji* (Oriya), ed. by A. Mohanty, Utkal University, Bhubaneswar, 1940.
61. B.M. Barna, *Old Brahmi Inscriptions*, pp. 7-30.
62. T.E. Donaldson, "Bhubaneswar (Ekāmra-Kṣetra): Temple Town and Cultural Centre", *Marg*, p. 13.
63. *Ibid.*
64. *Kapiḷa Saṁhitā*, Chapter-10, 7.
65. K.C. Panigrahi, *History of Orissa*, p. 51.
66. *JRASB*, Vol. XI (1945), pp. 1-9.
67. B. Mishra, *Orissa under the Bhauma Kings*, pp. 10-11.
68. K.C. Panigrahi, *Archaeological Remains at Bhubaneswar*, p. 231.
69. *OHRJ*, Vol. XIII, pp. 1-14.
70. K.C. Panigrahi, *History of Orissa*, p. 105.
71. *JASB*, Vol. VII (1838), pp. 557-562.
72. *Mādalā Pāñji*, p. 7.
73. S.N. Rajaguru, *Inscriptions of Orissa*, Vol. III, Part-II, p. 302.
74. *Mādalā Pāñji*, p. 43.
75. M.M. Chakravarti, *JASB*, Vol. LXII, 1893.
76. S. Tripathy, *Navajīvana* (Oriya), No. 9, 1970, pp. 563ff.
77. K.B. Tripathy, *The Evolution of Oriya Language and Script*, 1962, pp. 293-294.
78. B.B. Majumdar, *Caitanya Cariter Upādān* (Bengali), Calcutta, 1959, p. 354.
79. A. Stirling, "Religion, Antiquities, Temples and Civil Architecture", in *A History of Orissa*, ed. by N.K. Sahu, Vol. II, Delhi, 1980, p. 266.
80. A. Stirling, "An Account: Geographyical Statistical and Historical of Orissa Proper or Cuttack", *Asiatic Researches*, Vol. XV, 1825, pp. 326-333.
81. A. Stirling, "Religion, Antiquities, Temples and Civil Architecture", *op. cit.*, p. 267.
82. James Fergusson, *Picturesque Illustrations of Ancient Architecture in Hindostan*, London, 1847, p. 24.
83. William F.B. Lourie, *Orissa: The Garden of Superstition and Idolatry*, London, 1850, pp. 113-114.
84. *Ibid.*, p. 118.
85. Rajendra Lala Mitra, *Antiquities of Orissa*, Vol. II, Calcutta, 1961, p. 99.
86. *Ibid.*
87. *Ibid.*, p. 100.
88. *Ibid.*, p. 101.
89. *Ibid.*, p. 102.
90. *Ibid.*
91. L.S.S. O'Malley, *Puri: A Gazetteer*, New Delhi, 1984, p. 234.
92. *Ibid.*

93. *Ibid.*
94. K.M. Patra and Bandita Devi, *An Advanced History of Orissa (Modern period)*, Ludhiana, 1983, p. 319.
95. *Orissa Lagislative Assembly Proceedings*, Vol. II, 1946, p. 963.
96. K.M. Patra and Bandita Devi, *op. cit.*, p. 319.
97. *Hindustan Standard*, Calcutta, April 14, 1948, quoted by Ravi Kalia, in *Bhubaneswar: From a Temple Town to a Capital City*, p. 157.
98. Quoted by Ravi Kalia, in *Bhubaneswar: From a Temple Town to a Capital City*, p. 156.
99. *Ibid.*, p. 164.

II

THE MAIN TEMPLE COMPLEX OF LIṄGARĀJA

The main temple complex consists of a sanctuary (*deula*), porch (*jagamohana),* hall of dance (*nāṭa-mandira*), and hall of offering (*bhoga-maṇḍapa*). The sanctuary and the porch were integral parts of one architectural scheme, while the other two structures were later additions. The sanctuary is a fully developed Orissan *rekhā* temple and its attached porch is a *pīḍha* temple with its superstructure in the form of a stepped pyramid in two tiers (Pls. 1-10).

DEULA (Pls. 11-60)

Bāḍa: The *deula* rises from the ground and it is not built over a low *piṭha.* The *bāḍa* is *pañca-ratha* on plan and has five horizontal mouldings namely, *pābhāga,* lower *jaṅghā, bandhanā,* upper *jaṅghā* and *varaṇḍa.*

Pābhāga: The *pābhāga* of the *kanikā* and *anuratha* of the *bāḍa* have five mouldings, i.e., *khura, kumbha, paṭṭa, kaṇi,* and *basanta*. The *khura,* i.e., the bottom moulding, is carved with *vajra-muṇḍi* with its niche containing figures and scenes in the centre with flanking female figures. The *khurā* niche is crowned by a *vajramuṇḍi* design. The plain *kumbha* is relieved with ornate *campaka*-leaf design and scrollwork. The *paṭṭa* has scrollwork and the *kaṇi* is quite plain, while the *basanta* is relieved with foliated leaf. The *paṭṭa, kaṇi* and *basanta* are joined at intervals by vertical bands carved with female figures, placed one above the other or *mithuna* figures.

Lower *Jaṅghā:* The lower *jaṅghā* of the *kanikā* and *anuratha* contain a *khākharā-muṇḍi.* These *khākharā-muṇḍi,* instead of being formed of a series of horizontal mouldings, have a prominent *khākharā* design. The *muhanti* of the *khākharā-muṇḍi* is carved with scrollwork. The upper portion is relieved with *caitya*-window design. The niches of the *khākharā-muṇḍi* have flanking vertical bands relieved with scrollwork enclosing in their foils human and animal figures. The lintel of the *khākharā-muṇḍi* contains figures of Sarasvatī, Gaṇeśa and *bhāra rakṣakas.*

The niches of the *khākharā-muṇḍis* in the *kanika* contain seated *dikpālas*. They are Indra (east), Agni (south-east), Yama (south), Nirṛti (south-west), Varuṇa (west), Vāyu, (north-west), Kubera (north), and Īśāna (north-east). In the intermediary niches there are various scenes, such as royal figure holding a copper-plate, a group of figures in front of a woman, scene of Śiva's marriage and others.

The recesses between the *rathas* are filled with large *viḍālas* of various types: as lions shown rampant on elephants, some of them with body of the lion and having elephant trunks rampant over a human figure.

Bandhanā: The *bandhanā* is made of three mouldings, connected at intervals by vertical bands relieved with *mithuna* in the *kanika* and *caitya*-window motif connecting the two upper mouldings on the *anuratha.*

Upper *Jaṅghā:* The upper *jaṅghā* of the *kanika* and *anuratha* closely follow the lower *jaṅghā,* but in place of *khākharā-muṇḍis,* there are *pīḍha-muṇḍis.* The niches of the *pīḍha-muṇḍis* of the upper *jaṅghā* contain divinities, such as Śiva, Ardhanārīśvara, Pārvatī, Kārttikeya, Gaṇeśa, etc. In place of the *viḍālas* of the lower *jaṅghā,* the recesses in the upper *jaṅghā,* there are female figures or *alasa kanyās* in various poses.

Varaṇḍa: The *varaṇḍa* is composed of ten mouldings, all ornately carved with scrollwork, foliated leaf and friezes depicting animal figures, human figures, etc. The *varaṇḍa* mouldings provided a base for the soaring *gaṇḍi* without separating it from the *bāḍa.* In the local *śilpa śāstras,* the ten mouldings have their characteristic names and decorations, such as *khura, pheṇi, noli, paṭṭa, basanta,* etc.

Rāhā: The *rāhā* maintains the *pañcakama* pattern of the *bāḍa.* The construction of porches, locally called *niśā-deula,* in front of the *pārśva-devatā* images have partly obscured the layout of the *bāḍa* on the side faces of the *rāhā.* The *rāhā* of the *bāḍa* contains chlorite images of *pārśva-devatās,* Gaṇeśa in the south, Kārttikeya in the west, and Pārvatī in the north. The pyramidal porches in front of them are clearly later additions. The flanking pilasters of the *pārśva-devatā* images are carved with miniature *pārśva-devatās,* female figures, *mithuna* figures, etc. The niches below the *varaṇḍa* contain beautiful manifestations of Śiva, such as Andhakāsuravadha in the south, Naṭarāja in the west, Cāmuṇḍā in the north and Lakulīśa in the east. The *varaṇḍa* moulding on the *rāhā* has above it a *vajra-mastaka* motif crowned by a projecting lion.

Gaṇḍi: The curvilinear *gaṇḍi, pañca-ratha* on plan, has five *pāgās* on its four faces. The *kanika* is divided into ten *bhūmis,* each *bhūmi* surmounted by *bhūmi āmlās,* which are rounded at the corner and rectangular on the sides. The *kanika* wall is designed in two planes. The portion at the corner has been rounded and projected. The *anuratha* has a succession of four diminishing *rekhā-śikharas,* which add to the soaring quality of the *gaṇḍi.* There are also carved vertical lines, which are continued up to the top and accentuate the height. The base of the *rāhā* has a large *bho* or *vajra-*

Pl. I. Air view of the Liṅgarāja Temple.

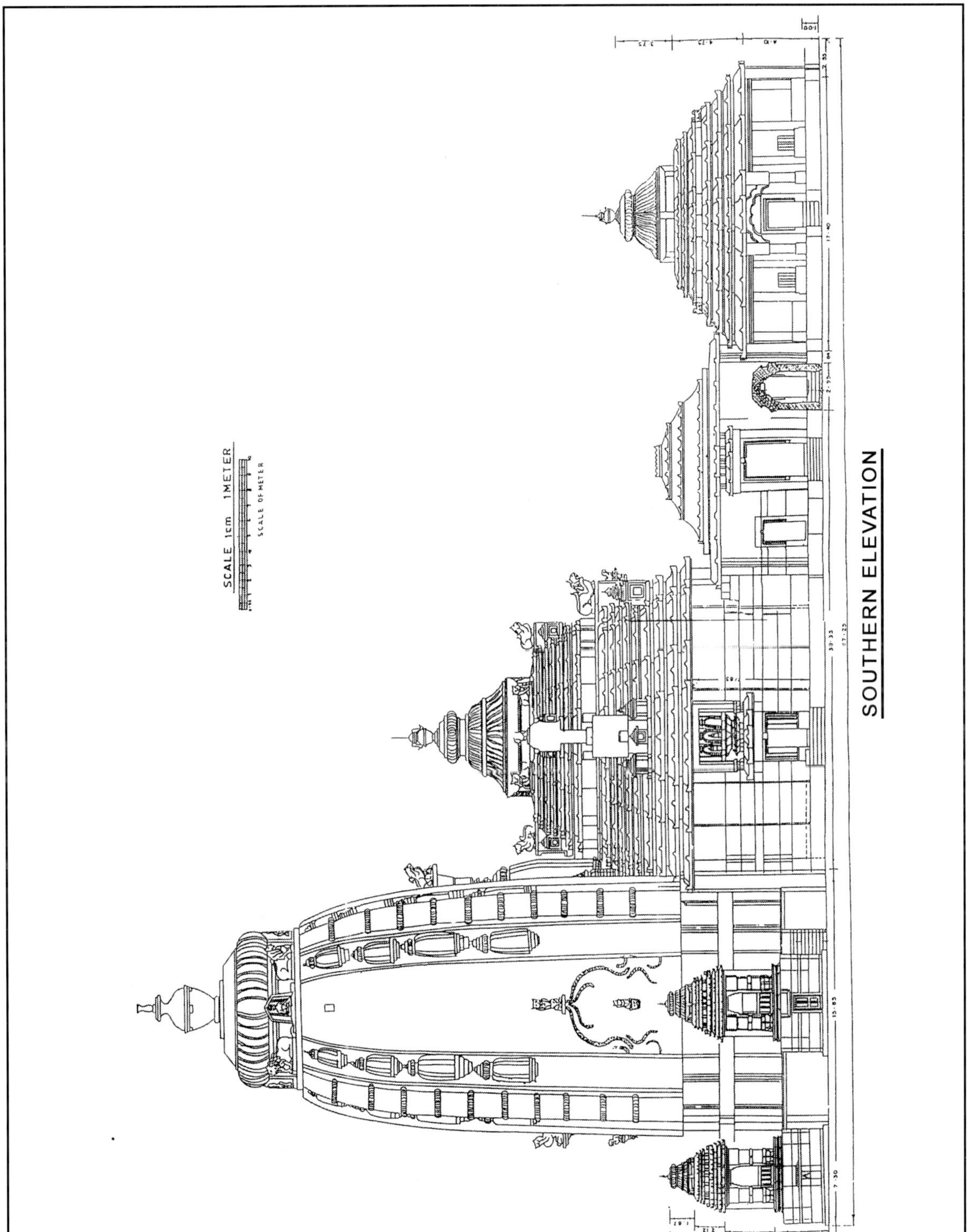

Fig. 5. Liṅgarāja Temple Complex: Southern Elevation.

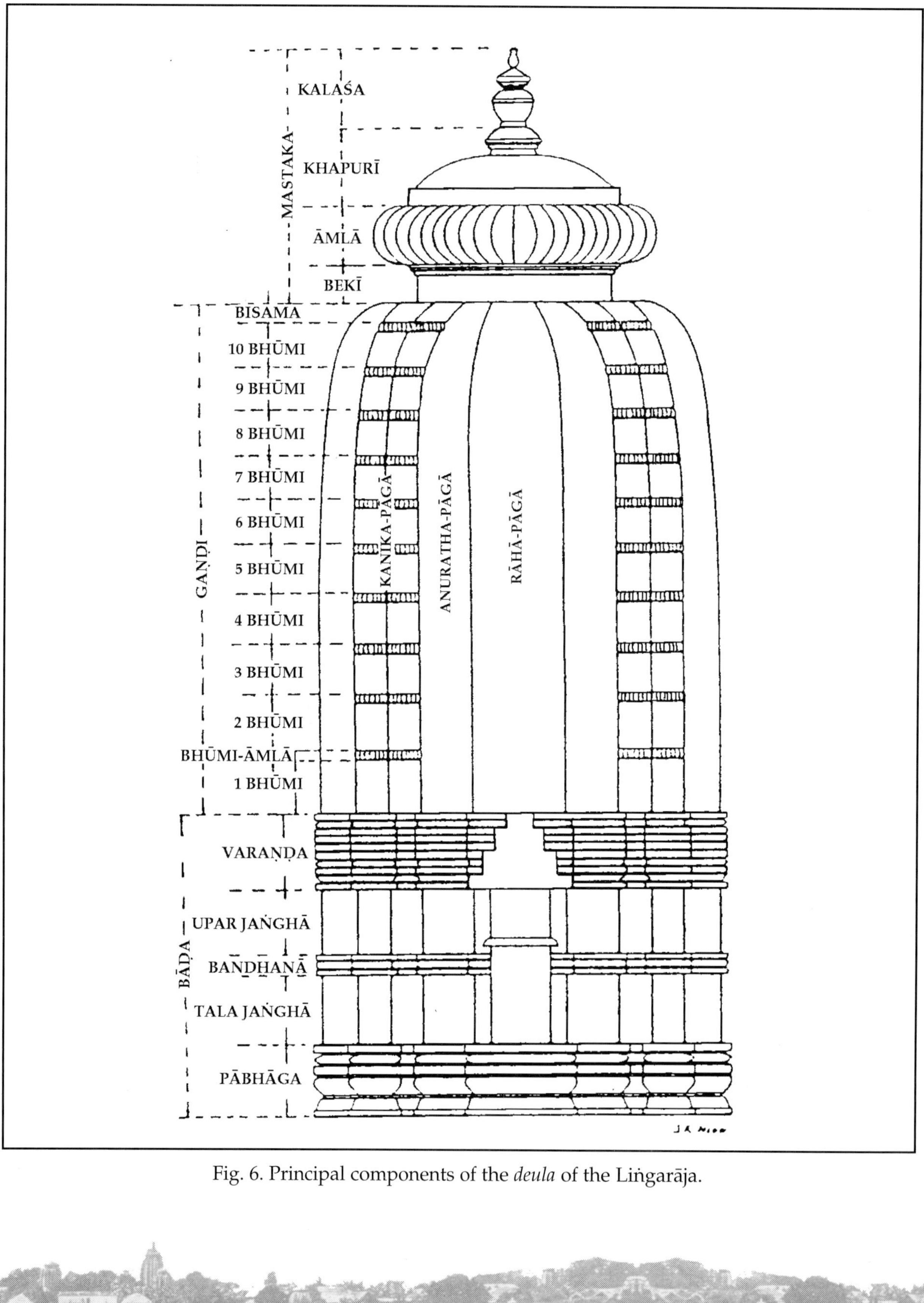

Fig. 6. Principal components of the *deula* of the Liṅgarāja.

mastaka design, which is placed above the smaller counterpart on the *varaṇḍa.* As usual, the design is flanked by *gaṇa* figures. In the centre of the design on each face, there are miniature figures of *pārśva-devatās;* Gaṇeśa on the south, Kārittikeya on the west and Pārvatī on the north. The *vajra-mastaka* is crowned with lotus and there is no *kīrtti mukha,* as at Mukteśvara temple. Above the *vajra-mastaka* occurs on each face a projecting lion rampant on an elephant. On the eastern side the *vajra-mastaka* is placed at a higher level than in other sides. The eastern *rāhā* is distinguished by a large *aṅga-śikhara* and the *vajra-mastaka* is placed above it. The decoration above the projecting lion consists of a series of *caitya*-windows. At the level of the top *bhūmi* each face of the *rāhā* has a small window. The *rāhā* has two vertical bands, which run up to the top of the *gaṇḍi.*

Mastaka: The crowning elements above the *gaṇḍi* consist of *bekī, āmlā, khapurī, kalaśa* and the *āyudha* or the emblem of the deity. The huge *āmlā* is supported by *dopicha-siṁhas* at the corners and seated figures above each *rāhā* representing forms of Śiva with trident being a characteristic feature. The seated figures are in the *padmāsana.* The eastern figure above the *rāhā* probably represents a figure of Śiva-Sūrya. Donaldson[1] believes that, "these images of the deity seated in *padmāsana* represent four aspects of Śiva, beginning with Hara/Sūrya on the east, so that the spire itself can be thought of as a *caturmukha-liṅga*". The *kalaśa* placed over the *khapurī* represents a later replacement as the original one was blown down in 1900. The *āyudha* on the top represents the emblems of both Śiva and Viṣṇu, symbolic of the identification of Liṅgarāja as Hari-Hara. The height of the *deula* is 45.11 mts.

Interior: The interior of the *deula* is plain, but it has been plastered. The floor has been paved with stone slabs. There is a huge Śivaliṅga located in the middle of the *sanctum* placed over a *liṅga pīṭha,* in which there is a channel to drain out the water. Access to the *sanctum* is provided through a passage leading to the interior of the *deula.* R.D. Banerjee noticed two different door frames of different sizes for which he believed that the *deula* and *jagamohana* were not built at the same time. The door frame on the eastern side is not lavishly carved like the chlorite door frame of the *jagamohana.* The base of the jambs contains figures of Śaivite *dvārapālas* and images of Gaṅgā and Yamunā.

Pārśva-devatā Shrines: The *pārśva-devatās* of the temple have a porch in front of each of them. The image is separated from the porch by a narrow strip. The *pārśva-devatā* porches are planned as full fledged *pīḍha* temples with *pīḍhas* arranged in two *poṭalas.* However, these are not integral parts of the original scheme, but are later additions. The super structure is supported by four pilasters in the corners. The base of the *pīḍha* temple is designed with *pābhāga, jaṅghā* and *varaṇḍa.* The inner room of the western complex is used as a *sanctum* for Jagannātha. The northern one serves as a drain being connected with the *sanctum sanctorum.* The inner cell of the southern complex serves as a subsidiary chamber. The pyramidal porches are approached by a flight of steps, which cover a part of the *pābhāga* of the *deula.*

JAGAMOHANA (Pls. 61-82)

The *jagamohana* (height 28.96 mts), is *pañca-ratha* on plan and it rises abruptly from the ground like the *deula.* The *bāḍa* closely follows the *deula* in its decorative programme. The *bāḍa* has five divisions. Its *pābhāga* consists of a series of five mouldings: *khura, kuṁbha, paṭṭa, kaṇi,* and *basanta.* The *jaṅghā* has been divided into two parts by a *bandhanā* composed of seven mouldings, at intervals connected

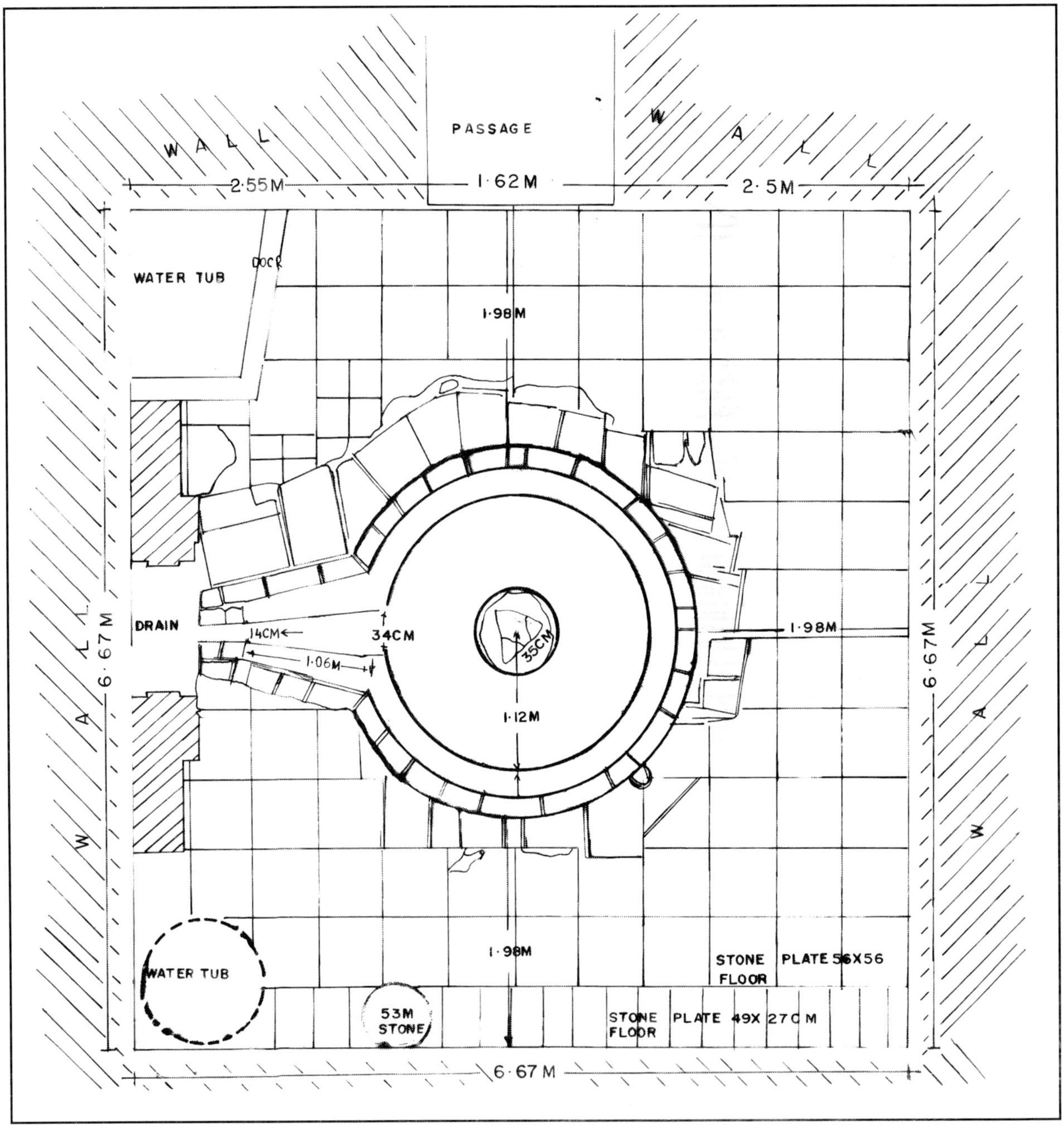

Fig. 7. Position of the Śivaliṅga in the interior of the *deula*.

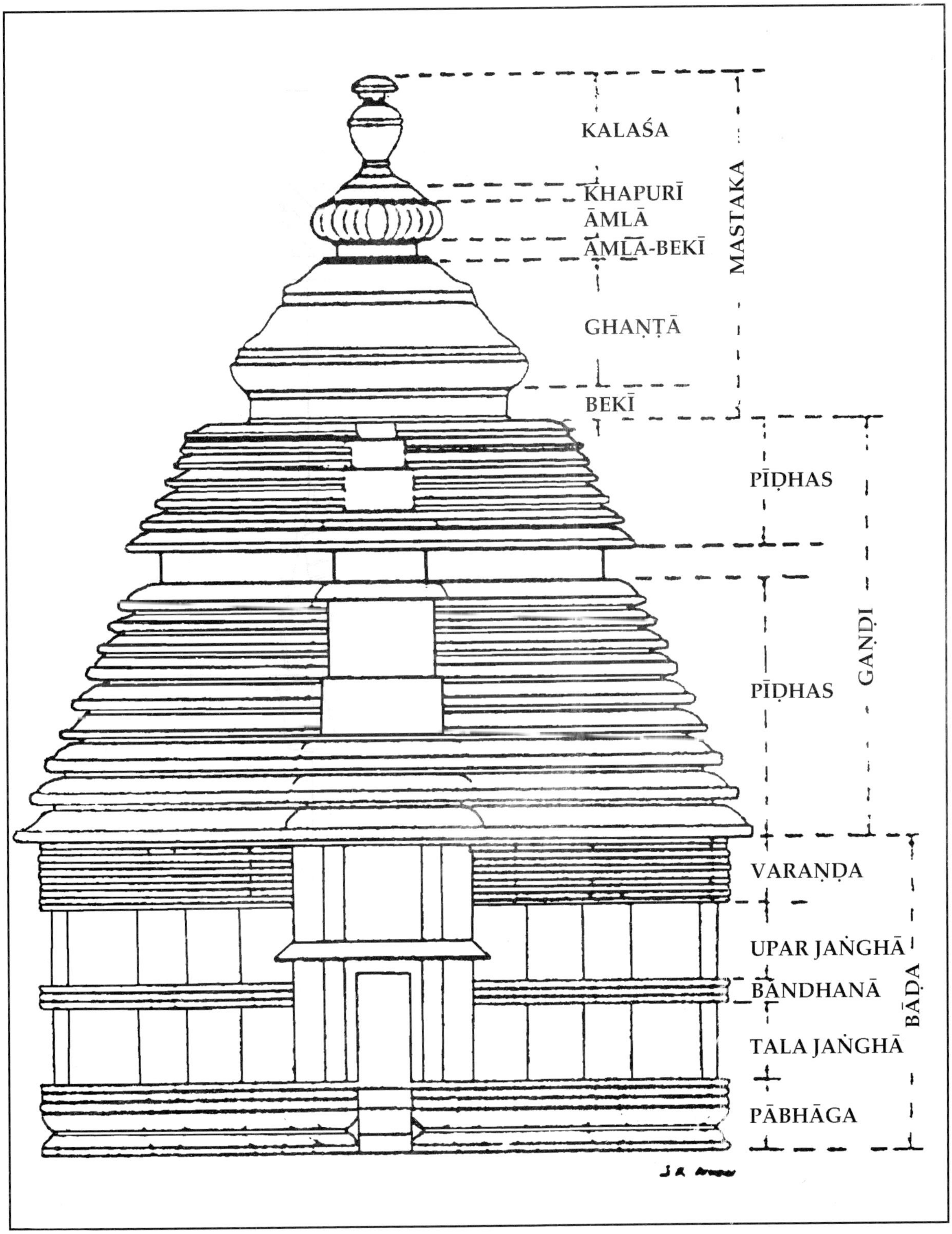

Fig. 8. Principal components of the *jagamohana* of the Liṅgarāja.

by vertical bands relieved with erotic couples. The lower *jaṅghā* contains *khākharā-muṇḍis* with a pilaster on either side. Th *khākharā-muṇḍis* carry the *bho*-motif on the central facet. In the niches are various figures and divinities, but *dikpāla* figure has not been depicted. In the recess between the *rathas* are rampant *vidālas.* These figures are depicted as lions shown rampant on elephants, while others are fashioned as hybrid figures, combining bodies of the lion and head of an elephant, standing over a human figure. The design of the upper *jaṅghā* duplicates that of the lower, but in place of *khākharā-muṇḍis, pīḍha-muṇḍis* have been inserted. Each *pīḍha-muṇḍi* consists of three *pīḍha* mouldings crowned by an *āmlā.* The niches of the *pīḍha-muṇḍis* are filled with cult icons and other figures. As in the lower *jaṅghā,* there are flanking pilasters on the either side of the *muṇḍis.* The *varaṇḍa* is made of mouldings.

The *jagamohana* originally had two balustraded windows, the one on the north is still intact. The balustraded window on the south has been converted into a door, probably when the *nāṭa-mandira* was added. As the eastern entrance was affected because of the erection of an additional structure in the front, a door on the south was thought of, to provide entry into the *jagamohana.* Each window had originally six balusters relieved with *alasa-kanyās* in high relief; three such balusters on the south were removed later on, when the window was converted into a door. The window is flanked on either side by *stambhas* decorated with a figure in high relief above the *pābhāga.* The *stambha* has a square capital depicted with figures of *gaṇas*. The central panel above the southern window depicts the marriage of Śiva and Pārvatī; the subject on the north side comprises a group of men in front of a preceptor. Above this, both on the south and north, there are three miniature *rekhā* temples separated from each other by an *alasa-kanyā,* but at each end, there is a male figure. This motif, though of inferior workmanship, also occurs above the side doors of the *nāṭa-mandira.*

The pyramidal *gaṇḍi* is in two tiers, each separated by a vertical wall known as *kaṇṭhi.* The facade of the *kaṇṭhi* is relieved with *khākharā-muṇḍis* and standing *alasa-kanyās*. In the bottom tier, there are nine gradually diminishing *pīḍhas* and in the top, there are seven *pīḍhas.* The *pīḍhas* are separated from each other by a narrow recess and have, at intervals, vertical projections called *tankus.* The vertical faces of the lower tiers are relieved with friezes representing processions of infantry, cavalry, elephants and other scenes. The *pīḍhas* in the upper tier are, however, plain. The *pīḍhas* maintain the *pañca-ratha* division of the *gaṇḍi.* Above the *ratha* of the bottom tier, at the level of the fourth moulding, there is a pediment containing a niche crowned by a projecting eave. It is flanked on the either side by *pīḍha-muṇḍis.* On the northern side, there is a scene of Śivaliṅga being worshipped by two ascetics. On the southern side, there are unidentified scenes in six panels. M.M. Ganguly[2] believed that, these represent scenes from the *Rāmāyaṇa* and the *Mahābhārata.* According to Ganguly, "the journey of the Pāṇḍavas to heaven has been depicted very faithfully. The lower right panel contains four human figures, two of which are armed with bows. The four figures represent Rāma, Lakṣmaṇa, Śitā and an attendant. Hanumāna and Bibhīṣana are walking in front. This scene probably refers to the release of Sītā from her captivity".[3] The *pīḍha,* in each *poṭala* in the *rāhā,* is crowned by a lion placed above a *bho*-motif. The *bho*-motif represents a bold *caitya*-window crowned by a *kīrtti mukha* with flanking *gaṇa* figures. In the bottom tier the *bho*-motif is surmounted by a lion on each of the *rāhā* at the level of the *kāṇṭhi.* The projecting lion is with uplifted paws. The *bho*-motif also occurs on the upper *poṭala* above the third mouldings and it is also crowned by a projecting lion placed on the *bekī*. Thus, on each *rāhā*, there are two ornamental *bho*-designs and two projecting lions. The upper *bho*-design is less ornamental than the lower one.

The *mastaka* of the *jagamohana* consists of a *bekī*, a bell-shaped member called *śrī* or *ghaṇṭā*, a second *bekī*, *āmlā*, *khapurī* and the *kalaśa*. The massive *mastaka* is supported by lion figures on the corners of the *bekī*. The double *ghaṇṭā* is divided into two parts by a central band; both the parts are relieved with a series of long *poṭalas*. The *bekī-āmlā* contains squatting *bekī-bhairavas*.

The eastern door of the *jagamohana* has an elaborate door frame, which is made of chlorite. Each jamb is divided into three *śākhās* relieved with scrollwork in the first *śākhā*, a vertical series of *vajra-muṇḍi* and *mithuna* in the second *śākhā*. At the base of the door jamb, there are two standing female figures possibly representing Gaṅgā and Yamunā. The third *śākhā* on the right is partially survived at the base. The central lintel contains the figure of seated Lakṣmī in the niche. In the horizontal facet of the lintel, among others, are depicted flying *vidyādharas* and other divine musicians. The adjoining walls on both the sides of the door jambs contain several inscriptions, which throw light on the history of the temple. The eastern entrance is provided with a wooden door.

The interior of the *jagamohana* is without any carving on the walls. Though earlier *jagamohanas* were of astylar plan, the *jagamohana* of the Liṅgarāja has in the interior four pillars dividing the hall into a nave and two aisles. These pillars are intended to support the weight of the roof. The roof is constructed in the usual bracket fashion; each course projects beyond the other and gives the appearance of an inverted pyramid. When the dimensions become narrow, a false roof is built and lintels are placed on the pillars to provide additional support to the roof.

NĀṬA-MANDIRA AND *BHOGA-MAṆḌAPA*

In front of the *jagamohana*, in the east-west axis, there are two structures, now known as *nāṭa-mandira* and *bhoga-maṇḍapa*, which are later additions. The early Orissan temple was represented by a *deula* and *jagamohana*. Later on with the elaboration of rituals and religious practices, new structures were added to the original architectural scheme. As late as mid-11th century, the *deula* of *rekhā* style and *jagamohana* of *pīḍha* order represented the standard temple complex. In the 11th century *devadāsīs* were dedicated to temples, as known from the Brahmeśvara temple inscription. In the Brahmeśvara temple, there is no separate structure for dancing purposes. A sculptural panel of the *jagamohana* of Brahmeśvara temple represents a scene of dancing, surmounted by a miniature *pīḍha* temple.[4] This could indicate that the *jagamohana* was used for various purposes, including dancing. With *devadāsī* system becoming increasingly popular and to meet the needs of religious festivals, a festive hall or *nāṭa-mandira* was conceived. The Dirghasi Inscription proves that by the late 11th century construction of a *nāṭa-mandira* was already in vogue. The layout and architectural design of the earliest *nāṭa-mandira* of Orissa is not known, but the remains at Konarak temple and Yameśvara temple indicate that in the 13th century, *nāṭa-mandira* was constructed as a detached structure in front of the *jagamohana*. The remains at Jaleśvara temple at Kalārāhanga, Paścimeśvara temple at Amangai, Sóbhaneśvara temple at Niali indicate that the *nāṭa-mandira* represented a pillared hall with a high platform.[5] At Liṅgarāja this general layout seems to have been followed and what is now called a *bhoga-maṇḍapa* (hall of offerings), originally represented a *nāṭa-mandira* (hall of dance and music). Subsequently, when a separate banquet hall was needed

Fig. 9. *Nāṭa-mandira* of the Liṅgarāja (R.L. Mitra, 1868).

in honour of the deity, the concept of *bhoga-maṇḍapa* developed. At Liṅgarāja the pillared hall directly facing the kitchen block was converted into a *bhoga-maṇḍapa,* sometime in the 16th century. The space between the *jagamohana* and the pillared hall was connected and this connecting hall came to be known as the *nāṭa-mandira.* It was not conceived as an independent hall and seems to be compressed between two more important structures, i.e., *jagamohana* and the structure now called *bhoga-maṇḍapa.* In other words, the Liṅgarāja temple consisted of three structures, i.e., *deula, jagamohana* and a pillared hall at a short distance from the *jagamohana.* Subsequently, a festive hall, called *nāṭa-mandira,* came into existence by placing it in the same axial alignment between the *jagamohana* and the isolated structure in front of it. The decorative programme indicates that it was a later structure, erected when the temple art of Orissa considerably declined.

NĀṬA-MANDIRA (Pls. 86-87)

The present *nāṭa-mandira* stands on a *pīṭha,* which connects the *jagamohana* and the structure now called *bhoga-maṇḍapa.* The facade of this platform is planned as a *bāḍa* consisting of *pābhāga, jaṅghā* and *varaṇḍa.* This hall being 15.84 mts. square, provided ample opportunity for dance and other festivities. The exterior of the platform is not highly ornamented; the *pābhāga* and *varaṇḍa* each consisted of three mouldings. The decorations in the *jaṅghā* comprise *khākharā-muṇḍis, pīḍha-muṇḍis* and female figures. The figures inside the *muṇḍi*s represent erotic or *alasa-kanyā*s.

Over the platform rises the structure of the *nāṭa-mandira.* The base is about 15.84 mts. long and 14.63 mts. wide. There is no beam on the east and the west. The *pābhāga* consists of five mouldings *(khura, kumha, paṭa, kaṇi* and *basanta).* The lower *jaṅghā* has *khākharā-muṇḍis.* Some of the niches of the *muṇḍis* contain figures. The *khākharā-muṇḍis* are flanked by a thin pilaster on each side. In the *bandhanā* are five mouldings. The decorative programme of the upper *jaṅghā* is similar to that of the lower one. The upper *jaṅghā,* however, has *pīḍha-muṇḍis* and flanking pilasters like the lower one. Most of the *muṇḍis* in the lower and upper *jaṅghā* are plain and devoid of ornamentation. The workmanship of the carvings is poor. In the *varaṇḍa,* there are ten mouldings. The *nāṭa-mandira* can be approached from all the four sides. The doorway on the eastern side connects the *nāṭa-mandira* with the *bhoga-maṇḍapa.* The walls on the south, west and north were provided with three doors. The dimensions of the side doors are smaller than the central ones. The principal door on the west connects it with the *jagamohana.* The *nāṭa-mandira* is approached by flight of steps in the central part in the northern and southern side. The side door on the north-east has been blocked due to abutment of the Vrisava temple in this side. The side door on the south-east served the purpose of the kitchen entrance.

The principal doorway on the north and south are surmounted by *navagraha* architrave. The *navagraha* slab is further crowned by *pīḍha-muṇḍis* and figure sculptures. Over the side doors, however, there are representations of three miniature *rekhā* temples kept apart by *mithuna* figures. This decorative programme recalls the treatment over the balustraded window of the *jagamohana.* The doorframes are comparatively plain except for the *dvārapāla* figures, which are placed at the base inside the *khākharā-muṇḍis.* The central door of the north has standing figures of Viṣṇu and Śiva in keeping with the Hari-Hara cult of the temple.

The roof of the *nāṭa-mandira* is sloping and is made of four tiers of *pīḍhas,* with *tankus* at interval. The structure ends with a flat terrace surmounted by battlement of crest tiles. This type of structure is known to local *sthapatis* as the *pīḍha mohana.* Unlike the *pīḍha* temple, it has no crowning elements, such as *bekī, ghaṇṭā, āmlā, khapurī* and *kalaśa.* The architectural style is similar to the *nāṭa-mandira* of the Jagannātha temple at Puri and seems to have provided the model for the latter.

The interior of the *nāṭa-mandira* is plain. There are four large pillars in the central part, arranged in a square. Each pillar rises over a plain pedestal, being made of *pābhāga,* lower *jaṅghā, bandhanā,* upper *jaṅghā* and *varaṇḍa.* The *jaṅghās* are divided into facets and recesses. The decorative programme of the columns continue till the springing point of the corbelled arches, which support the ceiling of the *nāṭa-mandira.*

BHOGA-MAṆḌAPA (Pls. 88-89)

The present *bhoga-maṇḍapa* is the eastern most structure, erected in east-west alignment in front of Liṅgarāja. It is constructed on a *pīṭha,* which is about 18.28 mts. square and 1 mt. high. The *pīṭha* rests over a low *upana* and is *pañca-ratha* on plan. The *pīṭha* has two mouldings both at the lower and the upper portion. The intervening space is filled with *vajra-muṇḍis* and human figures. The *jaṅghā* is decorated with *pīḍha-muṇḍis* and *khākharā-muṇḍis,* flanked by pilasters. In the niches of the *muṇḍis* are human figures either seated or in standing position. In between the pilasters, there are also *mithuna* figures. The *varaṇḍa* consists of a simple moulding crowned by a frieze work depicting rows of animals and other figures. A few fragments of this moulding are plain.

The *bhoga-maṇḍapa* rises over the platform. The layout of its *bāḍa* comprises of *pābhāga,* lower *jaṅghā, bandhanā,* upper *jaṅghā* and *varaṇḍa.* The wall in the *pābhāga* position is decorated with three rectangular panels and two *khākharā-muṇḍis* placed alternately below a horizontal band on the top. The band is originally decorated with a frieze of animal and cavalry procession. The *jaṅghā* is divided into two by a *bandhanā* of three mouldings. The lower *jaṅghā* has three rectangular panels relieved with *alasa-kanyās* in high-relief and two *khākharā-muṇḍis* arranged alternately with *nāga/nāgī-stambhas* placed between each. In the *khākharā-muṇḍi* niches, there are figures, such as *dikpālas,* divinities and female figures. The layout of the upper *jaṅghā* follows the decorative programme of the lower *jaṅghā,* but the *khākharā-muṇḍis* are replaced by *pīḍha muṇḍis* and in place of *alasa-kanyās,* there are *mithuna* figures. The *varaṇḍa* consists of seven mouldings, the top moulding being relieved with hunting scenes and animal procession. The pilasters, which framed the original openings, follow the design of the *bāḍa* with a *pābhāga* of six mouldings. The *jaṅghā* is divided into two registers by a *bandhanā* of three mouldings. The central facet of the shaft is relieved with *alasa-kanyā* or *mithuna.* The *varaṇḍa* consists of seven mouldings crowned by *bhāra rakṣakas.*

On the eastern face of the *bhoga-maṇḍapa,* in addition to the central doorway, there are two plain windows on each side, with two balusters on the left and three balusters on the right side. The two windows also exist on the northern and southern side, though the doorway on the northern side is blocked by a wall. The windows in northern and southern faces contain three plain balusters. The central doorways have arches rising from the flanking pilasters on either side. The arch formation gives a unique appearance to the *bhoga-maṇḍapa.* It recalls the use of *toraṇa* or arches at Gaṅgeśvarī temple at Bayālisbāṭi in Puri District which is assigned to the mid 13th century.

The roof of the *bhoga-maṇḍapa* is of *pīḍha* type. It is divided into two *poṭalas* with four *pīḍhas* in the lower and three *pīḍhas* on the upper. The *pīḍhas* are plain. A projecting lion is placed at the top

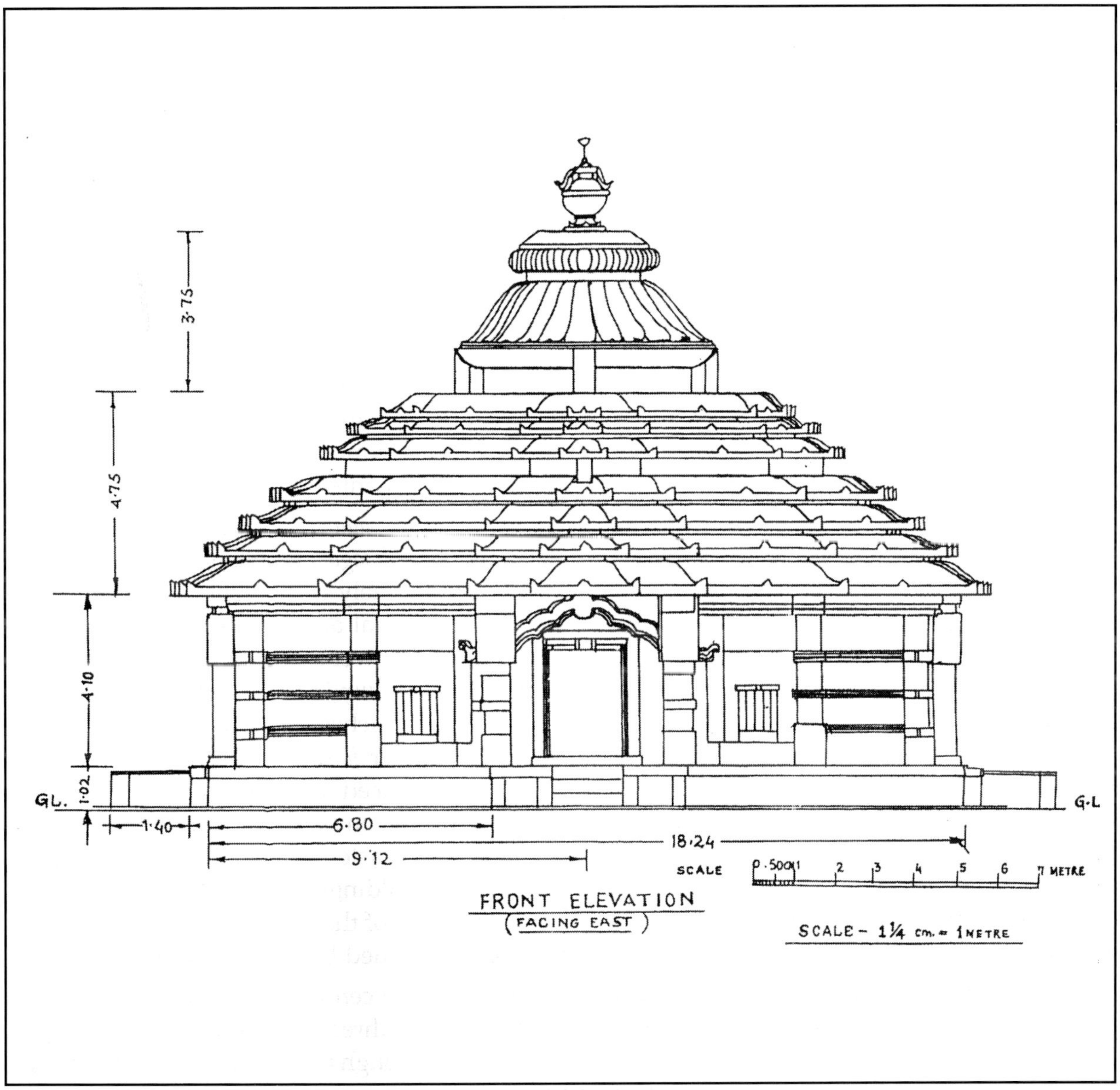

Fig. 10. *Bhoga-maṇḍapa* of the Liṅgarāja, front elevation.

of the first *poṭala,* one each in the central part of the four sides. The *mastaka* consists of a *bekī*, a bell-shaped member *(ghaṇṭā),* a second *bekī, āmlā, khapurī* and the crowning *kalaśa*. The *ghaṇṭā* is supported by lions.

The interior of the *bhoga-maṇḍapa* is approached by a flight of steps on the east and the south. On the north, there is a plain stair case consisting of three steps leading to a terrace in front of a small room, which houses the images of Lakṣmī-Nārāyaṇa. The stair cases cover a portion of the ornamented platform of the *bhoga-maṇḍapa.* In the interior of the *bhoga-maṇḍapa,* there are four large pillars, which divide the hall into a nave and two aisles. The pillars supported the massive ceiling of this structure. The structure was originally a pillared hall with openings in the four sides provided with arches. Later on, however, the openings were covered by walls. Thus the open pillared *maṇḍapa* became a closed chamber and served as the hall of offering. The pillars have five divisions of *pābhāga,* lower *jaṅghā, bandhanā,* upper *jaṅghā* and *varaṇḍa*. The *jaṅghās* are divided into facets and recesses relieved with various figures. The recesses in the lower *jaṅghā* contain lions rampant on elephants. The upper *jaṅghā* has figures of devotees, female figures, on the plain pilasters and the recesses.

VĀHANA-STAMBHA

At the end of the eastern stair case and in front of the *bhoga-maṇḍapa,* there is a monolithic free-standing pillar, *vāhana-stambha,* with couchant Vṛṣabha (bull) and figure of Garuḍa in kneeling posture. The pillar is 60 cms. in diameter and 6.09 mts. high. It has a square plinth at the base without any moulding. The pillar, however, is quite plain. This *vāhana-stambha* seems to have been erected at a later date and stylistically, it is no match to the *aruṇa-stambha* of the Sun temple of Konarak, which now stands in front of the *Siṁha-dvāra* of the Jagannātha temple, Puri. The workmanship of the pillar being quite inferior, it was erected at a time of the decline of artistic tradition.

BUILDER AND TIME OF CONSTRUCTION

The construction of a temple for Tribhuvaneśvara or Liṅgarāja is recorded in the traditions of the *Kṣetra Māhātmyas*, such as *Ekāmra Purāṇa, Svarṇādri Mahodaya* and *Kapila Saṁhitā*. The *Ekāmra Purāṇa,*[6] which is the earliest of these texts, records at different places that Candra, variously called Candramā and Śaśāṅka, is credited with the establishment of the *liṅgam* of Tribhuvaneśvara and construction of a temple in his honour. In Chapter 13, it says:

> "With the coming of the Kali Age, Candra will go to the earth and having become the lord of men, he will worship the *liṅgam.*"
>
> "He, who is of good determination, will cause a beautiful, white and purifying stone temple to be erected and a great worship performed."
>
> "He, who is famous, well-known, and engaged in the daily worship of Śiva, will establish this *liṅgaṁ* of Tribhuvaneśvara in accordance with my command."
>
> "O Brāhmaṇa, you know me to be this stone *liṅgam* that can neither be seen nor touched."
>
> "Śaśāṅka with his heart attached to Śiva, will be infinitely intelligent and will worship with diligence all the *liṅgams* that exist on the earth."

Pl. 1. Liṅgarāja Temple with the compound wall.

Pl. 2. Liṅgarāja Temple with the entrance porch, east.

Pl. 3. Air view of Liṅgarāja and Bindusāgara.

Pl. 4. Liṅgarāja Temple, view from Bindusāgara (R.L. Mitra, 1868).

Pl. 5. Liṅgarāja Temple from the north-east.

Pl. 6. Liṅgarāja Temple from the south-east.

Pl. 7. Liṅgarāja Temple from the north.

Pl. 8. Liṅgarāja Temple from the south.

Pl. 9. Liṅgarāja Temple from the west.

Pl. 12. Liṅgarāja: *pābhāga* details.

Pl. 10. Liṅgarāja Temple, view from the west with Parśvadevatā shrines.

Pl. 13. Liṅgarāja: *bāḍa*, south-east.

Pl. 15. Liṅgarāja: *deula*, lower *jaṅghā*, south-east flank.

Pl. 14. Liṅgarāja: *bāḍa*, south-west flank.

Pl. 11. Liṅgarāja: *deula*, *pābhāga*.

Pl. 16. Liṅgarāja: *deula*, lower *jaṅghā*, south-west flank.

Pl. 17. Liṅgarāja: *deula*, upper *jaṅghā*, south.

Pl. 18. Liṅgarāja: *deula, bāḍa,* west-south flank.

Pl. 19. Liṅgarāja: *deula, bāḍa*, west-north flank.

Pl. 20. Liṅgarāja: *deula, bāḍa*, north.

Pl. 21. Liṅgarāja: *deula*, lower *jaṅghā*, west.

Pl. 22. Liṅgarāja: *deula*, upper *jaṅghā* with *pīḍha-muṇḍi*, west.

Pl. 23. Liṅgarāja: *deula*, upper *jaṅghā* with *pīḍha-muṇḍi*, south.

Pl. 24. Liṅgarāja: *deula*, lower *jaṅghā* details, north.

Pl. 25. Liṅgarāja: *deula*, details of pilaster decoration, south.

Pl. 26. Liṅgarāja: *deula*, *alasa-kanyā*, upper *jaṅghā* recess, west.

Pl. 27. Liṅgarāja: *deula*, *alasa-kanyā*, upper *jaṅghā*, details.

Pl. 28. Liṅgarāja: *deula, gaṇḍi,* details.

Pl. 31. Liṅgarāja: facial expressions of female figures.

Pl. 29. Liṅgarāja: *deula,* decorative programme of *gaṇḍi.*

Pl. 30. Liṅgarāja: *deula*, *kanyā*, upper *jaṅghā* recess, west.

Pl. 32. Liṅgarāja: facial expressions of female figures.

Pl. 33. Liṅgarāja: facial expressions of female figures.

Pl. 34. Liṅgarāja: facial expressions of female figures.

Pl. 35. Liṅgarāja: *deula, kanyā* removing anklet, upper *jaṅghā*, north.

Pl. 36. Liṅgarāja: *deula*, female figure, *ḍākinī*, upper *jaṅghā* recess, south.

Pl. 37. Liṅgarāja: *deula*, Śiva as *yogī pīḍha-muṇḍi*, west.

Pl. 38. Liṅgarāja: *deula*, female figure with *triśūḷa* and *kapāla*.

Pl. 39. Liṅgarāja: *deula*, *pāṇigrahaṇa*, *khākarā-muṇḍi*, west.

"O Vivudheśvara (Brahmā), (Śaśāṅka's) temple (Kīrtti) will endure in this world. O Pitāmaha, it is difficult (for you) to do (i.e. to construct a temple for me); (so) your efforts are useless."[7]

The same tradition is recorded in the *Ekāmra Purāṇa* (47. 122-24) as follows:

कलौ मम स्फुटं लिङ्गं प्रासादगुणवर्जितम् ।
कलावतीतपादे च महीं यास्यति चन्द्रमा ॥

शासयेत् पृथिवीभागं मद्भक्तो नान्यमानसः ।
यावत् कलिङ्गपर्यन्तं शशाङ्कः पृथिवीपतिः ॥

ममोपदेश–कर्तासौ प्रासादं रुचिरं पृथुम् ।
श्रुत्वा देवेरितं सम्यक् श्रृतास्ते मुनिपुङ्गवाः ॥

"When one quarter of the Kali Age has passed away, Candramā will go to the earth."

"My devotee Śaśāṅka, the lord of the earth, with his mind fixed on none (except in me), will rule a portion of the earth extending up to Kaliṅga."

"According to my command, he will construct a massive and beautiful temple, hearing the voice of the gods. O the best of ascetics, you have (now) heard (this all) well."[8]

In Chapter 50 the story is told that Rāma during his visit to Ekāmra, wanted to construct a temple in honour of Śiva, but Vasiṣṭha advised him not to do that as "the past tradition is that Śaśāṅka will cause it to be done."[9] Chapter-61 also contains the statement that it will be done by Śaśāṅka (*Śaśāṅka kārayıṣyati*).[10] In Chapter-65, the construction of the temple is attributed to Candra, dropped down from the crown of Śiva (*lalāṭacandr vai bhrasta* ...). He worshipped the *liṅga* of Tribhuvaneśvara and by calling Viśvakarmā, King Candramā constructed the temple (*prāsādaṁ kārayiṣyati*).[11]

The tradition of the *Ekāmra Purāṇa* is repeated in the *Svarṇādrī Mahodaya, Ekāmra Candrikā* and the *Kapila Saṁhitā.* In the *Svarṇādri Mahodaya,* it is told that Brahmā wanted to build the temple (*Mandira*) of Bhubaneśa, but he was advised that it will not be done by him, "in the Kali Age Candra will do it" (*candra kariṣyati*).[12] The same statement is recorded in the *Ekāmra Candrikā* as follows: Śiva advised Bhīma, "Do not build the temple here; in the Kali Age Candra will do it" (*nātra prāsādakartāsi kalau candrah kāraiṣyati*).[13]

In the *Kapila Saṁhitā* Lord Tribhuvaneśvara refused the request of Himavat to construct a temple and told him, "Why have you asked for a thing which was not available to the gods such as Brahmā, Viṣṇu, Indra, Yama and Varuṇa? The temple (of mine) is impossible to be consturcted; in the Kali Age Candra will do it."[14]

K.C. Panigrahi identified Candra of the above-mentioned texts with Śaśāṅka, the king of Gauḍa. He believed that the earliest temple of Tribhuvaneśvara-Liṅgarāja was built by Śaśāṅka[15] in the 7th century.

In absence of corroborative evidence, we are not in a position however to accept his suggestion. The existence of a temple in the 7th century is probable but there is no conclusive evidence to connect it with Śaśāṅka. The tradition recorded in the *Sthala Māhātmyas* refers to Candra, who came to the earth being fallen from the crown of Śiva. This Candramā may be taken to be a king of the Somavaṁśī dynasty of Orissa.

The historical traditions of the *Mādalā Pāñji* refer to Lalāṭendu Kesarī as the builder of the temple of Krittivāsa. The statement runs as follows:

गजाष्टेषु मिते जाते शकाब्दे कृत्तिवाससः।
प्रासादं कारयामास ललाटेन्दु केसरी॥

In other words, the temple of Krittivāsa or Liṅgarāja was built by Lalāṭendu Kesarī in the Śaka year 588 (AD 666). R.P. Chanda was informed by an old Brāhmaṇa Pandit of Bhubaneswar that, "on a stone near the summit of the spire of the Liṅgarāja is engraved a stanza which says that the temple was built by Rājā Lalāṭendu Kesarī in the Śaka year 588 (AD 666)".[16] In reality no such stanza is inscribed on the top of the Liṅgarāja temple. This floating verse of uncertain origin, attributed to the *Mādalā Pāñji*, is to be found as early as 1807 in the *Journal of the Surveyor General Col. R.H. Colebrooke*.[17] Though the Sanskrit verse is not found in the Oriya version of the *Mādalā Pāñji*[18] the consecration of the Bhubaneswar temple is attributed to Śaka year 588 by Lalāṭa Kesarī. The Sanskrit versions of the texts, such as *Kaṭaka Rājavaṁśāvalī*[19] and the *Oḍra deśa Rājavaṁśāvalī* quote this stanza.

The construction of the temple by Lalāṭendu Kesarī reminds us the statement of the *Ekāmra Purāṇa* that in Kali Age Candra (moon) will go down to earth being fallen from the *lalāṭa* of Śiva and will construct the temple. U.N. Sarkar connects this couplet with the *Ekāmara Purāṇa* and remarks that, "Śiva is figured with a moon on its forehead; and the words *lalāṭa* and *Kesarī*, which form the Prince's name, signify forehead and lion, and this last term is used in Sanskrit for a superlative import."[20]

The *Śiva Purāṇa (Uttara Khaṇḍa)* refers to Śiva as Candra Śekhara.[21] Thus Candramā, of the *Ekāmra Purāṇa*, who built the temple of Śiva, may be considered identical with Lalāṭendu Kesarī and not King Śaśāṅka as believed by Dr. Panigrahi.

The *Mādalā Pāñji* contains conflicting statements regarding the construction of the Bhubaneswar temple. It is said to have been founded by Yayāti Kesarī. The construction is also attributed to Ananta Kesarī and finally it was consecrated by Lalāṭa Kesarī.[22] Thus three rulers were connected with this temple; Yayāti Kesarī laid the foundation, Ananta Kesarī continued the construction and Lalāṭa Kesarī or Lalāṭendu Kesarī completed it.[23] The *Mādalā Pāñji* further mentions a ruler called Surya Kesarī, before Ananta Kesarī, who was also associated with the construction of the Bhubaneswar temple[24] or K.C. Panigrahi is inclined to reject the name of Surya Kesarī on the ground that majority of the versions refer to three generations of kings as the builders of temple.[25] The legend about the construction of the temple by Lalāṭendu Kesarī follows the Shastrik injunction of the *Ekāmra Purāṇa.*

The *Mādalā Pāñji* mentions the Kesarī kings. But in inscriptions, the dynasty is said to have belonged to the Somakula. The inscription gives a very reliable genealogy[26] from Śivagupta to Karṇa. The only ruler bearing the Kesarī title is Uddyota Kesarī. The last ruler Karṇa, according to the *Rāmapālacarita,*[27] Sandhyākaranandī was called Karṇa Kesarī. Some other contemporary inscriptions mention names such as Bāla Kesarī[28] and Rāma Kesarī.[29] Thus the Kesarī dynasty of the popular traditions evidently represents the Somavaṁśī dynasty of Orissa. But in this dynasty, there is no ruler called Ananta Kesarī or Lalāṭa Kesarī. One cave of Khaṇḍagiri bearing the name Lalāṭendu Kesarī Guṁphā contains inscription of the time of Uddyota Kesarī.[30] In view of this, K.C. Panigrahi[31] suggested that, Ananta Kesarī and Lalāṭa or Lalāṭendu Kesarī were the variant names of Uddyota Kesarī. The *Mādalā Pāñji*[32] refers to Yayāti Kesarī as the founder of the Bhubaneswar temple. In the Somavaṁśī dynasty, there are two rulers bearing the name Yayāti: Mahāśivagupta I Yayāti I (AD 920-955) and Mahāśivagupta III Yayāti II (AD 1022-1040). It appears that the *Mādalā Pāñji* confused the two rulers as one. K.N. Mahāpātra believed that Yayāti I constructed the Liṅgarāja temple.[33] Considering the stylistic evolution of temples at Bhubaneswar, this theory may not be accepted. On the contrary, Yayāti II may be regarded as the founder of the Liṅgarāja temple and his successor Uddyota Kesarī seems to have completed this temple. This may be accepted as a reasonable hypothesis until definite evidence comes to light. A brief reference to the historical context[34] of the period may be helpful to understand this important monument. Janamejaya I (AD 880-920) was the first important ruler of the Somavaṁśī dynasty, whose coronation took place at Suvarṇapura (modern Sonepur). He fought against the Kālacuris and tried to expand eastward by interfering in the politics of Oḍra. His successor Yayāti I (AD 920-955) achieved success in this expansionist policy. In course of time, he could establish his sway over coastal Orissa. This is evident from the fact that Yayāti could grant a village in Dakṣiṇa Toṣālī. It seems that the Bhaumakaras suffered reverse and only continued in the holy tracts of Uttara Toṣālī. His successors, such as Bhīmaratha (AD 955-975) and Dharmaratha (AD 975-995) pursued the policy of expansion. Around AD 1022 Rajendra Chola defeated Indraratha of the Somavaṁśī dynasty. Yayāti II (AD 1022-1040), however, restored the fallen fortune of the family. He freed the kingdom from the invaders and brought about the unification of Kaliṅga, Kongoda, Utkala and Kośala. In the inscription he is spoken as "self-chosen husband" of Kaliṅga, Kongoda, Utkala and Kośala. Yayāti II was evidently a very powerful ruler of the family and his fame found expression in the local traditions. He seems to have ruled for about eighteen years.

Yayāti II was followed by Mahābhavagupta IV Uddyota Kesarī (AD 1040-1065). He was a Śaiva and one of his charters bears a figure of Nandī with a crescent above it.[35] His mother Kolāvatī was also a Śaiva and built the Brahmeśvara temple at Bhubaneswar.[36] His hold over Bhubaneswar is corroborated by his inscriptions engraved in the Lalāṭendu Kesarī cave at Khaṇḍagiri. A comparison of the Brahmeśvara temple and the Liṅgarāja temple[37] in respect of architecture, sculpture and iconography suggest that the Liṅgarāja temple was a close contemporary of Brahmeśvara temple built by Kolāvatī, during the 18th regnal year of Uddyota Kesarī. It is significant that a version of the *Mādalā Pāñji* mentions Tulāvatī (Sic. Kolāvatī) as the queen of Vasukalpa Kesarī and she is said to have built the Kṛttivāsa temple, when it got dilapidated.[38]

A fragment of *Mādalā Pāñji,* erroneously listed as *Konarka Kṣetra Māhātmya* and preserved in the India Office Library, London also connects Kolāvatī with the Bhubaneśwar (Liṅgarāja) temple. Therefore, it is reasonable to assign the Liṅgarāja temple to the second-half of the 11th century. Dr. Panigrahi places the temple of Brahmeśvara in about AD 1060[39] and the date of Liṅgarāja may not be far removed from this date.

In the inner sanctuary of the Liṅgarāja there is a fragmentary inscription of the 11th century which mentions Śrī Kīrttivāsa.[40] The *jagamohana* of the Liṅgarāja temple contains an inscription of Anantavarman Choḍagaṅga of the Eastern Gaṅga dynasty, which is dated in the Śaka year 1036 (AD 1114-15).[41] Choḍagaṅga is said to have donated lamp in honour of Kīrttivāsa. Anantavarman Choḍagaṅga conquered coastal Orissa some time between AD 1108 and 1115. The inscription of Anantavarman Choḍagaṅga on the Liṅgarāja temple proves beyond doubt that it was already in existence when Choḍagaṅga visited it in AD 1114. Evidently, it belonged to the 11th century and was probably built by Yayāti II and his successor Uddyota Kesarī. The statement of the *Mādalā Pāñji* that it was built in the Śaka year 588 (AD 666) cannot be accepted as a historical fact. If, however, Kīrttivāsa is accepted as a general name of Śiva, the existence of a Śiva temple in the 7th century seems probable. The pre-existing sanctity of the Ekāmra Kṣetra and the possible existence of a shrine for Tribhuvaneśvara led to the construction of a great temple in his honour in the 11th century. Building a temple and replacing it by a new one seems to have been a regular process, which is supported by archaeological evidence as at Siddheśvara[42] and by literary traditions. According to the *Ekāmra Purāṇa* the Brahmeśvara temple was rebuilt eleven times and the Liṅgarāja temple was rebuilt thirteen times.[43]

As already mentioned, *nāṭa-mandira* and *bhoga-maṇḍapa* were later additions. The eastern most structure now called *bhoga-maṇḍapa* was planned as a detached *maṇḍapa.* There is no inscription on this *maṇḍapa* to give us an idea about its probable date. An inscription on the *jagamohana* of the Liṅgarāja temple refers to a *maṇḍapa,*[44] which served as the venue for *parva, utsava* and other rituals. The inscription belongs to the reign of Anaṅgabhimadeva III (AD 1211-1238). The exact location of the *maṇḍapa* is not known from the inscription. In all probability, the present *bhoga-maṇḍapa* represents the structure under reference. If this suggestion is accepted, this structure now popularly called *Bhoga-maṇḍapa* was built in the 13th century, though it has undergone thorough renovation. The intervening structure between the *jagamohana* and the *bhoga-maṇḍapa,* now known as the *nāṭa-mandira,* was posterior to the *bhoga-maṇḍapa.* On grounds of style it may be assigned to about 15th century.

NOTE AND REFERENCES

1. Donaldson, *Hindu Temple Art of Orissa,* Vol. I, p. 332.
2. M.M. Ganguly, *Orissa and Her Remains,* p. 355.
3. *Ibid.*
4. See K.C. Panigrahi, *Archaeological Remains at Bhubaneswar,* Fig. 81.
5. For development of *nāṭa-maṇḍapa* in Orissan temple architecture, see T. Donaldson in J.G. Williams (ed.), *Kalādarśana,* pp. 35-46.
6. *Ekāmra Purāṇa,* 13.62-67; 32.57; 47.122-124; 50.46-49; 61.24; 65.7-15.
7. *Ibid.,* 13.62-67; English translation by K.C. Panigrahi, *Archaeological Remains at Bhubaneswar,* p. 30.
8. *Ibid.,* 47.122-124; English translation by K.C. Panigrahi, *Archaeological Remains at Bhubaneswar,* p. 30.
9. *Ibid.,* 50.46-49.
10. *Ibid.,* 61.24.
11. *Ibid.,* 65.7-15.
12. *Svarṇādri Mahodaya,* 14.7-10.

13. *Ekāmra Candrikā,* 9.112.
14. *Kapila Saṁhitā,* 16.55-56; English translation by K.C. Panigrahi, *Archaeological Remains at Bhubaneswar,* p. 31.
15. K.C. Panigrahi, *Archaeological Remains at Bhubaneswar,* pp. 29-31.
16. R.P. Chanda, *Annual Report of Archaeological Survey of India-1923-24,* p. 120.
17. U.N. Sarkar, "A Historical Account of the Temples in Orissa", in *Indian Historical Records Commission,* Vol. XXXII, Part-II, Patna, 1956, pp. 87-90.
18. A.B. Mohanty, *Mādalā Pāñji* (Oriya), p. 8.
19. *Kaṭaka Rājavaṁśāvalī,* (ed.) H.K. Kulke and G.C. Tripathy, p. 11.
20. U.N. Sarkar, *op. cit.,* p. 89.
21. *Śiva Purāṇa (Uttara Khaṇḍa),* 3.33.
22. A.B. Mohanty, *op. cit.,* pp. 5-8.
23. It is interesting to note that some years ago during the first ablution of Liṅgarāja, the names of Yayāti Kesarī and Lalāṭendu Kesarī are announced, as they were the traditional builders of the Liṅgarāja temple. Vide N.K. Bose *et al.,* "Organization of Services in the Temple of Liṅgarāja", p. 86.
24. A.B. Mohanty, *op. cit.,* p. 6.
25. K.C. Panigrahi, *Archaeological Remains at Bhubaneswar,* p. 165.
26. See Appendix-E.
27. Commentary on: 2.5.
28. *OHRJ,* Vol. 18, pp. 58-59.
29. S.N. Rajaguru, *Inscriptions of Orissa,* Vol. IV, p. 353.
30. K.C. Panigrahi, *History of Orissa,* p. 131.
31. K.C. Panigrahi, *Archaeological Remains at Bhubaneswar,* p. 166.
32. A.B. Mohanty, *op. cit.,* p. 6.
33. K.N. Mahāpātra, "Temples of Bhubaneswar", in M.N. Das (ed.), *Side Lights on History and Culture of Orissa,* pp. 547-549.
34. K.C. Panigrahi, *History of Orissa,* pp. 96-120; A.M. Shastri, *Inscriptions of the Sarabhapuriyās, Paṇḍuvaṁśīns and Somavaṁśīns,* Part-I, pp. 172-222.
35. See Mahā Kosala Historical Society's Plates.
36. *JRASB,* Letters, XIII, 1947, pp. 63-73.
37. K.C. Panigrahi, *Archaeological Remains at Bhubaneswar,* p. 164.
38. A.B. Mohanty, *op. cit.,* p. 20.
39. K.C. Panigrahi, *op. cit.,* p. 101.
40. *Annual Report on Indian Epigraphy for 1977-78,* ASI, Delhi, 1986, p. 85.
41. *Epigraphia Indica,* Vol. XXX, pp. 29ff.
42. K.C. Panigrahi, *Archaeological Remains at Bhubaneswar,* p. 18
43. *Ekāmra Purāṇa,* 63. 46.
44. *Epigrahia Indica,* Vol. XXX, pp. 17ff; see also Appendix-B. The inscription is dated in the *Aṅka* year 30 of Anaṅgabhimadeva III; which corresponds to 1236 AD.

III

Architectural Features

Built in the 11th century, the Liṅgarāja temple represents a typical Orissan temple at its best. The temple is built of fine grained khandolite stone in the traditional style of Orissan architecture. The principle of construction is based on traditional technique of corbelling. In erecting the temple, stone blocks have been placed one upon the other following the stacking technique. The masonry is of the dry order and mortar has not been used. Sometimes, iron dowels have been used to keep the stones in position. The *pārśva-devatā* images have been carved out of chlorite or *muguni* stone. The architrave and door jambs are also made of such stone. Precise information is not available on the foundation of the temple with regard to the materials used, the depth of foundation, its condition, horizontal extent, surrounding zone and other related issues.

The superstructure, as already mentioned, is based on corbelling principle and its stability depends upon the individual stones. To ensure structural stability, the architects adopted the device of tying the opposite walls of the tall temple by means of *mudas* or ceiling above the *sanctum.* The Liṅgarāja temple has at least three ceilings in its internal construction. During the repairs of the temple in 1924, the internal construction of the main temple came to light. R.D. Banerjee, who was deputed by the Archaeological Survey of India, reports as follows:

After the removal of the wooden ceiling from the interior of the *vimāna* it was found to be a tall chamber with a flat roof, composed of heavy slabs laid lengthwise. Over this there was another chamber, access to which was obtained by a steep staircase built through the thickness of the side of the *śikhara*. Mr. Sanat Kumar Rai Chaudhuri, the then Executive Engineer, Cuttack Division, ascended this staircase and found the upper chamber lighted by a window. A number of men, whose duty it is to ascend the *śikhara* on certain occasions, in order to place lamps on the top of the *āmalaka* state that they can see another window of another chamber over this one, but it is not known at the present day whether there is any method of ingress into it. It is, therefore, certain that the *śikhara* of the Liṅgarāja is a hollow pyramid and its interior consists of a number of superimposed chambers, gradually decreasing in size like those of the great temple at Bodh-Gaya and Konch, near Tikari, in the Gaya district of Bihar.[1]

In Orissan *Śilpa Śāstras* different names such as *garbha-muda, ratna-muda*, etc. are used to denote these ceilings. The ceiling immediately over the *garbha-gṛha* is known as *garbha-muda*. In large temples, such as the Jagannātha temple Purī the same system of *mudas* is followed. In the construction of the superstructure the architects used various devices to raise the blocks of stones to the required heights. It is believed that the temple was buried within the earth during the process of construction and stones were taken to great heights with the help of earthen ramps. The digging of the earth required for the construction of the temple, thus resulted in a large tank. It is believed that construction of the Liṅgarāja temple simultaneously resulting in Bindusāgara tank. This, however, does not appear to be correct as Bindusāgara existed in the 9th-10th centuries, evidently long before the construction of the Liṅgarāja. This is known from epigraphic evidence of Śāntikaradeva.

The temples of Śiva, according to the *Liṅga Purāṇa*,[2] are of three types: *Nāgara, Drāviḍa* and *Keśara (Vesara)*. The *Liṅga Purāṇa*[3] mentions temples, such as Kailāśa, Mandar, Meru, Himaśaila, Mahendrasáila, etc. The *Liṅga Purāṇa* records, "He who makes the temple called Kailaśa, rejoices happily in the aerial chariots of the shapes of Kailāśa peaks".[4] The tradition recorded in the *Mādalā Pāñji*[5] mentions that Yayāti Kesarī laid the foundation of Bhubaneswar temple in the form of "Kailāśa". As the peak of Kailāśa is the residence of Śiva, the tall *śikhara* of the temple dedicated in honour of Bhubaneswar, "the Lord of the World" is aptly called Kailāśa. The *Śilpa Sāriṇī*, an unpublished *Śilpa Śāstra* text of Orissa brought to light by Pandit Sadasiva Rathasarma and Alice Boner, designates the *deula* of the Liṅgarāja as Kailāśa variety of temple.

The Liṅgarāja temple broadly belongs to the *Nāgara* class, but it has certain individual features and is related to the Orissan style of architecture. The temple like the common Orissan temple, consists of a *sanctum*, surmounted by a curvilinear spire *(rekhā-deula)*, fronted by an audience hall *(mukhaśālā* or *jagamohana)* surmounted by a pyramidal roof *(pīḍha-deula)*. Both the temples, *rekhā-deula* and *pīḍha-deula*, are square in plan. Both the structures belong to one architectural scheme, but after the *deula* has been built to some height, the construction of the *jagamohana* walls seems to have been undertaken. This is suggested by the two different stone door frames, the sizes of which do not correspond as R.D. Banerjee has observed, "The stone lintel of the front door frame is much lower than that of the rear one, proving thereby that the *vimāna* and the *jagamohana* were not built at the same time".[6] Further, the carved front face of the *deula* is covered by the addition of the *jagamohana* in the front. The same building materials, style of carving and the decorative programme indicate that the interval between the dates of their erection could not have been long. Both the structures could have been conceived as one architectural plan and executed by the same school of sculptors. Both the monuments belong to the same period and the absence of a regular *kapili* of a juncture wall connecting the *sanctum* and the *jagamohana* gives the impression of an imperfect joint between the *deula* and the *jagamohana.* This seems to suggest that the Orissan architects adopted a different technique to join the two contrasting structures of different heights and forms.

In succeeding centuries two other structures were added at the front along the east-west axis. As already noted these are known as *nāṭa-mandira* and *bhoga-maṇḍapa.* The temple complex with four chambers essentially had functional purposes. The main temple or the *deula* housed the presiding divinity; the *jagamohana* was used for hall of assembly for the devotees, the *nāṭa-mandira* served as the festive hall and the *bhoga-maṇḍapa* located in front of the former was intended as the hall of offering (refectory). The large temple with spacious chamber and enclosed by high walls, gives the impression of a royal palace. The *Śiva Purāṇa* says, "The temple of Śiva shall be made like a royal palace with all the characteristics mentioned in the science of architecture. It shall be encircled by high walls with the ornamental gateway as lofty as a mountain".[7] The text also mentions that, "it shall contain thousands of courtesans in dance and music and those adept in playing on flutes and lutes."[8] By the 11th century, the tradition of presenting dancing girls to the temple was already in vogue and this *devadāsī* system gave rise to the construction of the *nāṭa-mandira* or a festive hall as an isolated structure. The present *bhoga-maṇḍapa* was originally a festive hall and later on, it was converted to a refectory.

The *deula* is *pañca-ratha* on plan with *pañcāṅga bāḍa.* The interior plan is square, though externally the wall is divided into five *pāgās* or *rathakas,* such as *kanikā, anuratha* and *rāhā. Deula* is of the *nirandhara* class, i.e., without ambulatory. In Orissa, temples with ambulatory (*sandhara* types) were never planned throughout the course of development. The elevation of the temple also reveals certain features. The *deula* is not erected on a *pīṭha* or a platform, but rises directly from the ground. The *deula* may be divided into three parts along the vertical plane and following the Orissan *Śilpa Śāstras,* these may be called *bāḍa, gaṇḍi* and *mastaka.* The *bāḍa* is of the *pañcāṅga* (five division) class with five principal parts, viz., *pābhāga, jaṅghā* subdivided into *tala* (lower) *jaṅghā* and *upara* (upper) *jaṅghā* by *bandhanā* and *varaṇḍa.* The *pābhāga* consists of a series of ornamental mouldings, such as *khurā, kumbha, paṭṭa, kani and basanta.* The *bandhanā* and the *varaṇḍa* have their distinctive ornamentations, the latter being placed in between the *jaṅghā* and the spire.

In elevation, the *jagamohana* closely follows the *rekhā deula.* There is virtually no difference between the *deula* and the *jagamohana* except in their relative dimensions. The *gaṇḍi* (trunk) or spire of the *deula* is different from that of the *jagamohana.* The *deula* is characterized by a curvilinear superstructure, while the *gaṇḍi* of the latter is in the form of a pyramidal superstructure with *pīḍhas* arranged in two tiers called *poṭalas.* The recessed vertical walls, which separate them from one another is called *kānthi* or *kānti.* The *gaṇḍi* is divided into five *pāgās* like that the *bāḍa.* The central projection is called *rāhā* and the projection flanking the *rāhā* are called *anuratha* and *kanika.* The projections and recesses on the temple produce a pleasing contrast of light and shade and add to the beauty of the spire. The *anuratha* has a succession of four miniature *rekhā* temples, which add to the vertical ascent of the *śikhara.* The *śikhara* surmounting the *sanctum* is beautifully conceived and is light and rythmic in treatment. In spite of massive dimension, it has shed the

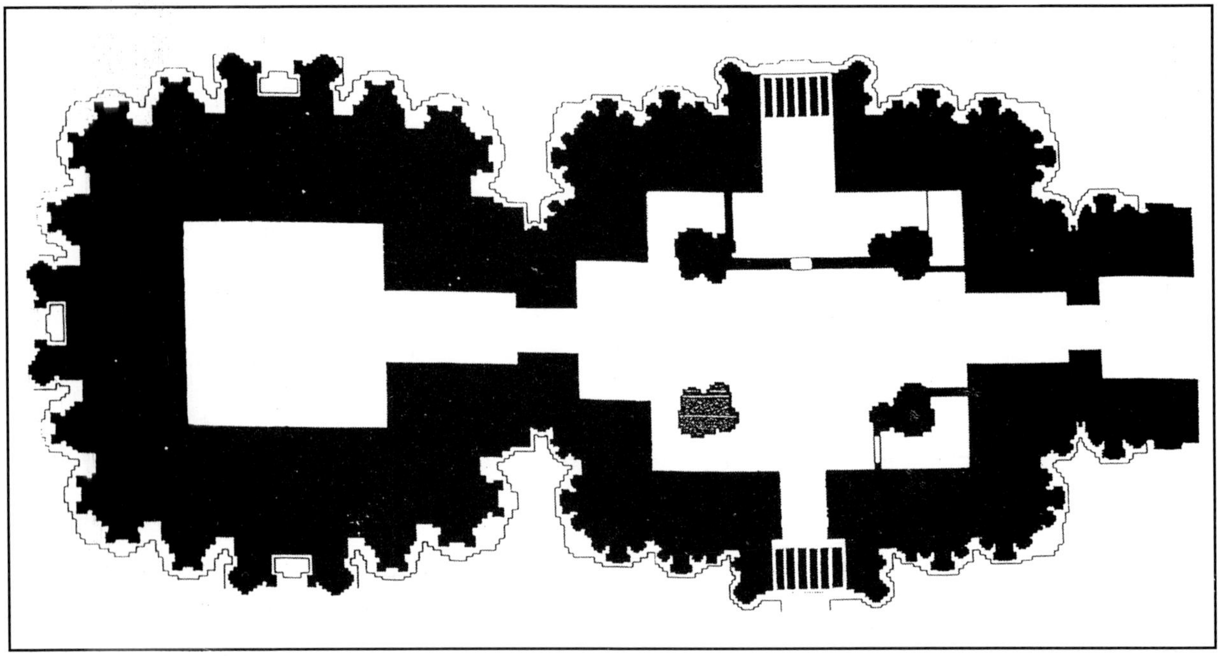

Fig. 11. Liṅgarāja Temple: Original plan of *deula* and *jagamohana*.

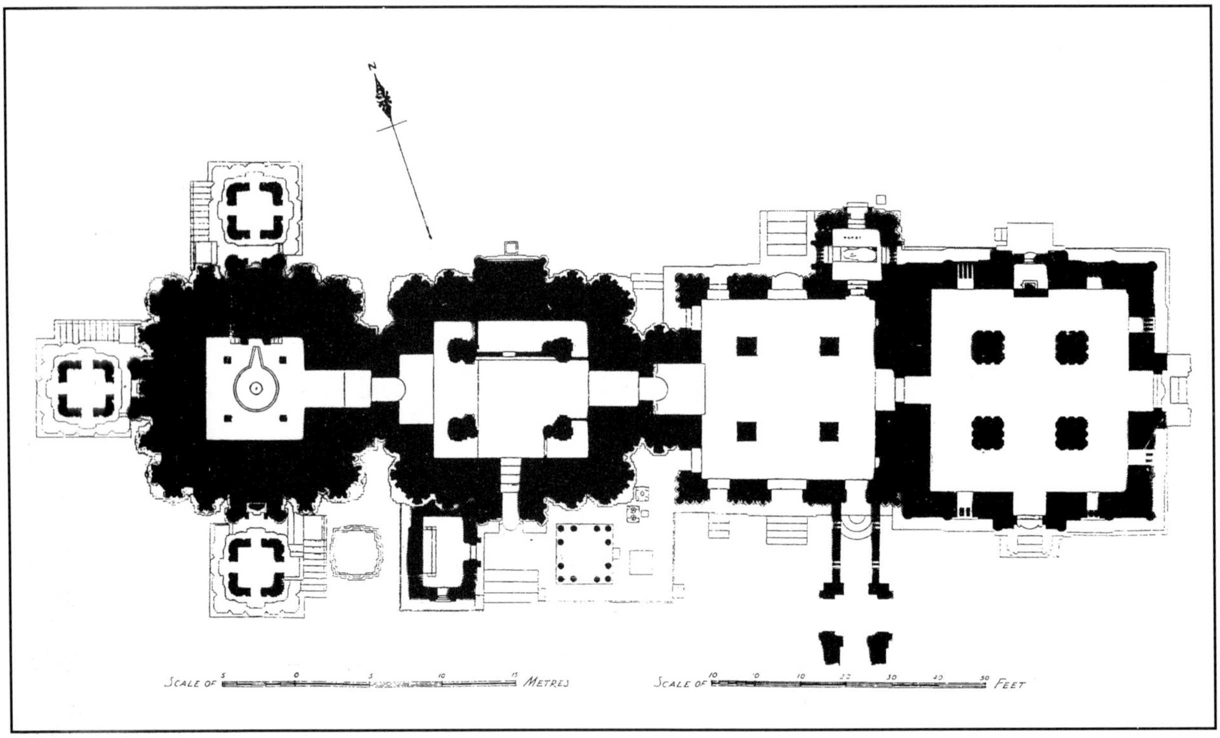

Fig. 12. Liṅgarāja Temple: Ground plan.

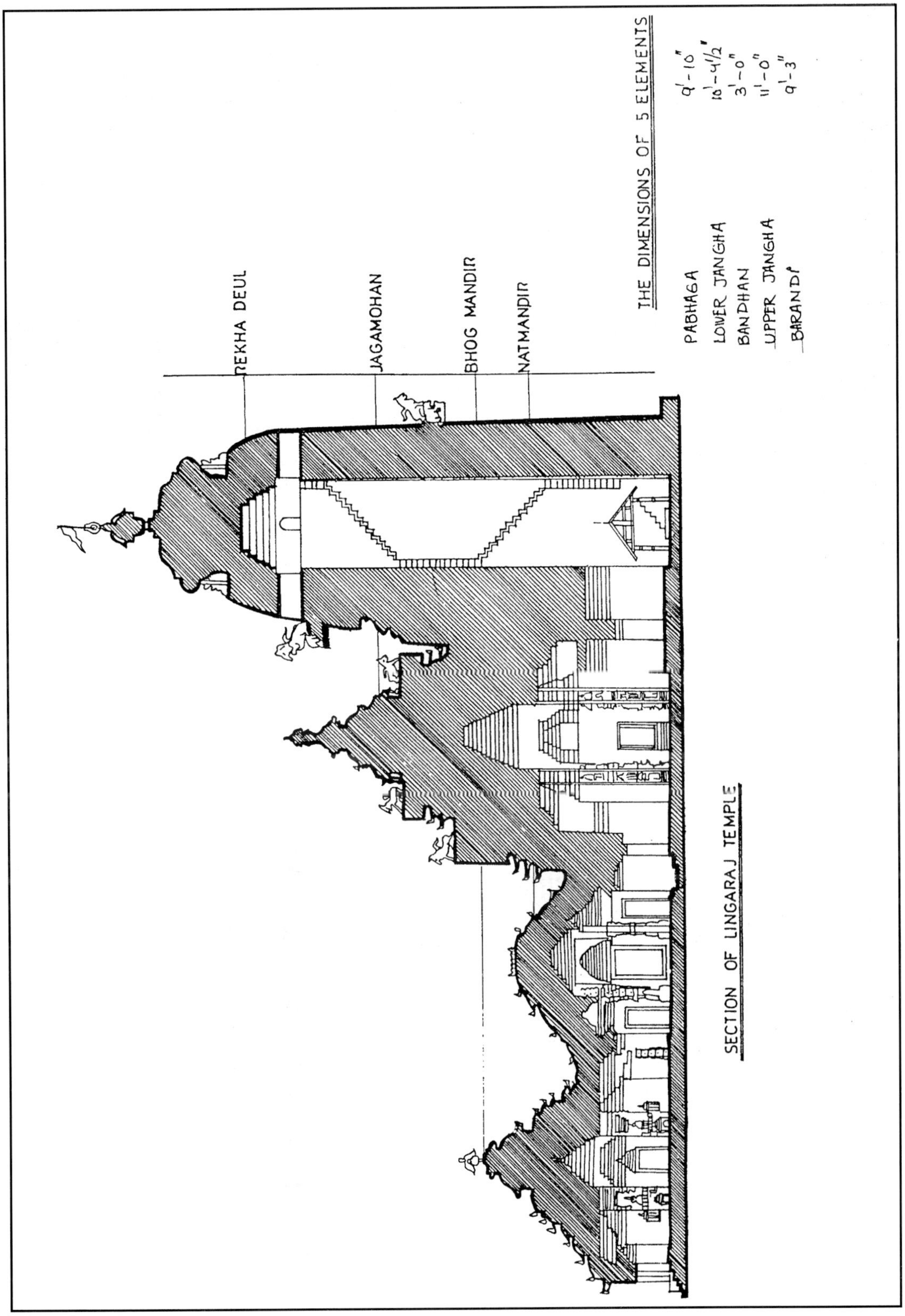

Fig. 13. Section of the Liṅgarāja Temple.

heaviness of the earlier epochs by its lyrical outline and elegant decorative programme. The *mastaka* of the *deula* is composed of *bekī, āmlā, khapurī, kalaśa* and the *āyudha.* The *mastaka* of the *jagamohana* is composed of *bekī, āmlā, khapurī, kalaśa* and *āyudha.* The dimension and height of the temple have increased and leaving behind a phase of modest dimension, the Liṅgarāja temple became the tallest of Bhubaneswar.

The *nāṭa-mandira* and *bhoga-maṇḍapa* were erected on platforms, that of the latter being comparatively high. The Orissan style of architecture is basically astylar in character, with its roof constructed on the corbel technique. The *nāṭa-mandira* and the *bhoga-maṇḍapa* had pillars inside, but the Orissan style did not develop pillar styles as in Karnataka, Madhya Pradesh and Western India.

In the earlier phase, there was no *prākāra* or enclosure wall. At the Mukteśvara temple, this feature started with a low enclosure. The temple of Brahmeśvara along with its subsidiary shrines in the four corners was enclosed by high walls. The Liṅgarāja temple constituted the same practice, which was followed in later temples. There are, however, no double enclosures as at the Puri temple. The construction of high *gopuram* was never favoured and entrances are surmounted by pyramidal porches of modest dimension, which never overshadowed the main shrine. The principal shrine called *deula* or *bāḍa-deula* was always the central focus and higher than the other structures located inside the enclosure.

The Liṅgarāja temple marks the culmination of the Orissan temple architecture and it provided the model for later temples to follow. The Indian *Śilpa Śāstra* texts and epigraphical evidence from Karnataka mention four styles of temples, viz., *Nāgara, Draviḍa, Vesara* and *Kaliṅga.* Kaliṅga in its geographical extent included present Orissan and adjoining areas of Andhra Pradesh and West Bengal. The inscriptions of Aśoka (3rd century BC) and Khāravela (1st century BC) mention Kaliṅga, which included Bhubaneswar area. In the 11th-12th centuries, however, Utkala meant coastal Orissa and by 14th-15th centuries the name Oḍisā had already become popular. In this context, the ancient name 'Kaliṅga' could have been used to denote the order of temples in Orissa in a broader sense. In general, the evolution of this Kaliṅga style can be divided into four phases, viz., early phase, middle phase, phase of maturity and the phase of ultimate climax. Temples of the early phase were represented either by the *sanctum* only or *deula* with a rectangular *jagamohana.* An important example of the latter is the Paraśurāmeśvara temple at Bhubaneswar. In this specimen the front wall of the *deula* served as the back wall of the *jagamohana.* By 10th century, as at Mukteśvara, the *jagamohana* had become an independent temple with pyramidal roof. The *ghaṇṭā,* however, has not yet appeared as a crowning member; the roof is crowned only by a *kalaśa.* In 11th century, with the construction of the Brahmeśvara temple, the *jagamohana* had become a full-fledged *pīḍha* temple with all its crowning elements. The *pīḍhas,* however, at Mukteśvara and Brahmeśvara are arranged in a continuous succession. The Liṅgarāja temple, as already noted, represents *rekhā-deula* with a *jagamohana* of the *pīḍha* order. It represents an improvement over the Brahmeśvara with its greater height and elegant curvature of the *deula* and arrangement of the *pīḍhas* of the *jagamohana* in two *poṭalas.* The *rekhā* is characterized by accentuated vertically and abruptly curves below the *mastaka* and this became the standard pattern in the mature phase. The crowning elements, such as *āmlaka-śilā, khapurī* and *kalaśa,* etc. however share pan-Indian features. The Liṅgarāja thus represents a typical Orissan temple with the *sanctum* as *rekhā-deula* and the audience chamber as the *pīḍha-deula.*

Pl. II. The Illuminated Liṅgarāja Temple at night.

In the early phase the temple of *tri-ratha* plan was favoured. In course of evolution *tri-ratha* developed into *pañca-ratha* and the Liṅgarāja shows the *pāgā* divisions of the *pañca-ratha* style. The *pañca-ratha* plan became the standard plan and it was followed at Jagannātha temple, Puri and Sun temple, Konarak. In course of evolution, however, *pañca-ratha* was elaborated into *sapta-ratha* and *nava-ratha.*

The Liṅgarāja also represents a *pancāṅga-bāḍa* with a *pañcakama pābhāga.* In comparison to the *pābhāga* of other Somavaṁśī temples, such as Mukteśvara, Rājarānī and Brahmeśvara, the *pābhāga* of the Liṅgarāja temple is very elegant as regards the ornamentation of the constituent elements, proportions and dimensions. The organic relationship between the *pañcakama* mouldings, such as *khura, kumbha, paṭṭa, kaṇi* and *basanta* imparts a rare beauty to the *pābhāga* than found in the *vedi bandhas* of temples in other parts of India. The division of *jaṅghā* into two by *bandhanā* moulding is a new feature found in the Liṅgarāja temple, which is akin to that of the Brahmeśvara temple. The placement of *khākharā-muṇḍis* in the lower *jaṅghā* and *pīḍha-muṇḍis* in the upper *jaṅghā* is also a common feature of the Brahmeśvara and the Liṅgarāja. The *varaṇḍa,* which separates the *bāḍa* from the *gaṇḍi* is made of a projecting moulding crowned by a sunken frieze. At Mukteśvara, the *varaṇḍa* representing a sunken panel continues the tradition of Mukteśvara. In the Brahmeśvara, the *varaṇḍa* is a single broad moulding. In the Liṅgarāja, it is made of ten carved mouldings. The *bāḍa* at Brahmeśvara has *khākharā-muṇḍis* in the lower *jaṅghā* and *pīḍha-muṇḍis* in the upper *jaṅghā.* This is also found at Liṅgarāja. The *jagamohana* of Brahmeśvara replaces the screen window of the Mukteśvara and has two balustraded windows and this is also continued at Liṅgarāja. The balusters are carved with graceful female figures in various poses.

The decorative programme of the *gaṇḍi* of *deula* is characterized by arrangements of *aṅga-śikharas*[9] in the *anuratha.* At Rājarānī, the *aṅga-śikhara* clustered round the spires is an experiment, which is found in the temples of Khajuraho. At Brahmeśvara, the *aṅga-śikharas* appear in the lower part of the *gaṇḍi.* After years of experiment, the architects of Orissa used the *aṅga-śikharas* at Liṅgarāja to enhance the vertical outline of the temple by placing them in the *anuratha* in a vertical succession. Among other features, the *gaṇḍi* of the Liṅgarāja temple has projecting lions, a feature which is found at Brahmeśvara temple. The *śukanāsā* so popular in North Indian temples, is found at Vaitāla, but in subsequent periods including at Liṅgarāja, it is not seen in the decorative programme of the *gaṇḍi.* The central projections are carved with *vajra-mastaka* motif.

The Liṅgarāja temple reflects the elaboration of some of the architectural features of the earlier temples. The earlier phases represent experiments by the architects. The accumulated experiment and expertise resulted in the construction of the Liṅgarāja temple with its architectural and decorative features in a standardised format. The selective choice of earlier features coupled with innovative designs make the Liṅgarāja one of the finest temples in India.

The Liṅgarāja temple shows certain distinctive peculiarities of its own. The construction of two contrasting structures, *deula* with a curvilinear superstructure and the *jagamohana* with a pyramidal superstructure mode of receding *pīḍhas* and the latter being subordinate to the *bāḍa-deula* is quite peculiar to Orissa. The grandeur of the curvilinear spire surmounting the *sanctum* is hightened with the placement of a *jagamohana* of lower height. This is evidently different from other regional manifestations of the *Nāgara* style, where the superstructure of the *maṇḍapas* largely differs from the soaring quality of the spire over the *sanctum.* The Liṅgarāja temple is also different from the northern Indian style being a compact and closed structure as distinguished from the open pillared halls, which detract the vertical ascent of the spire of the *sanctum*.[10] Unlike the large temples at Khajuraho, there are no lateral transepts with balconied windows in the *maṇḍapa*. At the Liṅgarāja, there is no inner ambulatory around the *sanctum*. The *sandhara* configuration is totally absent in the Orissan style of temple architecture. The temple is a *nirandhara* one without any ambulatory. The Liṅgarāja temple is different from the Khajuraho temples, which are without any enclosure wall. The Khajuraho temples stand over high platform-terrace or *jagatī*. The *deula* of the Liṅgarāja temple rises abruptly from the ground without any platform at the base. Due to the balconied windows, the interior compartments at Khajuraho get more light and air than the Liṅgarāja, which in contrast represents a compact and closed structure without the abovementioned devices. The interior of the Liṅgarāja temple is plain without any decorative carvings as found in Khajuraho temples. In the architectural design of the superstructure and placement of the *aṅga-śikhara*, the Liṅgarāja temple follows a different design in placing the four *aṅga-śikharas* on the *anuratha*. The Liṅgarāja temple is *pañca-ratha* in plan and is different from the *sapta-ratha sanctum* of Khajuraho. At Khajuraho, in some large temples, there are subsidiary shrines in the four corners to make the temple a *pañcāyatana* one. At Liṅgarāja, there are three subsidiary shrines in front of the three *pārśvadevtā* images, but such structures are clearly later additions. In many respects the architectural and the decorative programme of the Liṅgarāja is clearly related to Orissan style.

NOTES AND REFERENCES

1. R.D. Banerjee, *History of Orissa*, Vol. II, p. 360.
2. *Linga Purāṇa*, 77.7.
3. *Ibid.*, 77.9-21.
4. *Ibid.*, 77.8.
5. *Mādalā Pāñji*, p. 6.
6. R.D. Banerjee, *History of Orissa*, p. 359.
7. *Śiva Purāṇa*, *Vāyavīya Saṁhitā*, 25.35-36.
8. *Ibid.*, 25.41.
9. T. Donaldson, "Decorative Programme of the Superstructure on the *OrissanRekha-deula*", in M.N. Das (ed.), *Sidelights on History and Culture of Orissa*, pp. 584-598.
10. Stella Kramrisch, *The Hindu Temple*, Vol. I, Calcutta, 1946, p. 217.

IV

Sculptural Features and Cult Images

The decorative programme of the Liṅgarāja temple may be divided into various categories, such as surface carvings, religious sculptures, secular sculptures, erotic sculptures, female figures, composite figures, animal figures, architectural motifs, etc. The whole of the temple, from the bottom to the top, is elegantly carved and it adds to the beauty and magnificence of the temple. The entire surface of the temple seems to be an integrated manifestation of sculptures; architecture is not mere architecture; it is sculpture on a magnificent scale. Both, architecture and sculpture supplement each other to make the structure a worthy abode of God. Sculptural art is mainly found on the exterior walls of the temple. The interior is plain, except for the *dvāra-śākhās,* the *navagrahas*, architrave, and pillars inside the *nāṭa-mandira* and *bhoga-maṇḍapa.* This is a feature which is found throughout the development of the Orissan style; only rarely as at Mukteśvara, Jaleśvara and Brahmeśvara, the ceilings have been carved. The material used for sculpture is primarily khandolite stone for the construction of the temple. In the Liṅgarāja, however, the *pārśva-devatā* images, such as Gaṇeśa, Kārttikeya and Pārvatī are made of *muguni* or chlorite stone. This feature, by and large, began in the developed phase during the Somavaṁśī period. The decorative programme was executed *in situ* after the stone blocks having been set up in their proper positions. This technique ensured proper proportion and integration of details, which could not have been possible if carved stones would have been placed one upon the other to build the temple.

The technique of carving is based on the method of incision. The evidence of the earlier temples indicates that the surface wall was first carved with sketches, which were later on given finishing to achieve the required themes. Sometimes, the surface ornamentation reaches the level of fine filigree works. The architect-sculptors were masters in different techniques, such as low-relief, high-relief and alto-relievo. By the time of the Liṅgarāja, the figure-sculptures appear to be bold and emerge out from the wall and niches of the temple. The placing of the individual sculpture has broadly evolved into a pattern which became the model for the later temples to follow. For example, the *pābhāga* of five ornamental mouldings, the two *jaṅghās* with *khākharā-muṇḍis* in the lower, and *pīḍha-muṇḍis* in the upper, *viḍālas* in the *pāgā* recesses in lower and figures of *kanyās* in the upper and *varaṇḍa* mouldings demarcating the *bāḍa* and the *gaṇḍi,* became conventional features in the evolved stage of the temples. The quality of sculptures of the Liṅgarāja is quite refined compared to the stylized pattern of the later temples. The sculptures of the Liṅgarāja temple found on the *deula* and *jagamohana* are similar to those of the Brahmeśvara, which suggest that they belonged to one school of sculptors.

ARCHITECTURAL MOTIFS

Miniature temple motifs: The Orissan temple style is broadly divided into *rekhā, pīḍha,* and *khākharā* types. In the decorative programme, however, miniature representations of such temple motifs are found in the *bāḍa* and the *gaṇḍi* portions. *Khākharā-muṇḍis* occupy the lower *jaṅghā* and the *pīḍha-muṇḍis* are placed in the upper *jaṅghā.* The miniature *rekhā* temples are usually seen on the *gaṇḍi* of the main temple.

Khākharā-muṇḍi: At Liṅgarāja, the *khākharā-muṇḍis* assume the standard pattern, which was followed in later temples. The *khākharā-muṇḍi* found in earlier temples, such as Mukteśvara and Brahmeśvara is made of a series of horizontal mouldings but at the Liṅgarāja, it consists of a single large *khākharā* design. This ornate *khākharā* motif is relieved with scroll-work on its *muhanti* and a *bho*-motif on its central facet. The lintel of the *khākharā-muṇḍi* niches are variously carved with figures of divinities, such as Gaṇeśa, Sarasvatī, etc. The niches of the *muṇḍis* have scroll-work on both sides. The *khākharā-muṇḍi* at the Liṅgarāja discontinues the earlier practice of the Brahmeśvara where *tri-ratha* niches of the *khākharā-muṇḍi* have female attendants in the flanking niches. At Liṅgarāja such flanking niches are absent. The base is relieved with male and female figures. In the *jagamohana* of the Liṅgarāja, however, the *khākharā-muṇḍi* has flanking pilasters with scrollwork. The lintel of the niches are without any sculptural frieze as in the *khākharā-muṇḍis* of the *deula.*

Pīḍha-muṇḍi: The *pīḍha-muṇḍi* on the upper *jaṅghā* portion of the *bāḍa* represents a niche crowned by a *pīḍha* roof, which is made of three *pīḍha* mouldings with an *āmalaka* at the top. The niches of the *pīḍha-muṇḍis* containing various divinities are framed with scroll-work.

Rekhā-śikhara: Miniature replica of *rekhā-śikhara,* called *aṅga-śikhara,* usually adorn the body of the *gaṇḍi.* At Liṅgarāja, the *deula* of a temple has a succession of four *aṅga-śikharas* on the *anuratha-pāgā* of the *gaṇḍi.* The superimposed *anga śikharas* diminish in size as they reach to the top. Each *aṅga-śikhara* represents a miniature *rekhā* temple with a miniature divinity on its *rāhā* niche. The *jagamohana* has, at the level of *varaṇḍa* portion on the south, three miniature *rekhā* temples as part

Pl. 41. Liṅgarāja: *deula*, Gaṇeśa as Pārśvadevatā, south.

Pl. 40. Liṅgarāja: *deula*, Ācārya, *khākarā-muṇḍi*, north.

Pl. 42. Liṅgarāja: *deula*, Kārttikeya as Pārśvadevatā, west.

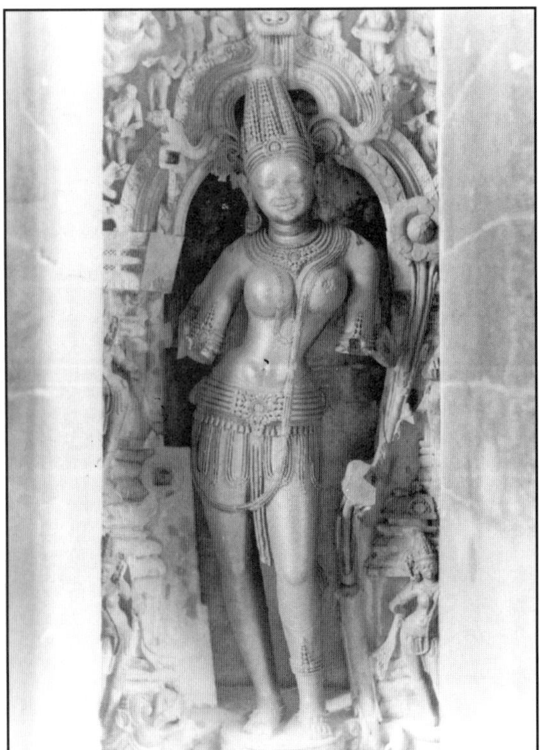

Pl. 43. Liṅgarāja: *deula*, Pārvatī as Pārśvadevtā, north.

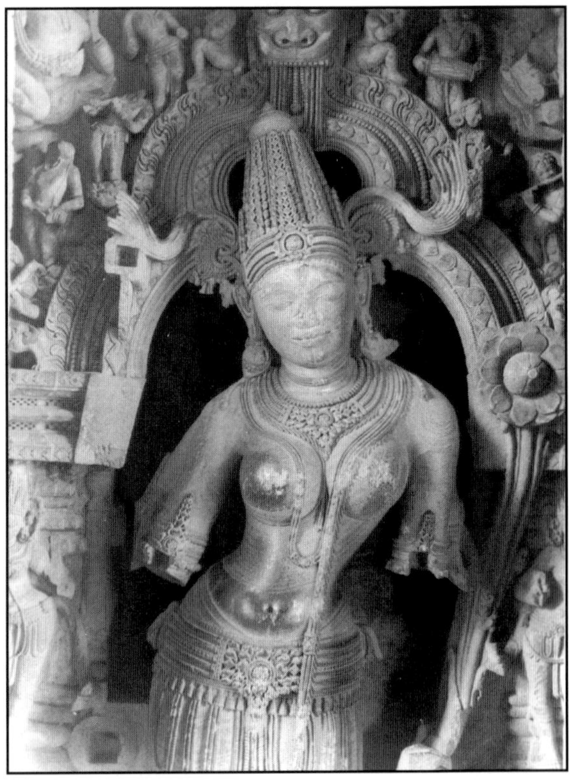

Pl. 44. Liṅgarāja: *deula*, Pārvatī, details.

Pl. 45. Liṅgarāja: *deula, dikpāla* Agni.

Pl. 46. Liṅgarāja: *deula, dikpāla* Niruthi.

Pl. 47. Liṅgarāja: *deula, dikpāla* Varuṇa.

Pl. 48. Liṅgarāja: *deula, dikpāla* Īśāna.

Pl. 49. Liṅgarāja: *deula*, a couple, pilaster left side of Pārvatī, north.

Pl. 50. Liṅgarāja: *deula*, churning of curd, *bāḍa*, south-east corner.

Pl. 51. Liṅgarāja: *deula*, domestic scene, *bāḍa*, south-east.

Pl. 52. Liṅgarāja: *deula*, Jagannātha, cell below Pārśvadevatā shrine, west.

Pl. 53. Liṅgarāja: *deula*, Lakulīśa, Rāhā, east.

Pl. 54. Liṅgarāja: *deula*, Andhakāsura-vadha-mūrtti, Rāhā, south.

Pl. 55. Liṅgarāja: *deula*, Naṭarāja Rāhā, west.

Pl. 56. Liṅgarāja: *deula*, Dancing Cāmuṇḍā, Rāhā, north.

Pl. 57. Liṅgarāja: *deula, gaṇḍi, vajra-mastaka* south.

Pl. 59. Liṅgarāja: *deula, gaṇḍi, vajra-mastaka* north.

Pl. 61. Liṅgarāja: *jagamohana*, south.

Pl. 60. Liṅgarāja: *deula*, Overlapping of *deula* and *jagamohana*.

Pl. 58. Liṅgarāja: *deula, gaṇḍi, vajra-mastaka* west.

Pl. 62. Liṅgarāja: *jagamohana*, south, 1868 (R.L. Mitra).

Pl. 63. Liṅgarāja: *jagamohana*, arrangement of *pīḍhas*.

Pl. 64. Liṅgarāja: *jagamohana*, details of *pīḍhas*, south.

Pl. 65. Liṅgarāja: *jagamohana*, *vajra-mastaka*, *gaṇḍi*, north.

Pl. 67. Liṅgarāja: *jagamohana*, *alasa-kanyā*, upper *jaṅghā* recess.

Pl. 68. Liṅgarāja: *jagamohana, staṁbha jāli gavākṣa*, north.

Pl. 66. Liṅgarāja: *jagamohana, bandhanā* and upper *jaṅghā*, north.

Pl. 69. Liṅgarāja: *jagamohana gavākṣa*, south.

Pl. 70. Liṅgarāja: Jaṅghā Miniature temple with flanking Kanyās, south.

Pl. 71. Liṅgarāja: Miniature temple with dancing Gaṇeśa and Naṭarāja.

Pl. 73. Liṅgarāja: *jagamohana Rāhu*, upper *jaṅghā*, north.

Pl. 72. Liṅgarāja: Pārvatī Pariṇaya scene, *gavākṣa*, south.

Pl. 75. Liṅgarāja: *jagamohana*, *kanyā* with attendants, south-west.

Pl. 74. Liṅgarāja: *jagamohana*, *gajavyāḷa*, south.

Pl. 76. Liṅgarāja: *jagamohana*, lady looking at the mirror, north-west corner.

Pl. 77. Liṅgarāja: *jagamohana*, *mithuna*, upper *jaṅghā*, south.

Pl. 78. Liṅgarāja: *jagamohana*, *mithuna*, upper *jaṅghā* recess, north.

Pl. 79. Liṅgarāja: *jagamohana*, man with sword, upper *jaṅghā*, south.

Pl. 80. Liṅgarāja: *jagamohana*, seated female figure with attendants, north.

Pl. 81. Liṅgarāja: *jagamohana*, *dvārasakhā*, north flank.

Pl. 82. Liṅgarāja: *jagamohana*, Pārvatī worshipped as Rāja Rājeśvarī.

Pl. 83. Liṅgarāja: *nāṭa-mandira*, seated Ardhanārīśvara.

Pl. 84. Liṅgarāja: *jagamohana*, Mahiṣamardinī.

of decoration. The same pattern is also repeated above the architrave of the side doorways of the *nāṭa-mandira.*

Vajra-muṇḍi: The *vajra-muṇḍi* motif is used at various places on the *bāḍa* and the *gaṇḍi.* It is an ornamental motif with its medallion, pear-shaped or circular in form. The design usually consists of two superimposed medallions placed one above the other, the lower one being comparatively smaller in size. The whole medallion is flanked by dwarfish figures on either side. In the niches of each medallion, there are figures of divinities and lotus. The *vajra-mastaka* is variously capped by a *kīrtimukha* or lotus. The *kīrtimukha* usually has a bell hanging down into the centre. The *vajra-mastaka* is found in the central facets of the *khākharā-muṇḍis* and on each face of the *rāhā* projection of the *gaṇḍi.* The design is highly ornate and bold; such motif is known as *bho* among the local artists. The depiction of the *bho* on the *rāhā* is comparatively larger and the one facing the *jagamohana* is at a higher elevation than to be noticed on the earlier temples, such as Mukteśvara and Brahmeśvara. The *bho*-motif is a typical feature of the developed phase of the Orissan *deula* and such occurance demarcates the early phase and the developed phase.

Window design: The window design as a part of Orissan temple architecture started in the 7th century in the stage of Paraśurāmeśvara. The windows of the *jagamohana* are in the form of screens. The lattice-window continued in the developing stage as at Mukteśvara to be replaced

Fig. 14. *Khākarā-muṇḍi* and *Pīḍha-muṇḍi.*

by balustraded windows of the Rājarānī and the Brahmeśvara. The windows of the *jagamohana* of the Liṅgarāja show the standard pattern of the balustraded windows with female figures on the balusters.

Projecting lion: The *rāhā* of the *deula* has projecting lions on each face of the *rāhā.* Such projecting lions appear in the developed phase as at Brahmeśvara and continue in the entire developed phase as at Liṅgarāja. Such figures of lion soar upward into the sky and have an elephant below them, making a composite motif of lion-on-elephant.

Decorative figures of the *bekī*: In the earlier phase, the *bekī* had no decorative figures; the lion figures placed on the *bekī* at Paraśurāmeśvara were later additions and not a part of the original design. Decorative figures, such as *deula-cārinīs, dopicha-siṁhas* and seated *bekī-bhairavas* appeared in the developed phase. At the Liṅgarāja, there are *dopiccha-Siṁhas* in the corners and seated *bekī-bhairavas* in the centre of the *rāhā.*

DECORATIVE MOTIFS

Viḍālas: The *viḍāla* motif, as known to the Orissan artists, is derived from *vyāḷa.* The composite motif was known to the artist of Khaṇḍagiri-Udayagiri during the Mahāmeghavāhana period (2nd-1st century BC). The composite lion-on-elephant motif is seen in the early stage at Paraśurāmeśvara. The motif of *meṣa-vyāḷa* appears in the Vaitāla temple of 8th century AD. The *aśva-vyāḷa* appears in the junction wall of the *jagamohana* and *deula* of the Mukteśvara. In the Liṅgarāja, in the recesses of the *bāḍa, vyāḷa* motifs appear in the lower *jaṅghā.* The composite figures represent lion-over-elephant or elephant-faced lion standing over demonic figures. The figures depicted in standing position and looking to the sides have emerging tongue, fiery eyes, twisted tails, lionine body and apparently convey the strength and power of a lion. As symbol of fertility and power, the *vyāḷa* motif continued in later temples in Orissa. In a pan-Indian perspective, the *vyāḷa* motif was limited to the Pallava phase in the Dravidian art. Various types of *vyāḷas* in several permutations and combinations appear in the temple art of Northern India including Orissa, Central India and Western India.

Nāga-Nāgi figures: *Nāga-nāgi* figures appear in the decorative programme from the Mukteśvara stage. They also adorn the entrance of the temple from the time of Rājarānī. Such *nāga-nāgi stambhas,* however, are not found at the door entrance of the Liṅgarāja. The decorative programme of the *bāḍa* does not include the *nāga-nāgi* figures as found at Mukteśvara; however, isolated *nāga-nāgi* figures are found on the Liṅgarāja temple complex. The *nāga-nāgi* pilasters occur on the lower *jaṅghā* of the *bhoga-maṇḍapa.* As symbols of fertility and auspiciousness, *nāga-nāgi* figures are found in large number at the Sun temple, Konarak.

Female figures: The female figures as a part of the decorative programme started in the early phase and continued in the developing and the developed phases of Orissan temple style. In the developing phase, however, it found supreme expression combining graceful and elegant postures. In the developed phase, as at Liṅgarāja, the female figures increased in number and size. Large-sized female figures, called variously as *kanyā*s, *apsarā*s, etc. on the *bāḍa* have a standard configuration being shown in the recesses of the *pāgās* in the upper *jaṅghā.* They are depicted in various roles, such as removing thorn from the foot, in the form of a *śālabhañjikā* holding the branch of a tree, holding a pet bird, removing anklet, looking at the mirror, adjusting drapery, and applying vermilion on her forehead. Each figure virtually is a masterpiece of Indian art, noted for its beauty and grace. The loving hand of the artists was particularly fond of carving lovely female figures in eternal youth, and often with vivid sensuousness. The temple figures have been depicted from different angles to reveal their voluptuous beauty in a variety of positions and postures.

Erotic sculptures: The *mithuna* sculpture started early in the 7th century and with the development of *kaula-kāpālika* sects, such motifs came to be depicted on the temples, such as Vaitāla. In the Liṅgarāja temple, such figures are generally found in the *bandhanā* portion of the *bāḍa,* which connects the lower and upper *jaṅghā.* The representations even include ascetics and bearded figures in the company of graceful female figures. The scenes representing various erotic postures and activities became an important feature of the Orissan temple art. The erotic sculpture increased at Konarak temple in the 13th century and at the *bhoga-maṇḍapa* base in the Liṅgarāja. Such representations are characterised by explicit and vivid depiction of love activities. Several interpretations have been given to explain their significance. Coomaraswamy observed, "Love and desire are part of life. Life is a veil behind or within which is God. The outside of the temple is an image of this life, *Saṁsāra,* and the carvings on it represent everything that belongs to *Saṁsāra* and perpetuate illusion, every bond and each desire of loveliness that binds men to the wheel of life and death". Symbolic or mere ornamentation, meaningful or purposeless, superstitious belief to ward off lightning, portrayal of tantric rituals or long standing customs, such youthful forms decorate the temple walls and the temple vibrates with life.

Secular figures and scenes: The secular figures included in the decorative programme consist of royal figures, *darbār* scenes, *śikṣādāna* scenes, procession of infantry, cavalry, elephants, etc. On the southern side in a niche of the lower *jaṅghā,* a standing figure seems to be reading from a copper-plate charter. The sword in his right hand and the *chatras* over his head, held by two attendants indicate his royal status. Royal figures surrounded by various attendants also appeared in the niches of the *pābhāga.* In a *muṇḍi* niche of the *deula,* a female figure, apparently a queen, is shown along with a number of female figures and three female attendants in the lower register. The niche has a seated figure of Sarasvatī in the centre and two seated Gaṇapati figures on either side. On the southern side of the *jagamohana,* there is an elaborate court scene of a royal figure, which some local people variously identify as *Indrasabhā* or a possible scene from the *Rāmāyaṇa.* Military scenes consisting of foot soldiers, cavalry, etc. are depicted in the *pīḍhas* of the *jagamohana.*

The *śikṣādāna* motif, which appears in the Brahmeśvara, is found in the northern side of the *deula.* The scene represents an *ācārya* and his disciples. There are also domestic scenes representing churning of curd, dressing of hair, marriage scene, etc. On the southern side of the *deula,* the scene representing churning of curd is usually identified as Yasodā along with child Kṛṣṇa and Nanda; the scene is similar to the depiction found on the north-east corner shrine of the Brahmeśvara temple. The marriage scene found in a niche in the western side of the *deula* vividly represents the *pāṇigrahaṇa* aspect of the marriage ritual. This scene, in view of the depiction in a Śiva temple, is sometimes identified as a scene of Śiva's marriage with Pārvatī.

Scroll-works: The scroll-works dominate the temple surface and are of various types, such as *vanalatā, patralatā, jīvalatā,* etc. The vertical frames are sometimes carved with rich foliage. The mass of leaves depicted together lend a swelling grace to the temple surface. Sometimes, in the foils of the scroll, leaves and flowers are enclosed giving the scrolls their characteristic names, such as *patralatā* and *phulalatā.* Sometimes, the scrolls enclose tiny figures of animals and birds and such motifs are locally known as *jīvalatā.* Of unique interest is a scroll-work with a man rowing a boat contained within limited space of a foil.

CULT IMAGES

An important category of sculptures consists of cult images. As already mentioned, the temple enshrines a massive Śivaliṅga in the *sanctum.* Being a Śiva temple, the outer wall is dominated by Śaivite *pārśva-devatās* in the cardinal directions and several manifestations of Śiva. An image of Gaṇeśa carved in chlorite adorns the southern niche of the *rāhā.* The image stands in a *tribhaṅga* pose holding broken tusk, rosary, *modaka pātra* and *kuṭhāra.* His *vāhana,* the mouse, appears on the lower right part of the base. The *toraṇa* at the back of the image is crowned by a *kīrtimukha.*

The over life-size image of Kārttikeya serves as the *pārśva-devatā* in the west. The four arms of the deity are missing. Kārttikeya is distinguished by his *śikhaṇḍaka* hair-do and a highly ornate arch as the back slab. His *vāhana*-peacock exists at the base.

The *pārśva-devatā* on the northern side is a beautiful image of Pārvatī. However, her arms are broken, but her attribute lotus is intact. The more than life-size image of Pārvatī stands majestically with a richly embellished *kirīṭamukuṭa* and other ornaments. Her rich lower garment is lavishly carved. The backslab of the image has an ornate arch similar to those of the two other images. The figure of a lion appears at the base to serve as the *vāhana.*

The upper *rāhā* niches on the south, west and the north contain an image of headed Andhakāsura-vadha-mūrtti, a dancing Śiva (mutilated) and image of Cāmuṇḍā, respectively. An image of Lakulīśa is placed on the eastern face of the *deula.* Miniature representations of seated Gaṇeśa, seated Kārttikeya and a dancing *devī* also occur inside the *vajra-mastaka* medallion on the upper *rāhā* on the south, west and north, respectively.

The iconographic programme of the *deula* on the upper *jaṅghā* includes divinities, such as Sūrya in the east, and figures of Ardhanārīśvara, Gaṇeśa, Kaumārī, dancing Bhairava in the south. The divinities in the west comprise Brahmā, Śiva in the yogic posture and Lakulīśa. On the north, there are representations of Pārvatī, Kāma flanked by his two consorts, standing Kārttikeya and others.

In the *jagamohana* also the iconographic programme consists of manifestations of Śiva and Pārvatī, Mahiṣamardinī, etc. Above the *gavākṣa* in the south, there is a sculptured frieze representing *Pārvatī pariṇaya* or the marriage of Pārvatī with Śiva.

The *deula* has seated figures of *dikpālas* in the *kanikā* niches, such as Indra (east), Agni (south-east), Yama (south), Nirṛti (south-west), Varuṇa (west), Vāyu (north-west), and Iśāna (north-east). Of these figures Agni has a flaming halo, while others have treefoil arches on their backside. In the *jagamohana,* however, the *dikpāla* figures are conspicuous by their absence, but the figure of Rāhu appears on the north.

The iconographic programme of the Liṅgarāja temple shows that, though a temple, its cult images are not confined to Śaiva pantheon. Religious syncretism has been a tradition in Orissa and shunning rigid sectarianism, the representations are broadly affiliated to Brāhmanical pantheon, covering Śaiva, Śākta and Vaiṣṇava denominations. We have already mentioned about the panel reminiscent of child Kṛṣṇa-Yasodā-Nanda episode. A possible depiction of Hanumān on the southern side of *deula* indicates its popular worship in the 11th century. The worship of Jagannātha on the western side enshrined inside the basement of the *pārśva-devatā* shrine indicates the influence of Jagannātha cult in this temple. The Vaiṣṇava transformation of Liṅgarāja is proved by Vaiṣṇava Jaya-Vijaya images placed as *dvārapāla*s at the entrance of the *nāṭa-mandira.* The worship of Lakṣmī-Nārāyaṇa in a separate shrine along the northern side of the *bhoga-maṇḍapa,* is yet another evidence of the influence of Vaiṣṇavism in the Gaṅga period. The erection of a temple in honour of Nṛsiṁha and two subsidiary shrines of Vaiṣṇava affiliation indicate the changing religious scenario and religious syncretism (Pl. 112).

The cult images depicted in the Liṅgarāja temple complex and other subsidiary shrines give us a broad idea of iconographic changes taking place over a period of time. The *deula* is adorned with family members of Śiva, such as Gaṇeśa, Kārttikeya and Pārvatī. In addition, there are independent shrines in the Liṅgarāja compound for the worship of Pārvatī, Gaṇeśa and Kārttikeya. The images of Gaṇeśa are of three types: seated, standing and dancing. The seated image of Gaṇeśa is found as the central deity of the Gaṇeśa temple and also as the *pārśva-devatā.* An early variety of detached image of Gaṇeśa is found in the Kārttikeya temple. The *sthānaka-mūrtti* of Gaṇeśa became the standard pattern for the *pārśva-devatā* in the developed phase. *Nṛtta-mūrtti* or dancing Gaṇeśa is noticed in the Liṅgarāja compound on the southern face of the Ekāmbareśvara temple (Pl. 94).

The images of Kārttikeya found in the Liṅgarāja compound can broadly be divided into two categories: standing and seated on his *vāhana* the peacock. An early form of the later type is noticed attached to the outerwall of a miner shrine. Standing images of the deity hold *kukuṭa* (cock) in the left hand, which is not noticed in the earlier phase. The *śrīkhaṇḍaka* mode of coiffure is generally noticed as a characteristic feature of this deity. A later representation of standing Kārttikeya is found in the *nāṭa-mandira* (Pl. 97).

Standing image of Pārvatī as the *pārśva-devatā* became a standard pattern in the developed phase replacing Mahiṣamardinī found in the temples, such as at Vaitāla and Jaleśvara. An early image of Pārvatī in standing pose is noticed in a minor shrine inside the Liṅgarāja compound. The iconographic features associated with Pārvatī are rosary, *nāgapāśā, ketakī* flower, *aṅkuśa,* etc. In the Pārvatī temple, the *devī* holds a lotus and a pot of gems in her right and left hand respectively. Her lion mount is shown in the pedestal on the right side.

The images of Mahiṣamardinī found inside the Liṅgarāja compound represent the demon issuing out from the decapitated body of the buffalo. This forms an important development from the earlier type representing the demon with a human body and a buffalo head. The Śākta images, apart from Mahiṣamardinī and Pārvatī, are represented by *mātṛkā*s, such as Cāmuṇḍā and Vārāhī (Pl. 85).

The images of Śiva include Naṭarāja, Andhakāśura-vadha-mūrtti, Hara-Pārvatī, Lakulīśa, Śiva as Mahāyogī, Ekapāda Bhairava and others. Lakulīśa formed a dominant motif in the early phase, but in the Liṅgarāja temple its representation has become very rare. In addition to *liṅga* of the *sanctum,* there are several scenes illustrating the worship of the *liṅga.* The *liṅga pūjā* scenes are shown at their best in the northern *gaṇḍi* of the *jagamohana.* Seated images of Śiva in *padmāsana* are also noticed in the Liṅgarāja. The composite forms of Śiva found in the Liṅgarāja compound include Ardhanārīśvara and Hari-Hara. Another composite form is Aja-Ekapāda. The image of Ekapāda Bhairava is noticed in the Bhairaveśvara temple. In the example of Hari-Hara form in the Liṅgarāja compound, the Hara part holds a trident with bull carved on the pedestal (Pl. 99).

The inclusion of Vaiṣṇava motif is found in the decoration of the early Śiva temples at Bhubaneswar. The Manibhadreśvara temple, for example, has representations of *avatāras* of Viṣṇu on the *bāḍa.* There are a few Vaiṣṇava temples inside the Liṅgarāja compound for worship of Lakṣmī-Nārāyaṇa, Nṛsiṁha and standing form of Viṣṇu. The images of Ananta, Ekānaṁśā and Vāsudeva trinity are also worshipped in the Liṅgarāja compound in a minor shrine. Detached images of Varāha, which evidently formed a part of the Viṣṇu temple, are noticed in the Liṅgarāja compound.

The *dikpālas,* as already mentioned, appear on the *deula* of the Liṅgarāja. But in later temples, in addition to *dikpālas,* their consorts appear in the *muṇḍi* niches of the upper *jaṅghā.* Among other divinities, Sūrya, Brahmā, Sāvitrī and Sarasvatī are depicted in the sculptural art of the Liṅgarāja.

Thus, the Liṅgarāja compound with its Śaiva, Śākta, and Vaiṣṇava temples, give an idea of not only the iconographic features of the images, but also the changing religious and cultural developments at Bhubaneswar and their impact on the Liṅgarāja temple.

V

Subsidiary Shrines and Structures

In the spacious compound of the Liṅgarāja, there are several shrines and structures belonging to different periods though most of them are later in date than the original temple complex comprising *deula* and *jagamohana.* In the original layout, the adjoining space around Liṅgarāja was left vacant. Subsequently, however, a number of temples were built in the courtyard.

The *Svarṇādri Mahodaya*[1] mentions some of the *liṅgas* located inside the *Prākārabhyantara* (compound) of the Liṅgarāja temple. The most important *liṅga* is Ekāmbareśvara, which was believed to be under a mango tree. In the northern side, there is Ugreśvara, the worship of which is considered highly meritorious. There is also Viśveśvara, which is another important *liṅga*. On the western side of Gaṇeśa, there are two *liṅgas* called Nandī and Mahākāla. These are also famous as Citragupteśvara. They were so named because the first worshippers of the *liṅgas* were a *gandharva* named Citra and a king named Gupta. Bhṛkuṭeśvara is located in front of Nandīśvara. The *liṅga* has been named Śabareśvara as it was first worshipped by a *Śabara* named Siddhabhūti. The *liṅga* called Laḍukeśvara, located in south-western corner, is considered to be the Lord of nine lakhs of *liṅgas*. This *bṛhatlinga* was first worshipped by Brahmā. It is round in shape like a *laḍu,* hence, it is called Laḍukeśvara. The *liṅga* named Śakreśvara was first worshipped by Śakra (Indra).

The *Svarṇādri Mahodaya*[2] mentions several *liṅgas* around the Liṅgarāja, such as Ugreśvara, Viśveśvara, Laḍukeśvara, Purveśvara, Sūkṣmeśvāra and Baidyanātha. In addition to these the text mentions other *liṅgas* of the Kṣetra, such as Kapileśvara, Iśāneśvara, Uttareśvara, Kedāreśvara and Jñyāneśvara, which may be located outside the Liṅgarāja compound. The *Kapila Saṁhitā*[3] mentions several temples inside the Liṅgarāja compound, such as Caṇḍeśvara, Vṛkṣarāja (Kalpavṛkṣa), Sāvitrī, Gaṇeśa, Himādṛjā (Pārvatī), Śikhidvaja (Kārttikeya) and Ekāmbareśvara.

The *Śiva Purāṇa*[4] *(Uttara Khaṇḍa)* also mentions temples, such as Ugreśvara (northern direction), Laḍukeśvara (south-west direction), Śakreśvara, Viśveśvara: the Lord of more than ten lakhs of *liṅgas*, Rudreśvara (east direction), Sūkṣmeśvara and Baidyanātha. Some of these shrines are still places of worship. Below is given brief description of the subsidiary temples and shrines in the Liṅgarāja compound. (Temples enlisted here are as per the site plan.)

GAṆEŚA TEMPLE (TEMPLE NO. 1)

The temple with its *deula* faces north. In front of the *sanctum,* there is a porch in place of a regular *jagamohana.* This structure again is not a part of the original plan, but is evidently a later addition. The *deula,* in the disposition of its *pāgās* of the *gaṇḍi,* gives the impression of a *sapta-ratha* temple. The *bāḍa* of the temple has five divisions. The *pābhāga* consists of five mouldings of which two upper mouldings are visible. The *jaṅghā* is divided into two registers by a *bandhanā* of three plain mouldings. The lower *jaṅghā* has *khākharā-muṇḍis,* which have empty niches. The upper *jaṅghā* is distinguished by *pīḍha muṇḍis.* The *varaṇḍa* is composed of seven plain mouldings. The central projections have in their niches, the images of Gaṇeśa as *pārśva devatās.* In the south, there is a two-armed seated image of Gaṇeśa while in the west a standing image of Gaṇeśa survives as a *pārśva devatā.* The niche on the east is empty (Pl. 114).

The temple is of modest dimension and its *gaṇḍi* has five *bhumis* in the *kanikā-pāgās*. The decoration of the *rāhā* consists of replicas of *rekhā deula* and a projecting lion. The treatment of the *rāhā* and the placement of the miniature temples is similar to other minor temples in the compound. The *anuratha* has a succession of two miniature temples. The *rāhā-pāgā* on the north is remarkable; in the arrangement of the miniature temples on its *gaṇḍi,* at the level of the *varaṇḍa,* there is a *pīḍha* type motif with two miniature *rekhā* temples, on either side. The *mastaka* consists of the *bekī,* the *āmlā* supported by *deula-cārinīs, khapurī* and the *kalaśa.*

The presiding deity of the temple is a two-armed seated figure of Gaṇeśa placed in a miniature *pīḍha* temple. The lintel above the doorway contains the figures of *navagrahas* with Ketu distinguished by upraised hands. On each side of the entrance, there are two *nāyikā* figures: one with folded hands and other playing a *vīṇā.* In front of the *deula,* there is a modest *vāhana stambha* surmounted by a rat. On the northern face of this column, there is a miniature figure of two-armed Gaṇeśa (Pl. 92).

In front of the temple there is a porch with a pyramidal roof made of five *pīḍhas.* The porch is open in all the sides with its doorways distinguished by decorated arches. The interior ceiling is carved with a lotus design. The over-sailing courses of the ceiling on the west depict Anantaśayī-Viṣṇu and the scene of the marriage of Śiva with Pārvatī (*Pārvatī pariṇaya);* while the northern face is relieved with a procession of infantry and elephants. The style of the ornamentation of the entrance pilasters and their arches suggest that the porch could have been added in the 13th century. On grounds of style, the temple however belongs to the late 11th-12th centuries. The temple of Gaṇeśa is first visited by devotees on entering the temple. The presiding deity of this temple is famous as Siddha-Lambodara or Siddha-Gaṇeśa. He is considered as Vighneśvara, the remover of obstacles.

LAKULĪŚA TEMPLE (TEMPLE NO. 3)

Adjoining the Gaṇeśa temple, on its eastern side, there is a small *pīḍha* temple made of laterite stone. Inside the *sanctum,* there is an image of seated Lakulīśa in the *dharma-cakra-pravartana-mudrā.* The two-armed Lakulīśa is depicted in *padmāsana.* The *lakuṭa* is found in his left hand. Lakulīśa is flanked by two devotees on either side (Pl. 108).

TWO RUINED ŚIVA TEMPLES NEAR GAṆEŚA TEMPLE (TEMPLE NOS. 5 AND 6)

There are two ruined temples to the south-east of the Gaṇeśa temple. Both the temples are built over a low platform. Each one of them faces the eastern direction. The northern temple (Temple No. 5) is of the *rekhā* order. Its *pābhāga* consists of five mouldings, *bandhanā* of three mouldings and *varaṇḍa* of seven mouldings. The lower *jaṅghā* has *khākharā-muṇḍis* and upper *jaṅghā* has *pīḍha muṇḍis.* The temple is *pañca-ratha* on plan. Its *rāhā* has a projecting lion. The *kanikā-pāgā* is demarcated by *bhūmi-āmlās.* The front *rāhā* has miniature temples as a part of its decoration. The *pārśva devatā* images are missing. On the whole, this small temple has a beauty of its own because of its decorative programme. On grounds of style, this may be assigned to the late 13th century (Pl. 115).

The other temple to its south (Temple No. 6) is also a *rekhā* temple. Though devoid of its crowning elements, this temple has a similar decorative programme. Its *bāḍa* has a *pābhāga* of five mouldings, *bandhanā* of three mouldings, and *varaṇḍa* of seven mouldings. *Pañca-ratha* on plan, its *gaṇḍi* has identical decorative carvings and has projecting lion on an elephant on the *rāhā.*

UNIDENTIFIED ŚIVA TEMPLE (TEMPLE NO. 8)

To the west of the Gaṇeśa temple, as the devotees ascend the steps and proceed towards the south, one comes across an abandoned Śiva temple, now used as a store for earthen pots to be used in the kitchen.

The temple, facing north, consists of a *deula* and *jagamohana.* The lower part of the temple is covered with debris. The *pārśva-devatā* niches are empty. The *bāḍa* has two *jaṅghās* with a *bandhanā* of a single moulding and *varaṇḍa* of five mouldings. The *gaṇḍi* is *pañca-ratha* on plan and it is plain. The projecting lions appear on the *rāhās.* The *rāhā* above the northern entrance, has three *rekha śikharas* below the projecting lion. The *mastaka* of the temple is missing.

The *jagamohana* is a *pīḍha-deula.* The lower portion of the *bāḍa,* like that of *deula,* is buried under debris. The *bāḍa* has two *jaṅghās* demarcated by a *bandhanā* of one moulding. The *varaṇḍa* above the upper *jaṅghā* has five mouldings. The *gaṇḍi* is made of two tiers of *pīḍhas*: four *pīḍhas* in the lower tier, while the upper tier is not complete and is without its crowning elements.

TEMPLES IN THE MALAYAGIRI AREA (TEMPLES NOS. 9 AND 10)

There are two temples in the south-east corner of the compound, located at a higher level, for which the area is called Malayagiri. Of these two temples, the one facing east is dedicated to Viṣṇu (Temple No. 10) and the other one facing west is a Śiva temple (Temple No. 9) (Pl. 116).

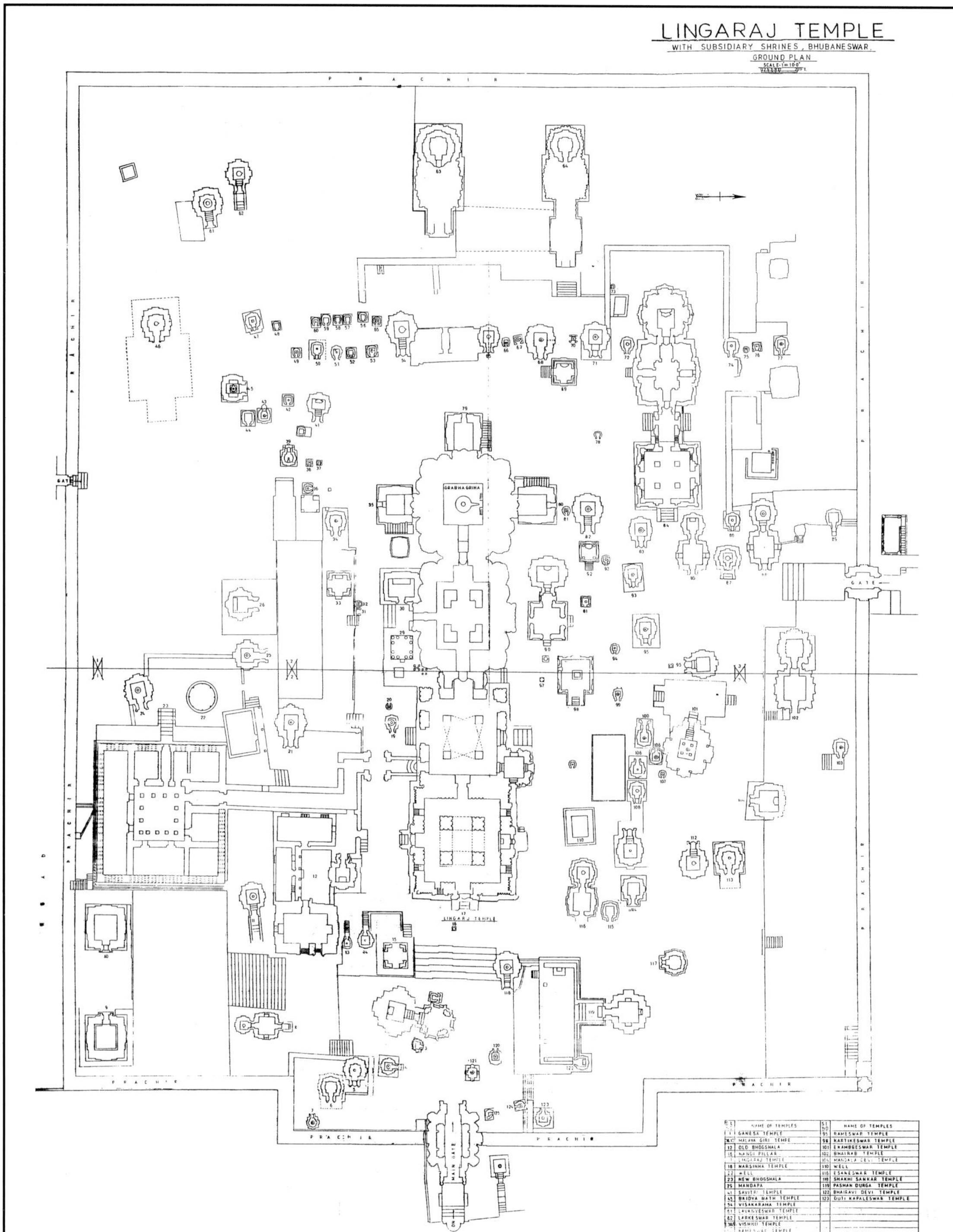

Fig. 15. Site Plan of Liṅgarāja Temple Compound.

(A) Viṣṇu Temple (Temple No. 10)

The east facing Viṣṇu temple is a temple of the *mukhaśālā* type with usual crowning elements. It is *pañca-ratha* on plan and stands over a high platform. The *bāḍa* is plain. Its southern niche is occupied by an image of Varāha and the western niche has a figure of Narasiṁha. The presiding deity of the temple is missing, but its Vaiṣṇava character is evident from its two surviving *pārśva-devatā* images. This temple may be assigned to the later Gaṅga period (Pls. 104-105).

(B) Śiva Temple (Temple No. 9)

This Śiva temple, facing west, is a *pīḍha* temple, which is very similar to the *mukhaśālā* of the Megheśvara temple. Like temple No. 10, it stands over a common platform ascended by steps on the north. The only surviving *pārśva-devatā* is a seated figure of Pārvatī on the north. The temple is *pañca-ratha* on plan and it is without any ornamental carvings. Originally, it was a Śiva temple and being identical with Temple No. 10, it also belongs to the later Gaṅga period.

The two temples, one dedicated to Śiva and other to Viṣṇu, being built over a common *pīṭha,* symbolize the cult of Hari-Hara, which became dominant at the Liṅgarāja temple. Some scholars believe that the temple No. 10 originally had Lakṣmī-Nārāyaṇa as its presiding deity. Later on, it was removed to a new shrine on the northern side of the *bhoga-maṇḍapa.*

The image of Ardhanārīśvara, which is placed inside the *nāṭa-mandira,* originally belonged to Temple No. 9 according to traditions.

UNIDENTIFIED ŚIVA TEMPLE NEAR THE KITCHEN BLOCK (TEMPLE NO. 11)

There is a Śiva temple (Temple No. 11) located in between the old and the new kitchen blocks. The temple built of khandolite stone is of the *rekhā* order. The *bāḍa* portion of the temple is covered with debris. The temple is *pañca-ratha* on plan and faces east. The *garbhagṛha* with Śivaliṅga is much below the ground level and is reached by descending steps. The *gaṇḍi* is plain and the projecting lions emerge into the air from the *rāhā.* The eastern face of the *rāhā* continues the usual tradition of placing a *khākharā-mastaka* in centre with flanking *rekhā-śikharas.* The doorway on the east has the usual decorative features, such as *dvārasakhas, dvārapālas,* Gaja-Lakṣmī in the lintel and the *navagrahas* architrave above it. The usual elements of *mastaka* of a *rekhā* temple, such as *bekī, āmlā, khapurī* and *kalaśa* are still intact.

THE TEMPLES OF CITREŚVARA AND GUPTEŚVARA (TEMPLE NOS. 13 AND 14)

The two temples, locally called Citreśvara (Temple No. 13) and Gupteśvara (Temple No. 14), stand to the south of the *Nāhikaṭā Maṇḍapa* (Temple No. 15) and east of Lakṣmī-Nṛsiṁha temple (Temple No. 18). The two temples face towards west and are of the *rekhā* order. The northern one is known as Citreśvara and to its south stands the temple of Gupteśvara. Both the temples are partly buried. Both the temples are *pañca-ratha* on plan and their *bāḍa* and *gaṇḍi* are quite plain.

In Citreśvara temple the figure of Gaja-Lakṣmī and the *navagraha*s are visible. The two temples are devoid of *kalaśa* on the *mastaka.*

LAKṢMĪ-NṚSIṀHA TEMPLE (TEMPLE NO. 18)

The temple of Lakṣmī-Nṛsiṁha is located on the southern side of the *Bhoga-maṇḍapa.* It stands on a high platform. The temple seems to have consisted of *deula* and *jagamohana,* of which only the *deula* facing west exists in a tolerable good condition. The *deula* is a *rekhā* temple. The *bāḍa* design is similar to the pattern followed in mature Orissan temples. Its *pābhāga* is of five plain mouldings, *bandhanā* of three mouldings and *varaṇḍa* has seven mouldings. The two *jaṅghas* are distinguished by *khākharā-muṇḍis* in the lower and *pīḍha-muṇḍis* in the upper respectively. In the recess of the upper *jaṅghā,* at places, female figures are extant. The *gaṇḍi, pañca-ratha* in style, has the usual projection with projecting lion on the *rāhā* and *bhūmi-āmalā* in the *kanikā-pāgā.* The *mastaka* of the temple has usual crowning elements. Its *āmlā* is supported by *dopicha-siṁhas* in the corners. The *pārśva-devatā* niches are empty. The temple, considering its plastic embellishment, may be assigned to the late 13th or 14th century. A modern hall in front of the *deula* indicates that there could have been a *jagamohana* adjoining the temple (Pl. 117).

The presiding deity of the temple is an image of Lakṣmī-Nṛsiṁha. The four-armed Nṛsiṁha is seated on a *padmāsana* in the *utkutika* posture with his legs kept in position by a *yogapaṭa.* His front two-hands are projected forward and are placed over his knees. The deity holds with his raised back hands a *cakra* and a *śaṅkha.* Lakṣmī is shown on his *yogapaṭa.* The image is flanked by *Śrīdevī* and *Bhūdevī.* The image can be assigned to the early 13th century. In Orissa there are excellent representations of Lakṣmī-Nṛsiṁha from Puri, Banpur, Jajpur and other places.[5]

MINOR SHRINES ON THE SOUTHERN SIDE OF THE *NĀṬA-MANDIRA* (TEMPLE NOS. 19 AND 20)

There are two minor temples on the south side of the *nāṭa-mandira* of the Liṅgarāja; one of the *rekhā* order and another of the *pīḍha* order. The *rekhā* temple (Temple No. 19), dedicated to Śivaliṅga, faces east. It is *pañca-ratha* on plan. The *bāḍa* consists of *pābhāga* of three mouldings, a *bandhanā* dividing the *jaṅghā* into two parts and a *varaṇḍa* of three mouldings. The *bāḍa* has the usual *pārśva-devatās* of a Śiva temple: Gaṇeśa on the south, Kārttikeya on the west and Pārvatī on the north. The plain *gaṇḍi* is distinguished by a projecting lion on the east. The *mastaka* has the usual components of a *rekhā* temple. The entrance has the usual motif of Gaja-Lakṣmī in the lintel and the *navagraha* slab.

The small *pīḍha* temple (Temple No. 20), situated towards the west of this *rekhā* temple, also contains a Śivaliṅga. This small *pīḍha* temple is *tri-ratha* on plan; its *bāḍa* is plain and its *gaṇḍi* is built of three *pīḍhas.* Its crowning elements are partly available.

UNIDENTIFIED ŚIVA TEMPLE ON THE NORTHERN SIDE OF KITCHEN BLOCK (TEMPLE NO. 21) (Pl. 118-120)

This unidentified Śiva temple is situated on the northern side of the kitchen block and eastern side of the *Bā-ā-khiā maṇḍapa.* It is a *rekhā* temple, which faces east. The *bāḍa* consists of a *pābhāga* of five mouldings, a *bandhanā* of one moulding dividing into two *jaṅghās* and a *varaṇḍa* of two mouldings. The *pārśva-devatā* niches on the *bāḍa* contain a broken standing Gaṇeśa on the south, standing four-armed Kārttikeya on the west and standing four-armed Pārvatī on the north.

Adjoining the northern *pārśva-devatā*, there is a miniature *pīḍha* temple, which seems to be a later addition. This *pīḍha* structure faces east and it has a standing four-armed figure.

The *gaṇḍi* of this temple is *pañca-ratha* on plan and distinguished by projecting lions on each *rāhā*. The *mastaka* has the usual components of a *rekhā* temple. The usual *deula-cariṇīs* are found in the middle of the *bekī* above each *rāhā*.

The eastern *rāhā* of the temple has an architectural design with five miniature temples; among these, the middle one is a *khākharā-muṇḍi* and the other four are of *rekhā* style. The doorway on the east has decorative *dvāra sakhās*, Gaja-Lakṣmī in the lintel and partly survived by *navagraha* slab architrave above it. Inside the temple, there is a Śivaliṅga which is under worship.

ŚIVA TEMPLE NEAR THE KITCHEN BLOCK (TEMPLE NO. 24)

Near the kitchen block in the southern part of courtyard, there are three temples all of the *rekhā* order. Of these, Temple No. 24 faces east. It has a *bāḍa* with the usual base mouldings, *jaṅghā* and *varaṇḍa*, which are partly buried. The *gaṇḍi* of the temple is plain: however, it has the usual projecting lions on the *rāhā* with *caitya*-window motif at the base. The eastern facade of the *gaṇḍi* has a miniature *khākharā-muṇḍi* in the centre and two flanking miniature *rekhā* temples on either side.

The *gaṇḍi* is *pañca-ratha* on plan and each *ratha* has a small *caitya* window motif at the base. The *pārśva-devatā* niches are empty. The eastern doorway is partly buried. It has the Gaja-Lakṣmī in the centre of the lintel and above it an architrave carved with *navagrahas*.

The *mastaka* of the temple has the usual elements, such as *bekī*, *āmlā*, *khapurī* and *kalaśa*. The *sanctum* has a Śivaliṅga, which is at a lower level.

UNIDENTIFIED ŚIVA TEMPLE ON THE EASTERN SIDE OF ANANTEŚVARA TEMPLE (TEMPLE NO. 25)

This unidentified Śiva temple is located on the eastern side of the Ananteśvara temple (Temple No. 26). It is a *rekhā* temple of the *pañca-ratha* plan. This temple faces north. The *bāḍa* consists of the *pābhāga* (fully buried), the plain *jaṅghā* divided into two parts by a *bandhanā* of one moulding and *varaṇḍa* of two mouldings. On the three sides of the *bāḍa*, there are *pārśva-devatā* niches, a four-armed standing Kārttikeya image on the west, a standing Gaṇeśa on the south and a four-armed standing Pārvatī on the east.

The curvilinear plain *gaṇḍi* is distinguished by projecting lions on each *rāhā*. The *mastaka* of this temple survives without *kalaśa*. The northern *rāhā* has projecting five miniature temples; the middle one is a *pīḍha* temple, other four are of *rekhā* style. The entranace doorway in the north has Gaja-Lakṣmī in the lintel and *navagraha* slab above it. The *sanctum* has a Śivaliṅga, which is now worshipped.

ANANTEŚVARA TEMPLE (TEMPLE NO. 26)

The Ananteśvara temple is located on the southern side of Liṅgarāja temple. It is a *rekhā* temple of modest dimension, which faces north. The temple, which consists of *deula* only, is *pañca-ratha* on plan. It rises on a low platform. Its *bāḍa* consists of *pābhāga* of five mouldings, a *bandhanā* of one moulding dividing the *jaṅghā* into two parts, and a *varaṇḍa* of four mouldings. Like the *bāḍa*, the *gaṇḍi* is plain. The usual projecting lion motif appears on the *rāhā*. The three *pārśva-devatā* niches are empty. Being built of laterite stone, the temple has no artistic carvings.

The unique interest of the temple lies in the worship of Baladeva, Ekānaṁśā and Kṛṣṇa in its *sanctum*. The image of Ekānaṁśā is placed in the centre. Baladeva (Ananta) stands in a *samabhaṅga* pose with two arms. Kṛṣṇa is four-armed. The arrangement of three figures seems to suggest that the arrangement could have been done later. The image of Baladeva is the largest among the three deities. His two hands are broken. The deity is distinguished by the serpent-hood over his head. The goddess Ekānaṁśā stands in *tri-bhaṅga* pose. Her right hand is in *varada* pose, while she holds a stem of lotus in her left hand. She is flanked by a female figure on the either side. Vāsudeva Kṛṣṇa evidently was four-armed, but the arms are now broken. The images of the Trinity may be assigned to the 13th century (Pl. 106).

MINOR SHRINE DEDICATED TO MAHIṢAMARDINĪ (TEMPLE NO. 31)

As a devotee comes out from the southern entrance of the *jagamohana* and proceeds towards the west, there is a small *pīḍha* temple, flanking the platform in which the *Bā-ā-khiā Maṇḍapa* has been erected. This minor shrine is of the *pīḍha* order and faces north. Its modest *gaṇḍi* has two *pīḍhas.* Inside the temple, there is a figure of eight-armed Mahiṣamardinī under worship. In this representation, the demon is shown as issuing out of the decapitated body of the buffalo.

SHRINE FOR UTSAVAVIGHRAHAS (TEMPLE NO. 30)

Near the southern entrance of the *jagamohana,* there is a structure for keeping the metal images of the temple. These images are used as *calanti pratimā* for various festivals and rituals. These images represent various Śaivite icons, such as Pañcavaktra Mahādeva, Candraśekhara, etc.

MINOR SHRINE (TEMPLE NO. 32)

There is a *rekhā* temple to the west of the Mahiṣamardinī shrine. This small temple faces north and has a Śivaliṅga for worship. The temple, *tri-ratha* on plan, is quite plain. The *bāḍa* of the temple contains *pābhāga* of one moulding, one *jaṅghā* and a plain *varaṇḍa.* Its *gaṇḍi* is distinguished by projecting lion. The *mastaka* has the usual components on a modest scale. The *dopiccha-siṁhas* appear on the *bekī.*

EKĀDAŚĪ MAHĀDEVA TEMPLE (TEMPLE NO. 34)

This Śiva temple is located on the southern side of the Liṅgarāja and just behind the *Bā-ā-khiā maṇḍapa.* The temple is of the *rekhā* order, and like many Śive temples, faces east. It is built over a low platform. The *deula* proper has *pābhāga* of five mouldings and two plain *jaṅghā*s connected by *bandhanā* of three mouldings. Above the upper *jaṅghā,* the *varaṇḍa* is made of seven mouldings.

The *gaṇḍi* divisions follow the *pañca-ratha* pattern. It has projecting lion on the *rāhā.* The *pārśva-devatā* niches in the *bāḍa* are empty. The eastern doorway has a Gaja-Lakṣmī in the centre of the lintel.

The presiding deity is a Śivaliṅga. It is specially auspicious to worship this *liṅga* on the day of *Ekādaśī*, hence, it is called Ekādaśī Mahādeva.

VĀRĀHĪ TEMPLE (TEMPLE NO. 39)

On the southern side of the Liṅgarāja compound, near the group of minor shrines, behind the *Bā-ā-khiā maṇḍapa* is a ruined *rekhā* temple, facing west. It is erroneously believed to be the Yamarājā temple. This temple stands on a low platform. The *bāḍa* of the temple has a *pābhāga* of five mouldings, two *jaṅghā* divisions, a *bandhanā* of three mouldings and a *varaṇḍa* of three mouldings. The *bāḍa* is virtually without any carving. The temple has *pañca-ratha* features on the *gaṇḍi*. A projecting lion appears on the northern facade of the *rāhā*. The upper portions of the *gaṇḍi* are missing along with all the components of the *mastaka*.

The presiding deity of the *sanctum* is the goddess Vārāhī. It is a four-armed Vārāhī image seated in *āliḍha* pose. Her upper right hand holds a fish and lower right is in *abhaya-mudrā*. She is holding a child in her lower left hand, while her upper left hand is broken. She is full of ornamentation and her hair-style is decorated. The mount buffalo is in the pedestal. It is wrongly identified by the local people as Yamarājā. Of the *Saptamātṛkā*s in Orissa, Vārāhī and Cāmuṇḍā are singled out for individual worship and individual temples are erected in their honour. The image of Vārāhī in the Liṅgarāja temple possibly belongs to a group of *mātṛkā*s. It may be mentioned here that outside the Liṅgarāja compound on the north-east, images of a group of three *mātṛkās* were recovered, while digging the foundation of a building, now known as the *Bhajana Maṇḍapa.* The worship of *matṛkā* indicates the popularity of the *Śakti* cult at Bhubaneswar (Pl. 109-110).

ṢAṢṬHĪ TEMPLE (TEMPLE NO. 40)

The Ṣaṣṭhī temple is located on the south-east corner of the Sāvitrī temple (Temple No. 41). It is a *pīḍha* temple, which faces north and stands on a platform. The *bāḍa* of the temple consists of *pābhāga* of one moulding, a single *jaṅghā* and a *varaṇḍa* of one moulding, all being without any workmanship. The temple is *tri-ratha* on plan and its superstructure consists of three continuous *pīḍhas.* The *mastaka* has the usual elements of a *pīḍha* temple.

The presiding deity of this temple is a four-armed standing female goddess, who is locally known as Ṣaṣṭhī devī.

SĀVITRĪ TEMPLE (TEMPLE NO. 41)

The temple of Sāvitrī situated on the south-west corner of the Liṅgarāja temple, is a modest *khākharā* temple facing east. Like the Bhubaneśwarī temple, this temple is distinguished by semi-cylindrical roof. Its exterior is without any plastic embellishment. This is due to the applied plaster at a later period. The *gaṇḍi* is dominated by four *caitya* windows on the four sides. The *sanctum* has a seated figure of goddess, who is worshipped as Sāvitrī. There are three *pārśva devatā*s on the exterior wall of the temple representing the forms of the goddess. The *mastaka* of Sāvitrī temple is surmounted by a *kalaśa.* The temple, being similar to Bhubaneśwarī temple, may be assigned to the 12th century (Pl. 121).

BAIDYANĀTHA TEMPLE (TEMPLE NO. 45)

Of the many minor shrines located in the southern side of the Liṅgarāja temple, the temple of Baidyanātha is remarkable for its sanctity and the power of the presiding Śivaliṅga to cure diseases. It is a *pīḍha* temple with five *pīḍhas.* The temple faces north. It seems that originally this temple had entrances in all the four sides. Subsequently, except the northern one, other entrances have been closed. The temple has a *pañcakāma pābhāga,* a *bandhanā* of three mouldings, two *jaṅghā*s and *varaṇḍa* of five mouldings. Inside the *sanctum,* there is an impressive Śivaliṅga with its *liṅga pīṭha,* pointing towards the west. Some priests believe that this Śivaliṅga originally formed a part of the great Śivaliṅga, in the *sanctum* of the Liṅgarāja temple, and later on this was removed on the wake of the Viṣṇuisation of the Liṅgarāja. There is no credible evidence, however, to confirm this hypothesis.

RĀMALIṄGEŚVARA TEMPLE (TEMPLE NO. 46)[6]

The Rāmaliṅgeśvara temple (Pls. 122-129) is situated in the south-western side of the Liṅgarāja compound. The temple faces east and is *pañca-ratha* in design. The temple is built on a low platform. The facing stones are not in proper position. The *bāḍa* of the temple is made of five divisions: *pābhāga* of five mouldings, *bandhanā* of three mouldings and *varaṇḍa* of ten mouldings. The usual *khākharā muṇḍi*s and *pīḍha-muṇḍi*s occur in the lower and upper *jaṅghā* respectively. The *gaṇḍi* is distinguished by a miniature temple on the *anuratha* on all the sides. The *rāhā* has also a miniature temple above which there is a projecting lion on an elephant. The *mastaka* as usual has *bekī, āmlā, khapurī,* but the *kalaśa* is missing. The seated *dikpāla*s are found in the niches of *khākharā-muṇḍis* of the *kanikā pāgās* and the consorts of *dikpālas* are found in the *pīḍha-muṇḍis* of the upper *jaṅghā.* In spite of the ruined condition of the temple, *dikpāla*s such as Indra, Agni, Yama, Nirṛti, Varuṇa, Vāyu, Kubera and Īśāna and their consorts are extant. An interesting scene of a man fighting a lion is found in the *khākharā-muṇḍi* in the lower *jaṅghā* on the western side in the *anurāhā-pāgā.* The *pārśva-devatā* niches of the three sides are empty. Below such niches, there are elongated *khākharā-muṇḍis* flanked by *nāga/nagī* columns. Inside the temple, there is a Śivaliṅga, locally known as Rāmaliṅgeśvara. The doorway on the east has a *navagraha* slab over the lintel. Of the *grahas,* Rāhu holds half-moon and Ketu holds sword and shield, a feature common to *navagraha* slabs of the 13th century. The door jambs of the temple consist of three *sakhās.* On grounds of style, this temple may be assigned to the 13th century. The clearance of debris around the temple, by the Archaeological Survey of India, brought to light architectural fragments and sculptures among which an interesting panel depicts a *Rāmāyaṇa* scene (Pl. 124).

VIŚVAKARMĀ TEMPLE (TEMPLE NO. 54)

On the western side of the Liṅgarāja temple, there is a row of temples; the one on the southern side is locally called Viśvakarmā, who was responsible for the construction of the great Liṅgarāja temple. The temple is *pañca-ratha* in design and faces east. The enshrined Śivaliṅga, placed much below the ground level, is worshipped as Viśvakarmā. The *bāḍa* of the temple is composed of a *pābhāga* of five mouldings, *jaṅghā* divided into two parts by a *bandhanā* and *varaṇḍa* of two

Pl. 85. Liṅgarāja: Compound, Mahiṣamardinī in a minor shrine.

Pl. 87. *Nāṭa-mandira, vaiṣṇava dvārapālas.*

Pl. 89. Liṅgarāja: *bhoga-maṇḍapa*, Lakṣmī-Nārāyaṇa.

Pl. 90. Gaṇeśa, Viśvakarmā Temple.

Pl. 86 (a)

Pl. 86. Liṅgarāja: *nāṭa-mandira*: (a) *pīṭha* (b) miniature temple design in the *bāḍa*, south.

Pl. 86 (b)

Pl. 88. Liṅgarāja: *bhoga-maṇḍapas* with *vāhana staṁbha* in the foreground, east.

Pl. 91. Gaṇeśa, Caṇḍeśvara Temple.

Pl. 92. Gaṇeśa, Gaṇeśa Temple as Pārśvadevatā.

Pl. 93. Gaṇeśa, Kārttikeya Temple, detached image.

Pl. 94. *Nṛtta* Gaṇeśa, Ekāmbareśvara Temple.

Pl. 95. Kārttikeya in a minor shrine.

Pl. 96. Kārttikeya, Viśvakarmā Temple.

Pl. 97. Kārttikeya, *nāṭa-mandira*.

Pl. 98. Pārvatī, minor shrine.

Pl. 99. Dancing Bhairava, Liṅgarāja Temple.

Pl. 100. Ekapāda Bhairava, Bhairaveśvara Temple.

Pl. 101. Sūrya, Vṛṣabha Temple.

Pl. 102. Sūrya, Kalpataru *maṇḍapa*.

Pl. 103. Sūrya *pūjā*, Liṅgarāja compound.

Pl. 104. Varāha, Lakṣmī Nṛsiṁha Temple.

Pl. 105. Nṛsiṁha, Viṣṇu temple, Malayagiri sea.

Pl. 106. Vāsudeva trinity, Ananteśvara temple.

Pl. 107. Hari-Hara, detached image, Liṅgarāja compound.

Pl. 108. Lakulīśa, in a minor shrine.

Pl. 109. Mātṛkā, Indrāṇī image recovered from *Bhajana maṇḍapa*.

Pl. 110. Mātṛkā Cāmuṇḍā from *Bhajana maṇḍapa*.

Pl. 112. Caturdhāmūrtti of Jagannātha fixed on the outer compound wall, east.

Pl. 111. Standing goddess, Liṅgarāja Temple.

Pl. 114. Gaṇeśa Temple: Gaṇḍi design, north-west.

Pl. 113. View of the minor shrines in Liṅgarāja compound, north.

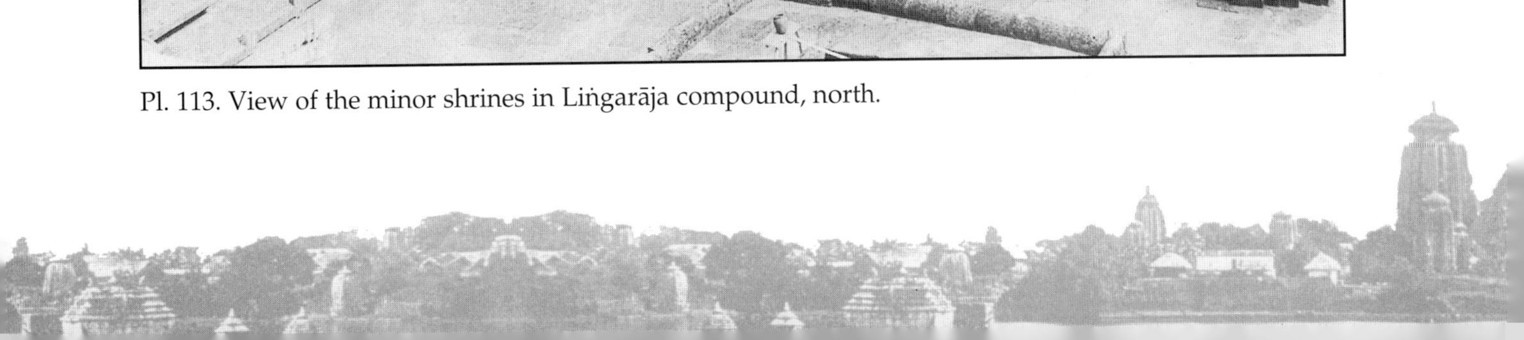

Pl. 115. Two ruined Śiva Temples to the South-east of Gaṇeśa Temple.

Pl. 116. Viṣṇu Temple, Malayagiri area.

Pl. 117. Lakṣmī Nṛsiṁha Temple.

Pl. 119. Śīva Temple near the kitchen block.

Pl. 118. Kitchen Block, Liṅgarāja Temple.

Pl. 120. Vajra-mastaka: Śīva Temple near the kitchen block, western *rāhā*.

Pl. 121. Sāvitrī Temple.

Pl. 123. Rāmaliṅgeśvara Temple, north.

Pl. 122. Rāmaliṅgeśvara Temple, east.

Pl. 124. Rāmaliṅgeśvara compound, *Rāmāyaṇa* scene.

Pl. 125. Lavaneśvara and Laḍukeśvara Temples.

Pl. 126. Viṣṇu Temple: Southern side.

Pl. 127. Vaiṣṇava Temple: north of No. 126.

Pl. 128. *Makara maṇḍapa*.

Pl. 129. Pārvatī Temple, north.

Pl. 130. Pārvatī Temple, south.

Pl. 131. Pārvatī Temple: *pīṭha* and *pābhāga*, west.

mouldings. The *bāḍa* is without any ornamentation. On the three sides of the *bāḍa,* there are *pārśva-devatā* niches: a four-armed Kārttikeya image on the west, a standing four-armed Pārvatī on the north and a four-armed standing Gaṇeśa on the south. The curvilinear *gaṇḍi* has projecting lions on the *rāhā.* The upper portion of the *gaṇḍi* has disappeared, but it has been made water-tight, as a result of conservation by the Archaeological Survey of India. The projecting wall on the east has a doorway with flanking *pīḍha-muṇḍi* on the sides, Gaja-Lakṣmī in the lintel and *navagraha* slab above the doorway (Pl. 90, 96).

The eastern face of the *gaṇḍi* of the temple is noted for its arrangement of miniature temples in the pattern of Laḍukesvara, Lavaṇeśvara, etc. In front of the temple, there is a small figure of Nandī, made of chlorite stone gazing at the Śivaliṅga of the temple.

LAVAṆEŚVARA TEMPLE (TEMPLE NO. 61)

The Lavaṇeśvara temple situated close to the Laḍukeśvara temple on its north is similar in design to the former. It faces east. The *bāḍa* consists of *pābhāga* not fully exposed, *jaṅghā* divided into two by a single moulding. The *varaṇḍa* consists of two broad mouldings with a sunken panel, which divides it from the *gaṇḍi.* The *gaṇḍi* is distinguished by a cluster of miniature temples on the eastern *rāhā,* the arrangement being identical to that of the Laḍukeśvara temple. The upper portion of the *gaṇḍi* is now missing. The *garbhagṛha,* which enshrines a Śivaliṅga, is much below the ground level. A four-armed standing Gaṇeśa on the south and a standing four-armed Pārvatī on the north constitute the usual *pārśva-devatā*s of this Śiva temple. The western niche meant for Kārttikeya is now empty.

LAḌUKEŚVARA TEMPLE (TEMPLE NO. 62)

On the western side of the Liṅgarāja compound, among the two ruined temples, locally called Laḍukeśvara and Lavaṇeśvara – the Laḍukeśvara temple, the northern one of the two, is in a better condition. The temple, which faces east, consists of only the *deula.* The temple rises abruptly from the ground level without any *pīṭha.* It is *pañca-ratha* on plan. As usual, the *pābhāga* consists of five mouldings, *bandhanā* of three mouldings, and *varaṇḍa* of five mouldings. *Khākharā-muṇḍis* and *pīḍha-muṇḍis* occur in the lower *jaṅghā* and the upper *jaṅghā* respectively. The *gaṇḍi* is without any decoration. On each *pāgā,* there is projecting lion on an elephant above a *kīrttimukha* base. The temple projects forward near the entrance and the eastern *rāhā* is distinguished by a cluster of three miniature temples, one *khākharā-muṇḍi* in the centre and two *pīḍha-muṇḍis* on the sides. The temple has the usual *pārśva-devatā* images; a four-armed standing Gaṇeśa in the south, a standing Kārttikeya in the west, and the northern niche which evidently had an image of Pārvatī, is now empty. The *pārśva-devatā*s are made of sandstone.

TWO TEMPLES IN THE WESTERN COURTYARD OF LIṄGARĀJA TEMPLE (TEMPLE NOS. 63 AND 64)

There are two richly ornamented temples in the western side close to the enclosure wall of the Liṅgarāja temple. These temples are not under worship and their religious affiliations are not clear, as *sanctums* and *pārśva-devatā* niches are all empty. It seems that both the temples had *jagamohanas* in the front, but in course of time these have disappeared. According to local traditions, these were Vaiṣṇava temples which enjoyed worship for a considerable period of time. There were separate kitchens for these temples, the remains of which are believed to exist towards the eastern side of the temples. Considering their rich decorative programme and architectural features, these two temples were a part of the cognate group and belong to the 13th century.

(A) Southern side Temple (Temple No. 63) (Pl. 126)

Of these, the southern temple (Temple No. 63) stands over a ornamented *pīṭha,* whose facing stones are not intact. Originally the temple consisted of the *deula* and *jagamohana* raised over a common *pīṭha.* As stated earlier, the *jagamohana* has disappeared and only the *deula* survives. The *deula* is *sapta-ratha* on plan. The *bāḍa* follows the conventional divisions of a mature medieval temple of Orissa. The *pābhāga* is made of five mouldings, *bandhanā* of three mouldings and *varaṇḍa* of nine mouldings. The lower *jaṅghā* has *khākharā-muṇḍis* on the *kanikā* and the *anuratha;* the corresponding parts in the upper *jaṅghā* have *pīḍha-muṇḍis.* The *pratiratha* is decorated with scroll-work. There are seated *dikpālas* in the *khākharā-muṇḍis* on the *kanikā* and the consort of the *dikpālas* appear in the corresponding *pīḍha-muṇḍis.* The *alasa-kanyās* are depicted in the *muṇḍi* niches of the *anuratha.* The recess of the *pāgās* in the lower *jaṅghā* are filled with the *viḍālas* and *alasa-kanyās.* The *rāhā* niches originally contained *pārśva-devatās,* which are not extant. Its *tala-garbhikā,* below the niche, is composed of an elongated *khākharā-muṇḍi* with flanking pilaster on either side. The niche itself is capped by a *pīḍha* moulding along with *kani* and *basanta.* Above the *basanta,* there are niches with flanking pilasters.

The *gaṇḍi* division also indicates the *sapta-ratha* plan. The *kanikā* is divided into ten *bhūmis,* demarcated by *bhūmi-āmlās.* The *kanikā* itself is disposed off in two planes. The *anuratha* is decorated with four *aṅga-śikharas* and diminishing in size, they enhance the vertical ascent of the temple. The *rāhā* is dominated by a major *vajra-mastaka,* above which is to be seen the projecting lion, rampant on an elephant. The *bekī* of the *mastaka* has *dopiccha-siṁhas* at the corners and figures of Garuḍa, placed on the *rāhā,* support the *āmlā.*

The *sanctum* is empty. The eastern doorway is made of three *dvāra-sakhās,* with *dvārapālas* in the *khākharā-muṇḍis* at the base and Gaja-Lakṣmī in the lintel.

(B) Northern side Temple (Temple No. 64) (Pl. 127)

The temple (Temple No. 64), situated to the north of temple No. 63, is virtually identical to the latter in architectural and decorative design. It is *saptaratha* on plan with the projection, such as *rāhā, anurāhā, anuratha,* and *kanikā.* The temple has a five-fold division in the *bāḍa, pābhāga* made of five mouldings, *bandhanā* of three mouldings and *varaṇḍa* of nine mouldings. The *jaṅghā* is divided into two registers. The lower *jaṅghā* has conventional *khākharā-muṇḍis* and the upper *jaṅghā,* as usual, the *pīḍha-muṇḍis.* The recesses between the *rathas* have *viḍālas* in the lower *jaṅghā* and female figures in the upper *jaṅghā.*

The *gaṇḍi* continues the *sapta-ratha* plan of the *bāḍa.* Above the *varaṇḍa,* however, there is no lower *vajra-mastaka* motif. The usual projecting lion appears on the *rāhā.* On each face the *rāhā* has a major *vajra-mastaka* surmounted by lion rampant on an elephant. On the eastern facade, in the place of *vajra-mastaka,* there is a large *aṅga-śikhara* with surmounting lion-on-elephant motif on the upper *rāhā.* The *kanika-pāgā* is disposed on two planes, has ten *bhūmis,* demarcated by *bhūmi-*

āmlās. The decoration of the *anuratha* presents a new feature; instead of a succession of *aṅga-śikharas,* there are eight stylized *vajra-muṇḍis* extending up to the *bisama.* The *pratiratha* has a succession of discs which enhance the height of the *śikhara.*

The *mastaka* consists of the *bekī,* the *āmlā* supported by *dopiccha-siṁhas* in the corners and images of Garuḍa above the *rāhās.* The main entrance in the east has Gaja-Lakṣmī in the lintel, three-fold division in the door jambs with *dvārapālas* in the *khākharā muṇḍis* at the base.

On grounds of style, this temple may be assigned to the 13th century. There are other temples in Bhubaneswar, which are similar in the disposition of the *gaṇḍi.* For example a ruined temple, locally called Vijayeśvara temple, closely follows this temple in the decoration of the *gaṇḍi* with similar succession of discs in the *pratiratha.*

RĀMA-SĪTĀ TEMPLE (TEMPLE NO. 65)

At a short distance to the north of the Viśvakarmā temple is the Rāma-Sītā temple facing east. It is a temple of the *rekhā* order with *pābhāga* of four mouldings, a plain *jaṅghā* and a *varaṇḍa* of two mouldings. The *gaṇḍi,* built in the *pañca-ratha* style, is conspicuous by the absence of any decoration except the projecting lion. The eastern face of the *rāhā* has three miniature temples with two flanking *aṅga-śikharas.* The treatment is similar to that of the Viśvakarmā temple. Inside the *sanctum,* there is a Śivaliṅga; in addition, there are metal images of Rāma and Sītā. The temple has a *navagraha* slab over the doorway. Being basically a Śiva temple, it has Śaivite *pārśva-devatās,* a four-armed standing Kārttikeya on the west and a four-armed Pārvatī image on the north. In front, in the absence of a *vāhana-stamba,* a Nandī has been installed on the pavement.

ŚIVA-KĀLĪ TEMPLE (TEMPLE NO. 68)

The minor temple, to the north of the Rāma-Sītā temple, is known as the Śiva-Kālī temple. It represents a *deula* of the *rekhā* order, which is *pañca-ratha* on plan. The temple faces east. The *bāḍa* has a *pañca-kama pābhāga,* two *jaṅghās* separated by a *bandhana* of three mouldings and a *varaṇḍa* of five mouldings. The *bāḍa* is quite plain and usual *khākharā-muṇḍis* and *pīḍha-muṇḍis* are absent. The *gaṇḍi* has in its *rāhā* projecting lion over the *kīrtti-mukha* pedestal. On each face of the temple in the *rāhā,* there are three miniature temples; in addition the *anuratha* has also a miniature *śikhara.* The entrance doorway of the east has Gaja-Lakṣmī in the lintel and *navagraha* slab above the doorway. In the *garbhagṛha,* a Śivaliṅga is worshipped. In front of the temple as usual there is a Nandī. The usual *pārśva-devatās* of a Śiva temple appear in the exterior niches in standing position; Gaṇeśa on the south, Kārttikeya on the west and Pārvatī on the north.

MINOR SHRINE WITH KĀRTTIKEYA FIGURE (TEMPLE NO. 70) (Pl. 95)

A miniature *pīḍha* temple on the western side of the Liṅgarāja is of unique interest. This shrine is evidently of a later date. But it has an early image of Kārttikeya fixed on its wall. This figure of Kārttikeya could have belonged to a temple of about 7th century AD, but its provenance is not known. Kārttikeya sits on the peacock. The outspread tail of the peacock is shown at the back. Kārttikeya is two-armed and holds a *śakti* in his left hand. Among the two divinities on either side of the image, one may be identified as Brahmā (on the right); the image on the left is broken.

KĀŚĪVIŚVANĀTHA TEMPLE (TEMPLE NO. 71)

The temple of Kāśīviśvanatha is situated in between the Śiva-Kālī temple and Pārvatī temple. It is located behind the *Svayaṁbara Maṇḍapa.* The temple is a *rekhā-deula* of *pañca-ratha* style. The *bāḍa* of the temple consists of a *pābhāga* of five mouldings, a *bandhanā* of one moulding dividing the plain *jaṅghā* into two parts and *varaṇḍa* of two mouldings. The *gaṇḍi* is also plain, but projecting lion is seen on the *rāhā* projection. The eastern *rāhā* has, like other temples such as Viśvakarmā, Rāma-Sītā, Śiva-Kālī, etc., five *aṅga-śikharas,* three on the central flank and two on the sides. The doorway, located in the east, carries Gaja-Lakṣmī in the lintel and *navagraha* slab above it. The *mastaka* consists of the usual architectural elements, such as *bekī, āmlā, khapurī* and *kalaśa.* Being a Śiva temple, it has the usual *pārśva-devatās,* such as Gaṇeśa on the south, Kārttikeya on the west and Pārvatī on the north, all shown in the standing position.

The presiding Śivaliṅga of this temple is regarded as Kāśīviśvanātha. According to the traditional texts, Ekāmra is regarded as Guptakāśī.

PĀRVATĪ TEMPLE (TEMPLE NO. 84) (Pls. 129-130)

The Pārvatī temple is located in the north-west corner of the Liṅgarāja compound. Being dedicated to Pārvatī, the consort of Śiva, this temple has a special religious significance. From the point of view of architecture and sculpture, it is also a magnificent temple. The temple consists of the *vimāna, jagamohana, nāṭa-mandira* and the *bhoga-maṇḍapa.* The *vimāna* and the *jagamohana* formed parts of the original scheme and belong to the same period. The *nāṭa-mandira* and the *bhoga-maṇḍapa* are clearly later additions.

R.L. Mitra[7] believed that the Bhagavatī temple (same as the Pārvatī temple) was erected by Vijaya Kesarī, although he did not assign any date. According of him the temple was built about two centuries later than the Liṅgarāja temple. M.M. Ganguly[8] also subscribed to the same view. A comparative study of the architectural and sculptural features of this temple and the Liṅgarāja temple confirm that the temple was posterior to the *vimāna* and the *jagamohana* of the Liṅgarāja temple. This view is also confirmed by the epigraphic evidence brought to light in 1954.[9] The inscription, in two lines engraved on the *pīṭha* of the temple, refers to gift of two earthen pots filled with cakes by Bhīma Bahika to goddess Umā Devī in the 13th *aṅka* of Śrī Bhānudeva who may be identified with the Gaṅga monarch Bhānudeva I, who ruled Orissa from AD 1264-1278. Thus it is evident that the temple was already in existence in AD 1274, which corresponds to the 13th *aṅka* year of Bhānudeva. This small inscription is significant in fixing the upper limit of the temple. On grounds of style, however, the temple may be regarded as a monument of the Gaṅga dynasty, which succeded the Somavaṁśī dynasty in coastal Orissa. Its stylistic features are similar to those of the Lakṣmī temple within the compound of the Jagannātha temple at Puri. The exuberance of the decorative details and the propensity for over ornamentation seem to suggest the date of the construction in the 13th century.

The above-mentioned inscription refers to Umā Devī, who was evidently the presiding deity. At present the presiding goddess of the temple is variously called Bhagabatī, Annapūrṇā and Pārvatī. The goddess is two-armed and she holds a lotus in her right hand and a pot of gems in the left hand. She is seated in *lalitāsana* on a *viśvapadma*. She wears a bejewelled *kirīṭa-mukuṭa*. The image is placed below a tri-foil arch with a *kīrttimukha* at the apex and *makaras* at the sides. Her *vāhana*, the lion is present to be seen in the right side, while kneeling devotees are seen on the left side. H.K. Shastri[10] mentioned about the iconography of Saubhāgya Bhuvaneśvarī and Annapūrṇā. The goddess of the temple conforms to Saubhāgya Bhubaneśvarī, who holds a pot of gems in one hand and a red lotus in the other hand. Pārvatī is also called Umā. Therefore, in later period the presiding goddess was called Umā or Pārvatī. B.V. Nath[11] believed that the original image of Umā Devī has been destroyed and has subsequently been replaced by a new one, which is now called Pārvatī. In our opinion, there is no justification for this suggestion and the original presiding deity is still *in situ* in the *sanctum.*

Deula (Pls. 131-137)

The Pārvatī temple, originally built with the *deula* and *jagamohana,* stands on a *pīṭha* of three mouldings with a narrow ledge around the base. The *pīṭha* mouldings follow the *pañca-ratha* plan of the *deula* and the *jagamohana.* The facade of the platform (about 9.60 mts. high) is richly carved. The bottom moulding is relieved with lotus petals on the upper portion, scroll-work on the *muhanti* and, at places, *caitya*-window motif. The middle moulding *kaṇi* is plain. The top moulding *basanta* is relieved with creepers and scroll-work. The exterior wall of the *bāḍa* is embllished with elongated *khākharā-muṇḍis, nāga/nāgī-stambhas, alasa-kanyās,* scroll-works, etc. The profusion of sculptural art makes the *bāḍa* one of the most ornamented of its type in Orissan temple art. The *bāḍa* is made of *pābhāga, jaṅghā* and *varaṇḍa.* It is *pañca-ratha* on plan. The *pābhāga* consists of five mouldings. The decorative programme of the *bāḍa* recalls that of Mukteśvara and Gaurī temple. The *kanika pāgā* is relieved with scroll-work and its central facet is embellished with female figures. The *anuratha* is treated with elongated *khākharā-muṇḍis* flanked by *nāga/nāgī-stambhas* on the *anuraha* recesses. The placement of the *nāga* and *nāgī* on the pilasters, show an upward movement. The *viḍāla* at the base is of single type, rather than the double *viḍālas* to be seen at Mukteśvara.

The central projection had in their niches the images of the *pārśva-devatās*. The niche is treated like a *khākharā-muṇḍi* with a pilaster surmounted by a mainiature *khākharā-muṇḍi* on either side. A projecting eave is found above the niche. Below the niche, there is a design of the elongated *khākharā-muṇḍi* crowned by a *bho*-motif. There were images of *pārśva-devatās* in the south, west and north niches. All of these represented a form of goddess. At present, only a chlorite image of the goddess Pārvatī is *in situ* in the northern niche. The four-armed standing goddess holds *triśūla* and a water jar in her upper hands, while the lower hands are broken. She stands against an ornamental *makara-toraṇa.* She is flanked by female attendants near her feet. The *pārśva-devatā* image of Pārvatī in the south side niche is made of khandolite stone and it seems to be a later replacement. The goddess stands in *sama bhaṅga* posture and holds *triśūla* and an indistinct object in her upper hands. The lower hands are missing. The western niche is empty and its *pārśva-devatā* image is also missing.

The *varaṇḍa* consists of a projected moulding, crowned by a recess separating the *bāḍa* and the *gaṇḍi.* The recess is relieved with *jāli* work. The upward thrust of the *gaṇḍi* is not disturbed by the *varaṇḍa.*

The *gaṇḍi,* like the *bāḍa,* is *pañca-ratha* on plan and has five divisions. In addition, the *anuratha* is provided with two *anurāhā* recesses covered with super-imposed *vajra-muṇḍis.* The *kanika* is divided into ten *bhūmis* and demarcated by *bhūmi-āmlās.* The *kanikā* is not disposed in two planes as in the case of the Liṅgarāja, but is rounded at the corner. The *anuratha* is carved with three vertical rows of *caitya*-windows and not replicas of the *rekhā-śikhara* as in the case of the Liṅgarāja.

The decoration of the *rāhā* consists of an elaborate *bho*-design, which starts immediately above the *varaṇḍa* recess. The *caitya*-window is relieved with an elongated miniature *khākharā-muṇḍi.* The flanking dwarfs give a distinct appearance to the *bho*-motif. The motif is surmounted by a projecting lion rampant on an elephant. On the eastern facade, the decoration of the *rāhā* has a miniature *śikhara* below the projecting lion, which is seen at a higher level. The *rāhā* decoration above the projecting lion includes five vertical bands of scroll-work reaching almost the top. Over the *biṣama,* there are the usual crowning elements with a trident at the top. The *āmlā* is supported by *dopiccha-siṁhas* at corners and seated figures of Devī, one each above the *rāhā.* The *deula* is about 17.98 mts. in height.

As in case of the other Orissan temples, the walls of the interior are plain. The door frame of the temple is surmounted by an architrave carved with figures of the *navagrahas.* Surya holds lotus in each hand. Chandra, Maṅgala, Budha, Bṛhaspati, Śukra and Śani carry in their left hand water pot and in the right hand rosary. Rāhu represented in upper half only, holds a crescent in each hand. Ketu holds a sword and shield and the lower part of his body is in the form of a serpent.

Jagamohana (Pls. 138-141)

The *bāḍa* of the *jagamohana* follows closely the ornamentation of the *deula.* It has a *pābhāga* of five mouldings, a *jaṅghā* and a *varaṇḍa* of two mouldings. The additional feature to be noticed in the *jagamohana* is the provision of *anuratha* being flanked by a *nāga/nāgī-staṁbha* with a pilaster on each side. The *kanikā* has pilaster with an *alasa-kanyā.* The *nāga/nāgī-staṁbhas* are similar to those of the *deula,* but without crowning *bhāra rakṣaka* figures. Originally, the *jagamohana* had two balustraded windows. The one on the north is still there, but on the south, it has been converted into a door, probably during the addition of the *nāṭa-mandira* and the *bhoga-maṇḍapa,* as in the case of the Liṅgarāja temple. The lintel over the balustraded window is carved with a procession of elephants. The five balusters on the north are relieved with female figures in high relief.

The *jagamohana* originally had images of *dikpālas* in the niches of the *khākharā-muṇḍis.* This is evident from an image of seated Īśāna, which is found in a niche of the *khākharā-muṇḍi* in the north-east corner. The seated image is placed on a bull but his hands are broken.

The pyramidal roof of the *jagamohana* is made of eleven *pīḍhas* arranged in two tiers; six on the lower and five on the upper. The usual crowning components are all in position. The *ghaṇṭā* is supported by *bekī-bhairavas.*

Nāṭa-Mandira and *Bhoga-Maṇḍapa*

The *nāṭa-mandira* and *bhoga-maṇḍapa* are stylistically later than the *vimāna* and *jagamohana* of the Pārvatī temple. It appears that, originally, the *bhoga-maṇḍapa* was built as an isolated structure. It was probably an open-pillared *maṇḍapa* and subsequently the openings were closed with walls. The *nāṭa-mandira* came up later than the *bhoga-maṇḍapa* by connecting the *jagamohana* with the *bhoga-maṇḍapa.* This connecting hall is about 5.18 mts. long and 4.26 mts. wide. In the *nāṭa-mandira,* there are two doorways, one on the north and another on the south provided with flight of steps. In addition, on each side there is a balustraded window with three balusters. The roof of the *nāṭa-mandira* is built of three *pīḍha* mouldings.

Both the *nāṭa-mandira* and the *bhoga-maṇḍapa* stand on a *pīṭha,* which is higher than that of the *vimāna* and *jagamohana.* The face of this platform is in the form of a *bāḍa* with *pābhāga, jaṅghā* and *varaṇḍa.* The *jaṅghā* is embellished with *muṇḍi* designs. Such ornamentations in the *bhoga-maṇḍapa* are more ornate than those of the *nāṭa-mandira.* The *bhoga-maṇḍapa* is built as a *pīḍha* temple. Its pyramidal roof is made of five *pīḍhas* and is crowned by the usual *mastaka.*

The *bhoga-maṇḍapa* has openings on north and south and an entrance in the east. In addition, there are balustraded windows – two each in south, north and west. Inside the *bhoga-maṇḍapa,* there are four pillars arranged in a square. The roof of the structure rests on the four pillars. In the interior of the *bhoga-maṇḍapa,* there are two detached chlorite images, a four-armed standing Kārttikeya and a two-armed standing female figure fixed on the inner side of the eastern wall.

CAṆḌEŚVARA TEMPLE (TEMPLE NO. 82)

The temple of Caṇḍeśvara, situated to the north of the main temple of Liṅgarāja, consists of *deula* only. It is devoid of any artistic merit. It is *pañca-ratha* on plan and faces east. The *deula* is a *rekhā* temple with its *pābhāga* composed of five mouldings, which are connected by vertical bands at intervals. Its *jaṅghā* is divided into two parts, i.e., lower *jaṅghā* and upper *jaṅghā* with the usual *khākarā-muṇḍis* and *pīḍha-muṇḍis,* with their niches being empty. The *bandhanā* consists of three mouldings and the *varaṇḍa* has five mouldings. An image of four-armed standing Gaṇeśa (Pl. 91) adorns the southern niche of the *bāḍa* as the *pārśva-devatā.* The *gaṇḍi* is conspicuous by the absence of any decorative programme, except the projecting lions of the *rāhā.* The eastern face of the *rāhā* has five *aṅga-śikharas* on the *gaṇḍi* including two on the sides. The treatment recalls the series of temples located in the western side of the courtyard, such as the Viśvakarmā, Kaśī-Viśvanātha, Śiva-Kālī temple and others. The temple has a *tri-sakhā* doorway on the east with Śaivite *dvārapālas,* placed in the niche of the *pīḍha-muṇḍis.* The facade of the sill of the doorway is in the form of a moon stone. The presiding Śivaliṅga of the *sanctum* is called Caṇḍeśvara as Caṇḍa is included as one of the eleven incarnations of Śiva.[12]

GAURĪ-ŚAṄKARA TEMPLE (TEMPLE NO. 83)

This temple is situated to the east of *bhoga-maṇḍapa* of the Pārvatī temple. The temple is so called because in addition to the usual Śivaliṅga in the *sanctum,* there is a standing four-armed figure of Pārvatī attached to the back wall of the temple.

The temple is of the *rekhā* order and faces east. It has *bāḍa* with five divisions; *pābhāga, jaṅghā* divided into two registers by a *bandhanā* of one moulding and *varaṇḍa* of two mouldings. The outer niches of the *bāḍa,* meant for the *pārśva-devatās,* are empty. The *bāḍa* is devoid of any carving and architectural motifs, such as *pīḍha-muṇḍis* and *khākharā-muṇḍis.* The *gaṇḍi* is *pañca-ratha* on plan and has projecting lions on the *rāhās.* The upper portions of the *gaṇḍi,* including the crowning elements are missing. The front face of the *rāhā* is decorated with a central *khākharā-muṇḍi,* flanked by miniature *rekhā-śikharas* on either side. The doorway in the east has *dvārapālas* at the base, Gaja-Lakṣmī in the lintel and the *navagraha* slab architrave above it.

SATYANĀRĀYAṆA TEMPLE (TEMPLE NO. 85)

In front of the Pārvatī temple, there is a later temple locally called Satyanārāyaṇa, worshipped as the presiding deity. The image is a four-armed standing figure of Viṣṇu holding *śaṅkha* and *cakra* in upper right and left hands respectively. The lower right hand holds a lotus, while the lower left hand rests over the mace *(gadā).* The top corner of the deity is flanked by *vidyādharas* and on either side of the deity, there are two female figures of Śrī Devī and Bhū Devī. The image stands on a lotus pedestal and Garuḍa is seen in the kneeling position near the right side of the image. The deity may be identified as Keśava-Viṣṇu.

On grounds of style, the image belongs to the late 12th or early 13th century. The temple facing east consists of *deula* and *jagamohana.* The *deula* without any carving is *pañca-ratha* on plan. Its *bāḍa,* as usual, has a *pābhāga,* a plain *jaṅghā* and a *varaṇḍa* of four mouldings. The *gaṇḍi* is plain and has the usual crowning elements. The projecting lions appear on the *gaṇḍi.* The *pārśava-devatā* niches of the *deula* are all empty.

The *jagamohana* is a *pīḍha* temple with seven *pīḍhas* without any *poṭala* division. The *bāḍa* of the temple is plain.

UNIDENTIFIED ŚIVA TEMPLE (TEMPLE NO. 86)

This Śiva temple located in the north-western side of the Satyanārāyaṇa temple, is a *rekhā* temple built of laterite stone, which explains the plain character of this structure. It is *pañca-ratha* in design and stands over a low platform. The temple faces east. Its *bāḍa* has a *pābhāga* of three mouldings, one plain *jaṅghā* and *varaṇḍa* of three mouldings. Its *pārśva-devatā* niches are empty.

The *gaṇḍi* of the temple is devoid of any architectural beauty. The temple has, as usual, crowning elements such as *bekī, āmlā, khapurī.* The eastern doorway has a Gaja-Lakṣmī in the centre of the lintel and above it the *navagraha* slab. The *sanctum* has a Śivaliṅga for worship.

TĀRAKEŚVARA ŚIVA TEMPLE (TEMPLE NO. 87)

There is a ruined Śiva temple close to the north of the Satyanārāyaṇa temple. The temple faces east and is of the *rekhā* order. It is built on a low platform and its loose stones are still extant. The temple is of modest dimension and the design and carvings indicate that it could have belonged to the 13th or early 14th century. The temple proper stands over a *pīṭha* of three mouldings. The *bāḍa* of the temple is made of *pābhāga* of five mouldings, *jaṅghā* divided into two registers by a *bandhanā* of three mouldings. The *varaṇḍa* is made of five mouldings. The *gaṇḍi* has projecting lions on the *rāhā.* The *kanikā pāgā* is demarcated by *bhūmi-āmlās.* The *pārśva-devatā* niches of this temple, however, are empty. The *kalaśa* of the temple is now missing. The *navagraha* slab is noticed above the eastern doorway. There is no trace of the *jagamohana.*

UGREŚVARA TEMPLE (TEMPLE NO. 88) (Pl. 142)

To the north of the ruined Tārakeśvara Śiva temple (Temple No. 87), there is a *rekhā* temple of laterite stone, which is locally called Ugreśvara. As one enters the premises of the Liṅgarāja temple through the northern entrance, this temple is the first temple located on the right-hand side. It is virtually devoid of any architectural or decorative significance.

The temple, facing east, consists of *deula* and *jagamohana.* The *deula* is *pañca-ratha* on plan. Its *bāḍa,* as usual, has *pābhāga* of five mouldings, which is not fully visible. Its *jaṅghā* is divided into two parts, i.e., lower *jaṅghā* and upper *jaṅghā* with the usual *khākharā-muṇḍis* and *pīḍha-muṇḍis.* The *bandhanā* consists of three mouldings and the *varaṇḍa* has five mouldings. There is a projecting lion on each *rāhā,* while the *pārśvadevatā* niches are empty. The *mastaka* has, as usual, *bekī, āṁlā* and *khapurī.*

The *jagamohana* is a *pīḍha* temple consisting of two tiers. The lower tier has four *pīḍhas,* while the upper tier has three *pīḍhas.* The *bāḍa* has a *pābhāga* of five mouldings, *bandhanā* of three mouldings and *varaṇḍa* of four mouldings. The lower *jaṅghā* is adorned with *khākarā-muṇḍis* and upper *jaṅghā* with *pīḍha-muṇḍis* respectively. The balustraded windows, consisting of four balusters, are found in the south and north side of the *jagamohana.* The main entrance in the east has Gaja-Lakṣmī in the lintel of doorway and *navagrahas* are placed above it.

GOPĀLINĪ (BHUVANEŚVARĪ) TEMPLE (TEMPLE NO. 90) (Pl. 143)

The temple of Gopālinī or Bhuvaneśvarī is situated on the northern side of the Liṅgarāja temple. As the Devī, according to the legends, subdued the two demons Kīrtti and Vāsa (*kīrttivās vimardinī*) in the guise of a Gopālinī, the temple of the consort of Śiva (Bhuvaneśvarī), is famous as Gopālinī. The temple consists of a *deula* and *jagamohana.* The *deula* is of the *khākharā* variety, while the *jagamohana* is of the *pīḍha* order. The *deula,* oblong on plan, is surmounted by the semi-cylindrical roof. The *bāḍa* of the *pābhāga* consists of four mouldings, instead of the usual five mouldings; a plain *jaṅghā* and recess separate the *bāḍa* and the plain *gaṇḍi.* The *khākharā-mastaka* is distinguished by a *kalaśa,* flanked by lions on both sides. The front *rāhā* of the temple is dominated by three miniature *rekhā* temples. The *pārśva-devatā* images of the temple are standing figures of Pārvatī placed in the niches on the south-west and the north.

The *jagamohana* is a *pīḍha* temple and like the *deula,* is devoid of decorative details. Built on a low platform, its *bāḍa* is plain. The *jagamohana* has two entrances, one on the east and another on the north. The pyramidal superstructure has five *pīḍhas.* The *mastaka* consists of the usual components, such as the *bekī, ghaṇṭā, āmlā, khapurī* and *kalaśa.*

The *khākarā-deula* of Bhuvaneśwarī is at a lower level than the Pārvatī temple, which belongs to the 13th century. The temple, which is very close to the Liṅgarāja, could not have existed in the 11th century when the main temple of the Liṅgarāja was erected. It seems that this *khākharā* temple was erected in the 12th century.

RUINED ŚIVA TEMPLE (TEMPLE NO. 93)

This Śiva temple, which bears no special name, stands over a low platform. It consists of *deula* only, which is of the *rekhā* order. Facing to the east, it is *pañca-ratha* in design. The *bāḍa* of the temple has a *pābhāga* of five mouldings, *bandhanā* of three mouldings, and *varaṇḍa* of five undecorated mouldings. The two *jaṅghās* are also plain. The three *pārśva-devatā* niches on the *bāḍa* are now empty.

The *gaṇḍi* has a miniature *rekhā-śikhara* on the eastern face of the *rāhā.* The top portion of the *gaṇḍi* is missing. The eastern doorway has a Gaja-Lakṣmī in the centre of the lintel and above it, there is the conventional *navagraha* slab. The *sanctum* has the usual Śivaliṅga.

MINOR SHRINE WITH FIGURE OF PĀRVATĪ (TEMPLE NO. 94) (Pl. 98)

A small shrine in the Liṅgarāja compound on the northern side, close to the *Kalpataru Maṇḍapa,* is significant because of a figure of Pārvatī dating back to about early 7th century AD. This minor structure is apparently of a later period but for construction of its wall an early sculpture of Pārvatī has been attached. Pārvatī usually is seen as a *pārśva-devatā* of a Śiva temple and this detached sculpture of Pārvatī evidently belongs to an early temple. The figure of Pārvatī is four-armed. She holds rosary in the upper right hand and *ketaki* flower in the upper left, while her lower right hand is in the *varada* pose and the lower left hand holds a small vase. Apart from ornamentations and top-knot hair-do, the goddess wears *yajñopavīta* of deer skin. She is flanked by two attendants on either side with basket full of offerings on their heads.

KĀRTTIKEYA TEMPLE (TEMPLE NO. 95)

The temple of Kārttikeya is located in the northern side just in front of the temple of Ekāmbareśvara. The temple is of the *rekhā* order and faces south. As in a typical Orissan temple, *deula* has five-fold divisions in the *bāḍa.* Its *pābhāga* consists of five mouldings, *bandhanā* of three mouldings, and *varaṇḍa* is composed of five mouldings. The plain lower *jaṅghā* has *khākharā-muṇḍis* and in the upper *jaṅghā* there are *pīḍha-muṇḍis.* The *gaṇḍi* is devoid of carvings. The temple is *pañca-ratha* on plan with five projections on each side. The projecting lion is seen on each face of the *rāhā.* The *deula* has the usual crowning elements, such as *bekī, āmlā, khapurī* and *kalaśa.* The northern niche has a standing figure of Kārttikeya as the *pārśva-devatā,* the western niche is empty and the eastern niche contains a standing female figure as the *pārśva-devatā* and her hands are not intact. The central southern *rāhā* has three miniature temples and one miniature temple on each of the two sides. The temple has no *jagamohana.* The *vāhana-stambha,* located in front of the entrance at a short distance, is surmounted by a peacock. The presiding deity of this temple is a standing figure of Kārttikeya, whose upper part is only visible. He is distinguished by *śikhaṇḍaka* hair style and *Mayūra vāhana.*

UNIDENTIFIED ŚIVA TEMPLE NEAR THE TEMPLE OF KĀRTTIKEYA (TEMPLE NO. 96)

There is a *rekhā* temple to the south-west of Kārttikeya temple dedicated to Śiva. The temple faces east and is built on a low platform. It is *pañca-ratha* in design and has a *tri aṅga bāḍa.* The three divisions of the *bāḍa* are *pābhāga* of four mouldings, a plain *jaṅghā* and *varaṇḍa* of two mouldings. The *bāḍa,* in its outer niches, has *pārśva-devatā* images of standing four-armed Gaṇeśa in south, standing four-armed Pārvatī in north, while the western niche meant for Kārttikeya, is empty.

The plain *gaṇḍi* has projecting lions on the *rāhās*. The eastern face of the *rāhā* is carved with a *khākharā-muṇḍi* in the centre flanked by two miniature *rekhā* temples. The temple has the usual crowning elements. The eastern doorway is now devoid of usual figures of *dvārapālas,* Gaja-Lakṣmī and *navagraha* slab. The *sanctum* has a Śivaliṅga, which is now under worship.

EKĀMBAREŚVARA TEMPLE (TEMPLE NO. 101) (Pl. 144)

The Ekāmbareśvara Śiva temple is located in the northern side of the courtyard of the Liṅgarāja temple. According to the *Śiva Purāṇa (Uttara Khaṇḍa),* the Ekāmbareśvara *liṅga* facing west was located under the shade of a mango tree in the forest, called the Ekāmravana. Therefore, it was called Ekāmbareśvara *liṅga* and it is praised as an excellent *jyotirliṅga.* It is said that in the Ekāmra Kṣetra were three deities, namely, Ekāmbareśvara, Tribhuvaneśvara and Gopālinī.[13]

The temple is a *rekhā-deula* and is *pañca-ratha* on plan. The *bāḍa* consists of *pābhāga* of five mouldings, *bandhanā* of three mouldings connecting the lower and upper *jaṅghās* and *varaṇḍa* is of seven mouldings. The *bāḍa* is virtually plain, but the *pāgā* divisions are well articulated. The *pārśva-devatā* niches on the north and east are empty; an eight-armed dancing Gaṇeśa adorns the niche of the south. There are *aṅga-śikharas* at the base of the *gaṇḍi* on each *pāgā.* In addition, there are *aṅga-śikharas* above the flanking pilasters of the *rāhā.* On each face of the temple, there are seven *aṅga-śikharas;* the one on the *rāhā* is the tallest of all. The arrangement of *aṅga-śikharas* in the base of the *gaṇḍi* recalls the treatment at the Dākrā-Bhimeśvara temple. The clustering of the *aṅga-śikharas* at the base of the *gaṇḍi,* however, does not aid to the soaring quality of the temple. The *kanikā pāgā,* above the *aṅga-śikharas,* is divided into four *bhūmis.* The treatment of *aṅga-śikharas* of this temple is different from those of the Rājarānī temple, where the crowding of the *aṅga-śikharas* highten the vertical thrust of the temple. The flattened *aṅga-śikharas* arranged horizontally at the base of the *gaṇḍi* provides a different model, which laid the foundation for the development at the Brahmeśvara temple. Another peculiarity of Ekāmbareśvara is the depiction of one large miniature temple on the front facade of the *rāhā,* instead of two miniature temples as in other sides. The projecting lion on the front facade is therefore very large compared to its counterparts in other sides. The *gaṇḍi* terminates with a *biṣama.* The usual components of the *mastaka* are found. The *bekī,* however, has *bekī-vairavas* in the *rāhā* and *dopiccha-siṁhas* on the corners, this arrangement being the first of its type in the evolution of Orissan *rekhā-deula,* a feature which is repeated in the *deula* of the Liṅgarāja temple. In front of the main entrance on the west, there is an open platform meant for rituals. It is said that, Rājā of Puri used to visit the temple on the *Śivarātrī* and royal *Saṁskāra*s are held on this platform.

The Ekāmbareśvara temple, considering its affinity to Rājarānī and Dākrā Bhimeśvara, may probably be assigned to the 11th century and could be earlier than the Brahmeśvara and Liṅgarāja temple. Ekāmbareśvara is the first Śivaliṅga of the *kṣetra.* In view of the great sanctity and popularity, it finds mention in several texts such as *Ekāmra Purāṇa, Ekāmra Candrikā* and *Śiva Purāṇa (Uttara-Khaṇḍa).* The *Oriyā Mahābhārata* of Sāralā Dās (15th century) also refers to the Ekāmbareśvara in the Ekāmra Kṣetra.

BHAIRAVEŚVARA TEMPLE (TEMPLE NO. 100)

The Bhairaveśvara temple, so called because of an Ekapāda Bhairava image, is located quite close to the northern boundary wall inside the compound, a little away from the northern entrance. The temple originally consisted of *deula* and *jagamohana.* The *deula* has disappeared and only the *jagamohana* remains. The *jagamohana* is a *pīḍha* temple, *pañca-ratha* on plan and built on a raised ground. The *bāḍa* of the temple has the usual decorative programme with *khākharā-muṇḍis* in the lower *jaṅghā* and *pīḍha-muṇḍis* in the upper *jaṅghā.* The *dikpāla*s and their counterparts still survive at places, in spite of the lack of conservation. In the interior on the southern flank, there is an image of Ekapāda Bhairava, the source or origin of which is not precisely known. The *jagamohana* faces east and is provided with balustraded windows. The entrance on the west originally led to the *garbhagṛha* of the main temple, has not survived. The temple may be assigned to the 13th century.

MAṄGALĀ TEMPLE (TEMPLE NO. 104)

Of the subsidiary temples dedicated to Śakti worship, Maṅgalā temple is situated on the northern side of the Liṅgarāja compound, to the north of the Ekāmbareśvara temple. The temple is a *pīḍha-deula.* It is made of laterite stone.

The pyramidal *gaṇḍi* consists of two tiers with four *pīḍhas* in lower and three *pīḍhas* on the upper. On each face, the *gaṇḍi* has a bell-shaped member *(ghaṇṭā),* thus converting the temple into a *pañca-ghaṇṭā* type *pīḍha-deula.* The temple faces south and its presiding goddess is locally known as Maṅgalā.

She is an eight-armed female figure seated in *padmāsana.* The image is of sandstone and holds in her hands *triśūḷa, nāgapāśa, daṇḍa, mālā,* etc. She has the lion mount in the pedestal.

VṚṢABHA TEMPLE (TEMPLE NO. 111)

Vṛṣabha is intimately connected with Śiva as his *vāhana.* On the northern side abutting the wall of the *nāṭa-mandira,* there is a *pīḍha* temple dedicated to Vṛṣabha. The temple stands on a low platform of three mouldings. The temple has five-fold divisions in the *bāḍa.* The *pābhāga* and the *bandhanā* consist of five and three mouldings respectively. There are *khākharā-muṇḍis* in the lower *jaṅghā* and *pīḍha-muṇḍis* in the upper *jaṅghā.* The recesses in the *bāḍa* have *vyālas* and *kanyās.* The balustraded window on the west is plain, the eastern one has a figure of Sūrya placed in a chariot, which is drawn by four horses. The figure of four-armed standing Kārttikeya on the western face of the temple is noteworthy for its iconography. The *varaṇḍa* of the temple consists of seven mouldings. This Nandī shrine has its entrance on the north with *dvārapālas* showing Vaiṣṇavite attributes such as *śaṅkha, cakra,* etc. (Pl. 101).

The superstructure of the temple is of the *pīḍha* type. The *pīḍhas* are arranged in two tiers, with four *pīḍhas* in lower and three *pīḍhas* in the upper portion. Inside the temple, there is a colossal monolithic figure of a squatting bull. The floor on which it rests is about one metre below the ground level of the courtyard. M.M. Ganguly praises this bull as, "a well proportioned and nicely carved example of the animal"[14] (Pl. 145).

ĪŚĀNEŚVARA TEMPLE (TEMPLE NO. 116)

The Īśāneśvara temple is located to the north-east of the *bhoga-maṇḍapa,* quite close to the Garā well (No. 110 of the side plan). The temple, which faces east, consists of two structures. The main temple is of the *rekhā* order, while its frontal porch is of the *pīḍha* order.

The temple complex stands on a platform of four mouldings. The *rekhā* temple has a *pābhāga* of five mouldings. *Jaṅghā* is divided into two parts by a *bandhanā* of one moulding. The *varaṇḍa* above the upper *jaṅghā* consists of five mouldings. The curvilinear *gaṇḍi* is distinguished by projecting lion on each *rāhā.* The one on the east has a miniature temple below the lion motif. The *mastaka* has the usual components of a *rekhā* temple. The *dopichha-siṁhas* adorn the corners of the *bekī.* The usual *deula-cāriṇīs* are found in the middle of the *bekī* above each *rāhā.* The *pārśva-devatā* niches on the *bāḍa* contain the standing four-armed figure of Gaṇeśa on the south, Kārttikeya on the west and Pārvatī on the north.

The *jagamohana* is a *pīḍha* temple which is *pañca-ratha* on plan. Its *bāḍa* consists of the *pañcakarma-pābhāga,* two *jaṅghās,* a *bandhanā* of one moulding and a *varaṇḍa* of five mouldings. The superstructure consists of *pīḍhas* in two tiers; the lower with four *pīḍhas* and the upper having three *pīḍhas.* The *mastaka* has the usual components of a *pīḍha* temple.

Both the temples, being built of laterite stone are without any artistic elements.

SĀKṢĪ-ŚAṄKARA TEMPLE (TEMPLE NO. 118)

This Śiva temple, locally called Sākṣī-Śaṅkara, is located on the northern flank of the steps leading to the *vāhana-staṁbha* of the Liṅgarāja temple. The temple, now partly buried, is of the *pīḍha* order. It is made of laterite stone. The visible portions of the temple indicate that its *bāḍa* consists of *pābhāga,* one plain *jaṅghā* and *varaṇḍa* of three mouldings. Of the *pārśva-devatā* niches, the one in the south contains a standing image of Gaṇeśa.

The pyramidal superstructure consists of five continuous *pīḍhas* and it is crowned by *bekı, āmlā, khapurī* and *kalaśa.* The entrance on the east has the usual planet slab as the lintel. Inside the *sanctum,* the usual Śivaliṅga was worshipped.

PĀSĀṆA-DURGĀ TEMPLE (TEMPLE NO. 119)

Among the Śākta shrines in the premises of the Liṅgarāja temple, the Pāṣāṇa-Durgā temple deserves brief mention. It is a pyramidal temple, *pañca-ratha* on plan, which is located on the north-east part of the courtyard. The temple faces south. Its *bāḍa* is made of *pābhāga,* a single plain *jaṅghā* and *varaṇḍa* of three mouldings. The *bāḍa* is provided with balustraded windows, each with three plain balusters.

The *gaṇḍi* has five continuous *pīḍhas* and the *mastaka* is survived by *bekī, āmlā* and *khapurī.* The presiding deity is a standing figure of mother goddess, variantly called Pāṣāṇa-Durgā or Kanaka-Durgā.

DAKṢIṆA-KĀLĪ TEMPLE (TEMPLE NO. 122)

This Śākti shrine is located in the north-eastern part of the courtyard, quite close to the eastern boundary wall. It is a *pīḍha* temple which stands on a platform. The *pīḍha* temple is quite plain with a *pābhāga, jaṅghā* and a *varaṇḍa.* The pyramidal superstructure consists of three continuous *pīḍhas.* The *mastaka* consists of *bekī, āmlā* and miniature *kalaśa.* The *pārśva-devatā* niches are all empty.

The four-armed presiding goddess holds *padma, triśūla, cakra* and *khaḍga.* The goddess stands over a prostrate male figure. This modest shrine is an important *pīṭha* for tantric worship.

KAPILEŚVARA TEMPLE (TEMPLE NO. 123)

The small Kapileśvara temple, adjoining the eastern *prākāra,* is a *pīḍha* shrine facing west. It stands over a low platform. The main temple has a plain *bāḍa,* a *gaṇḍi* of diminishing five *pīḍhas.* The *mastaka* consists of the usual components of a *pīḍha* temple. The *pārśva-devatā* niches are empty. Inside the temple a Śivaliṅga, locally called Kapileśvara, is still in worship.

CHRONOLOGY OF THE TEMPLES

The Liṅgarāja temple was built in the 11th century and thereafter, a number of temples were erected in the Liṅgarāja compound. The temples belong to *rekhā, pīḍha* and *khākharā* order. There are two *khākharā* temples dedicated to *śākti* worship, i.e., Bhuvaneśvarī and Sāvitrī. The *pīḍha* temples, as usual, represent the *jagamohana* and form an integral part of a scheme consisting of *deula* and the *jagamohana.* Sometimes, however, in the later period, *pīḍha* temple also formed the main temple to enshrine the presiding deity or the Śivaliṅga. In some examples, the temple proper is of the *rekhā* order and has no *jagamohana.* The subsidiary temples inside the Liṅgarāja compound belong to different centuries. On grounds of architectural and sculptural features, the chronology of the temples inside the enclosure may be tentatively fixed as follows (Pl. 113):

Detached sculptures and architectural fragments (Since their provenance is not clearly known, it is difficult to say whether there was any temple inside the Liṅgarāja compound datable to 7th century AD)	: 7th century
Ekāṁbareśvara temple	: late 11th century
Gaṇeśa temple	: late 11th or 12th century
Gopālinī (Bhuvaneśvarī) temple	: 12th century
Sāvitrī temple	: 12th century
Laḍukeśvara temple	: 12th century
Lavaṇeśvara temple	: 12th century
Viśvakarmā temple	: 12th century
Caṇḍeśvara temple	: 12th century
Pārvatī temple	: 13th century
Rāmaliṅgeśvara temple	: 13th century
Two Viṣṇu temples	: 13th century
Bhairaveśvara temple	: 13th century
Two ruined Śiva temples near Gaṇeśa temple	: 13th century
Lakṣmī-Nṛsiṁha temple	: late 13th or 14th century
Tārakeśvara temple	: late 13th or 14th century

Temples in the south-east corner of the compound, locally called Malayagiri : 14th century

MAṆḌAPAS IN THE COURTYARD OF LIṄGARĀJA TEMPLE

In addition to the temples, there are a few *maṇḍapas* which have ritual significance. Of these, the following *maṇḍapas* deserve special mention.

1. *Nāhikaṭā Maṇḍapa* (No. 15)

This *maṇḍapa* is noticed on the left side as the devotees proceed from the *vāhana-staṁbha* towards the west keeping the *bhoga-maṇḍapa* on the right side. This *maṇḍapa* has ritual-connection with the celebration of Śrī-Kṛṣṇa *Janmāṣṭamī.*[15] The celebration of birth ceremony of Kṛṣṇa, usually performed in Viṣṇu temples, seems to have started in the Liṅgarāja temple when Liṅgarāja came to be regarded as Hari-Hara. The symbolic ritual of *nābhi chedana* (cutting of navel) is performed in this *maṇḍapa* on the night of *Janmāṣṭamī.*

2. *Beheraṇa Maṇḍapa* (No. 29)

It is situated quite close to the *jagamohana* of the Liṅgarāja towards its south. This pillared *maṇḍapa* originally had a thatched roof, which was replaced later on. The important rituals held here are the *Puṣyābhiṣeka* and the *Śītalāṣa ṣṭhī.*

A small *maṇḍapa* to its east is called *Thālikaṭā Maṇḍapa* as *prasāda thālis* of Liṅgaraja, after being offered to Pārvatī, are placed here.

3. *Bā-ā-Khiā Maṇḍapa* (No. 33)

This small *maṇḍapa* stands in the north-western part of a long *maṇḍapa.* It is an open *maṇḍapa* provided with arches. The platform inside is used during the *candana yātrā* of the deity, which continues for twenty-one days from the day of *akṣya tritīyā.* The god enjoys dance and music from this *maṇḍapa.* During summer, the deity comes out from the temple to enjoy cool air (*bāpavana*), therefore, it is also called *Pavanakhiā Maṇḍapa.*

4. *Ratha Maṇḍapa*

This *maṇḍapa*, situated to the south of the main temple, is survived by its plinth only. A notable feature is the provision of the wheels, which seems to suggest that it was conceived as a chariot like the *Alaṅkāra Maṇḍapa* of the Siṁhāncala temple. Its ritual significance, in the context of a Śiva temple, is not quite clear.

5. *Somabāra Maṇḍapa* (No. 69)

This *maṇḍapa* is situated on the north-western side of the Liṅgarāja temple near the Śiva-Kālī temple (Temple No. 68). It has a special significance in connection with the rituals of Lord Liṅgarāja held on Monday *(Somabāra),* which is an auspicious day for Śiva. This Monday festival is locally known as *Somabāra bedhā* and it is celebrated every Monday. The *utsava vigrahas* of the Liṅgarāja are taken out in a procession and placed on this *maṇḍapa* for ritual worship.[16] The ritual ends with circumambulation *(pradakṣiṇa)* of the temple. A notable feature of this *maṇḍapa* is the provision of arches.

6. MAKARA MAṆḌAPA (NO. 92): (Pl. 128)

The *Makara maṇḍapa* is situated on the northern side of the Liṅgarāja temple, immediately to the east of the Candeśvara temple (Temple No. 82). It consists of a high platform, provided with four pillars on the four corners. It is open to the sky. The approach to this *maṇḍapa* is on the east through a stair case, consisting of five steps. The *maṇḍapa* is used in connection with the rituals on the *Makara Saṅkrānti.* On this day, the ceremony involves eating of the harvested paddy. After the procession of the Lord Liṅgarāja returns to the temple complex, milk is boiled on this *maṇḍapa* to prepare cream, which is used for the preparation of *makara* rice.[17] Therefore, this *maṇḍapa* is locally called *Makara maṇḍapa.*

7. KALPATARU MAṆḌAPA (NO. 98)

This ornamented *maṇḍapa* is situated in front of the temple of Gopālinī (Temple No. 90) on the northern side of the *jagamohana* of the Liṅgarāja temple. It is open to the sky. This structure is generally believed to be in honour of the Kalpataru of the temple, which is locally called a *Varuṇa* tree. A detached image of the Sun god has been placed near the sacred tree. Both the Sun god and the tree are placed inside a square pit. The Kalpataru is a wish-fulfilling tree and it represents the triple qualities of Śiva. The worship of the Kalpataru along with three circumambulations is an essential part of the *pradakṣiṇa* of the Liṅgarāja temple. The facade of the platform has been carved with workmanship of a later period. On the western side, the scheme of decoration includes a female figure which is reminiscent of the story of Pārvatī subduing the two demons Kīrtti and Vāsa. The platform is approached by a flight of steps on the eastern side (Pl. 102).

WELLS IN THE LIṄGARĀJA COMPOUND

There are three wells inside the premises of the temple. These are (1) Jemādei well, (2) Amaṇiā well, and (3) Garā well.

1. JEMĀDEI WELL (NO. 22)

The Jemādei well is located near the kitchen towards its western side. The well is of round shape and its low parapet is made of khandolite stone and the water is used for cooking purposes.

2. AMAṆIĀ WELL

The well near the south-western corner of the enclosure is locally called Amaṇiā well. This well is actually a big trench and there is no water in this well. When the sanctity of the temple gets polluted for some reason, the offerings meant for the deity are thrown into this well.

3. GARĀ WELL (NO. 110)

The Garā well to the south of the Ekāmbareśvara temple is rectangular in plan. The water of the well is used by the devotees and for the worship of the deities.

Pl. 132. Pārvatī Temple: *pābhāga*.

Pl. 133. Pārvatī Temple: *bāḍa*.

Pl. 134. Pārvatī Temple: Elongated *khākarā-muṇḍi*, north.

Pl. 135. Pārvatī Temple: *gaṇḍi* of the *deula*.

Pl. 137. Pārvatī Temple: Pārśvadevatā, southern *rāhā* of the *deula*.

Pl. 136. Pārvatī Temple: *vajra-mastaka*.

Pl. 138. Pārvatī Temple: *bāḍa* of the *jagamohana*.

Pl. 139. Pārvatī Temple: *bāḍa* of the *jagamohana*, north.

Pl. 140. Pārvatī Temple: *jagamohana, staṁbha, jāli, gavākṣa*, north.

Pl. 141. Pārvatī Temple: *jagamohana*, door-frame.

Pl. 142. Ugreśvara Temple.

Pl. 143. Bhubaneśvarī Temple.

Pl. 144. Ekāmbareśvara Temple.

Pl. 145. Nandī in the Vṛṣabha Temple.

Pl. 146. Eastern entrance porch of the Liṅgarāja Temple, west.

Pl. 147. Brahmā in the entrance porch, used as *sārathi* in the Car Festival.

Pl. 148. Liṅgarāja Temple, in 1868 (R.L. Mitra).

PĀDUKĀ CHANNEL

The water poured on the deity Liṅgarāja along with milk, coconut water, etc. is discharged through a channel which passes under the Niśā Pāravatī temple. The underground channel for draining water from the *sanctum* passes near the Caṇḍeśvara temple and moves towards the west and is connected with a *kuṇḍa* (reservoir), located on the south of Pārvatī temple. The path of the drainage is marked by a small *rekhā* temple to the west of the Caṇḍeśvara temple and another *pīḍha* temple on the west of the *pādukā kuṇḍa.* The underground channel is connected with the *Pāpanāśinī kuṇḍa* situated on the north-west of the Liṅgarāja temple. The paved courtyard is provided with inspection chambers along the path of the drainage channel.

ENCLOSURE OF THE LIṄGARĀJA TEMPLE

The main temple complex and the subsidiary shrines are protected by a high compound wall, as in the case of the Jagannātha temple at Puri. The total area of the courtyard is 158.49 mts. x 141.73 mts. with a 8.53 mts. projection on the northern side. The courtyard around the main temple complex is paved with khandolite stone. The compound wall is made of dressed laterite blocks. The wall is about 2.28 mts. thick. The high wall has a battlemented top. The walls are plain in both the sides, except a simple moulding below the coping. The coping is slopy to facilitate the drainage of rain water. The top portion of the wall is flat. At the north-eastern corner, there is a small pavilion approached by a flight of steps. The small structure is called *Cāhāṇi Maṇḍapa* or *Bheṭa maṇḍapa* and during the return Car festival, goddess Pārvatī comes to this platform to welcome Lord Liṅgarāja. This seems to have been a later practice and the original purpose of this structure is not known quite clearly.

There are entrances to the temple on the east, north and south side of the boundary wall.

1. Eastern Entrance (Pl. 146)

The main entrance of the Liṅgarāja temple in the east is called *Siṁhadvāra.* There are two lions as the guardian animals. Of the three entrances, the eastern one is the largest and is about 9.44 mts. in width. This entrance is surmounted by a *pīḍha* temple, which has nine continuous *pīḍhas.* The height of this *pīḍha* temple is about 15.24 mts. The *bāḍa* has a *pābhāga* of five mouldings, *bandhanā* of seven mouldings and *varaṇḍa* of ten mouldings. The lower *jaṅghā* is adorned with *khākharā-muṇḍis* and upper *jaṅghā* with *pīḍha-muṇḍis* respectively. The usual crowning elements of a *pīḍha* temple appear in the *mastaka.* In front of the eastern entrance, there is a road which is at a higher level. Therefore, the pilgrims have to descend down to enter the temple and after crossing the eastern entrance, they have to proceed again through an ascending flight of steps, which is 15.24 mts. broad from north to south and the east-west length is about 19.81 mts.

2. Northern Entrance

The eastern entrance, which is the main entrance of the temple, was used by the devotees for entering the temple but the northern entrance being close to Bindusāgara and the habitation zone, was used by the temple priests. The entrance is surmounted by a *pīḍha* temple, which is comparatively smaller in dimension than the structure in the east. The *bāḍa* of the temple is plain.

Fig. 16. Eastern entrance of the Liṅgarāja Temple (R.L. Mitra, 1868).

The *jaṅghā* is divided into two by a *bandhanā* of two mouldings. In this *pīḍha* temple, the *pīḍhas* are arranged in two tiers; having four *pīḍhas* in lower and three *pīḍhas* in the upper. The projecting lions are placed at the level of the upper tier. The usual crowning elements are also to be seen in this temple. The *dopichha-siṁhas* occupy the *bekī* at the corners.

3. Southern Entrance

Like the eastern and northern entrances, the courtyard of the temple can be approached through a gateway on the south. It is reported that, the palace complex was situated on the southern side and usually the monarchs visit the temple through the southern entrance. The southern gateway is comparatively small and represents a mere opening with two folding doors.

NOTES AND REFERENCES

1. *Svarṇādri Mahodaya,* Chapter 8; also see *Ekāmra Candrikā,* Chapter 4.
2. *Ibid.,* Chapter 19.
3. *Kapila Saṁhitā,* Chapter 13 .
4. *Śiva Purāṇa (Uttar Khaṇḍa),* 30.80-87.
5. T. Donaldson, *The Iconography of Vaiṣṇava Images in Orissa,* p. 130.
6. Described as Lavaṇeśvara temple No. 61 by T. Donaldson vide *Hindu Temple Art of Orisa,* Vol. II, pp. 706-707, See Fig. No. 1722 Liṅgarāja compound.
7. R.L. Mitra, *The Antiquities of Orissa,* Vol. II, p. 123.
8. M.M. Ganguly, *Orissa and her Remains,* p. 367.
9. B.V. Nath, "The Pārvatī temple Inscription at Bhubaneswar", *OHRJ,* Vol. III, p. 146.
10. H.K. Shastri, *South Indian Images of Gods and Goddess,* p. 218.
11. B.V. Nath, *op. cit.,* p. 148.
12. *Śiva Purāṇa, Śatarudra Saṁhitā,* 18.26-27.
13. *Śiva Purāṇa, (Uttara Khaṇḍa),* 30.16-17.
14. M.M. Ganguly, *op. cit.,* p. 365.
15. M.M. Mahāpātra, *Traditional Structure and Change in an Orissan Temple,* p. 84.
16. For details See M.M. Mahāpātra, *op. cit.,* p. 54.
17. For *Makara Saṁkrānti* festival on the Liṅgarāja temple, See M.M. Mahāpātra, *op. cit.,* p. 65

VI

Lord Liṅgarāja, Mode of Worship, Daily Ceremonies and Festivals

Lord Liṅgarāja, the presiding deity of the temple, is considered as *Sanātana liṅga* or the *liṅga* eternal. As the Lord of the twelve *Jyotirliṅgas,* he is called Liṅgarāja. He is identical with Sadāśiva, who gave rise to a crore of *liṅgas*.[1] Lord Liṅgarāja is visualised in his eight forms.[2] In the Ekāmra Kṣetra reference is made to *ekonakoṭi liṅgas*, i.e., 'one less to a crore' and a crore is completed when Liṅgarāja is taken into account. A crore of *liṅga* makes an integrated whole in the form of Liṅgarāja or Bhuvaneśa.[3] Hence, Liṅgarāja is the embodiment of a crore of *liṅgas*, and his worship is as good as the worship of one crore of *liṅgas*. The *Svarṇādri Mahodaya*[4] recommends the eighth day of dark fortnight of *Kārttika* for performance of *Kotiliṅgārcana*, which implies the worship of Bhuvaneśa. The Liṅgarāja is also called Tribhuvaneśvara,[5] i.e., 'the lord of the three worlds' (*svarga, martya* and *pātāla*).

Lord Liṅgarāja is famous as Kīrttivāsa. In the *Śiva Purāṇa,*[6] Śiva is mentioned as one with 'tiger's hide as the upper garment' and the 'wearer of elephant's hide'. The story relating to the former relates that once Śiva visited a forest in the guise of a mendicant and charmed the wives of the sages. The sages became angry and created a tiger to punish Śiva. However, Śiva slew the tiger and he used its skin as a garment. The story relating to elephant's skin is associated with

Gajāsura who oppressed the gods and sages. Śiva killed the *asura,* took out his hide and used it as cloth. Therefore, Śiva was known as Kīrttivāsa (one clad in elephant's hide).[7]

The *Ekāmra Purāṇa* uses the term Kīrttivāsa for the Liṅgarāja and associates two demons named Kīrtti and Vāsa to explain the name Kīrttivāsa. According to the story recorded in the *Ekāmra Purāṇa,*[8] Kīrtti and Vāsa were among the one hundred sons of a king of demons, named Drimila. As per the boon of the Brāhmaṇas, these two brothers could not be killed by any male human being. Kīrtti and Vāsa became very powerful and in course of time, they killed many of their brothers. Their father sent his army to kill them but due to the earlier boon the two brothers became victorious. Ultimately, King Drimila was able to drive them out of the kingdom. Subsequently, Kīrtti and Vāsa came to reside in the Ekāmra Kṣetra. Pārvatī came to Ekāmra in the guise of Gopālinī (cowherd woman). The two demons Kīrtti and Vāsa were charmed by her beauty and wanted to make her their wife. Gopālinī conveyed to Śiva the evil desire of the demons. Śiva told her that as they could not be killed by any male being, the goddess should kill them for the good of the gods and the world. Śiva instructed her to request the two demons to carry her on their shoulders and while being carried by them, she would crush them to death. The goddess followed Śiva's advice and succeeded in killing the demons Kīrtti and Vāsa by pressing them under her feet.[9] The place where they died is locally known as *Devi Pādaharā.* Due to the death of the demons Kīrtti and Vāsa, the *kṣetra* became famous as Kīrttivāsa Kṣetra.[10]

The *Śiva Purāṇa*[11] *(Uttara Khaṇḍa)* refers to the great significance of the Ekāmra Kṣetra and mentions the story of the demons Kīrtti and Vāsa and their destruction by the goddess Pārvatī in guise of Gopālinī. The *Oriyā Mahābhārata*[12] by Sāralā Dās (15th century AD) mentions the episode of *Kīrttivāsa Daitya Vadha* in connection with Lord Liṅgarāja of the Ekāmravana. In the story, however, the two demons are mentioned as the sons of King Saudās. The two demons were crushed by the feet of goddess Gopālinī, identical with Pārvatī. After the names of Kīrtti and Vāsa, Ekāmra was called *Kīrttivāsana tīrtha.*[13]

The presiding deity of the Liṅgarāja temple is mentioned as Kīrttivāsa, a corrupt synonym for Kṛttivāsa. The earliest inscription of the Liṅgarāja temple belonging to the reign of Annantavarman Coḍagaṅgadeva mentions the deity as Kīrttivāsa in place of Kṛttivāsa. Several other inscriptions of the Gaṅgas and the Gajapatis mention the name in the corrupt form. The corrupt pronunciation of the name Kīrttivāsa for Kṛttivāsa, indicate orthographical peculiarity of the inscriptions of Orissa in the early medieval period. Dr. Snigdha Tripathy explains this due to corrupt pronunciation of the Sanskrit word then prevalent in Orissa. It appears that the epithet Kīrttivāsa instead of Kṛttivāsa was based on the local pronunciation of the name Kṛttivāsa.[14]

The Liṅgarāja is *svayaṁbhu,* i.e., self-originated and self-manifested. His form resembles black, white and purple colours. He is *nāda svarūpa.* The *Ekāmra Candrikā*[15] has described him as follows:

लिङ्गानां वै ज्योतिषां द्वादशानां राजत्येतत् संस्थितं लिङ्गराजम्।
दिवैकाम्रे ब्रह्मलिङ्गं पुरानम् सितासितारूण नाद स्वरूपम्।।

He is identical with *Pūrṇa Brahma (Pūrṇa Brahma svarūpa)*. His form is made of *śphaṭika* in the bottom, *vaidurya* in the middle and *padmarāga* on the top. His effulgence is that of fire.

आमुलं स्फटिकाबद्धं मध्ये वैधुर्यसन्निभम्।
पद्मरागसमोर्द्धवं च ज्वलते अजसतुलम्।।[16]

Further, another description of the *liṅga* runs as follows:

मूलं स्फटिकसंकासं महानीलं च मध्यमम्।
माणिकाव्यां तदूर्ध्व च लिङ्गं त्रिभुवनेश्वरम्।।[17]

THE MODE OF WORSHIP

The mode of worship of the Liṅgarāja is Vedic and Tantric. The *Ekāmra Purāṇa* refers to *Śiva Saṁhitā* and *Śiva tantra.* R.C. Hazra believed that *Ekāmra Purāṇa* was a work of the *Agamic Pāśupatas.*[18] The worship is conducted by Brāhmaṇa devotees of Śiva, well-versed in the Veda, Vedānta and Śaivite scriptures. In the worship, *japa* of Śiva *mantra, dhyāna, homa, yajña, prāyascita* etc. play an important role. The five-syllabled *mantra* and texts such as *Śiva sūkta* have an important place in the worship of Śiva.

Lord Liṅgarāja is worshipped with sixteen *upacāras* or sixteen forms of homage, such as: 1. invocation *(āvāhana)*, 2. offering the seat *(āsana)*, 3. water offering *(arghya)*, 4. washing of the feet *(pādya)*, 5. water for rinsing the mouth *(ācamana)*, 6. oil bath *(abhyaṅga snāna)*, 7. offering of cloth *(vastra)*, 8. sandal wood paste *(gandha)*, 9. flowers *(puṣpa)*, 10. incense *(dhūpa)*, 11. lamp *(dīpa)*, 12. food offering *(naivedya)*, 13. waving of lights *(nirājanā)*, 14. offering of betel leaves *(tāṁbūla)*, 15. obeisance *(namaskāra)*, and 16. mystical discharge and conclusion *(visarjana).*[19] In the use of *upacāras* there is nothing peculiar to Śiva worship. Other deities are also worshipped with five or sixteen *upacāras.*

The *Śiva Purāṇa*, in *Vāyavya Saṁhitā,* mentions the sequence of the rituals of Śiva in an elaborate manner which include performance of *nyāsa*, purification of the holy materials, worship of Vināyaka, Nandī, Caṇḍa, Ādhāra Śakti, etc. In the rites a white lotus-seat is conceived with eight petals.[20] The eight petals represent eight attributes, such as *animā*, etc. The filaments represent *rudras* in the company of other *śaktis*; the pericarp is symbolic of greatest detachment and the stalk is the Śaivite knowledge.[21] It is interesting to note that a *kamala yantra* has been carved on the floor in front of a minor shrine enshrined with a *liṅga*. This lotus seat seems to have been used by a Śaivite *sādhaka* during the worship of Śiva (Pl. 103).

After offering *upacāras* and showing appropriate *mudrās*, Śiva is invoked along with the goddess. He is the cause of all worlds. He is the great Being, who prevades everything from within and without. He is without beginning, middle or end. He is the unchanging Lord. The *liṅga* or the phallic emblem is the image of Śiva. The *liṅga pīṭha* is usually of three types, i.e., circular, square and rectangular. The *liṅga pīṭha* of Liṅgarāja belongs to the circular type and the *liṅga* is regarded as *svayaṁbhu liṅga*.

An important feature of the worship is the ablution of Śiva. The *liṅga* is to be bathed with liquid *pañcagavya,* such as curd, milk, ghee, honey, butter and jaggery. Mere water with chanting of *mantra* can be used for the ablution of Śiva. In the worship of Liṅgarāja, the phallic emblem is conceived as a human being. He wakes up, brushes his teeth, takes bath and is dressed with flowers and ornaments, takes food eight times. The food items are drawn from the Oriya society and are a part of the typical food habits of the Oriyas. Boiled rice with curd (*dahi pakhāḷa*), puffed rice *(khai)* and betel leaves *(pan* or *tāṁbūla),* so popular in Orissa, are included in the food offerings. The Lord goes to bed shortly before midnight. His temple is built like a palace with audience chamber *(jagamohana* or *mukhaśālā)* and hall of dance *(nāṭa-mandira).* He has thirty-six functionaries to manage the temple with specific duties.

The original temple with its *pārśva-devatās,* such as Gaṇeśa, Kārttikeya, Pārvatī, Śaivite *dvārapālas* and host of Śaivite images on the temple walls clearly indicate that it was a temple dedicated to Śiva. The worship of Liṅgarāja also includes the worship of Gaṇapati, Kārttikeya, Nandī, *dikpālas, dvārapālas* and other manifestations of Śiva. Later on, however, the worship underwent major transformation and the presiding *liṅga* was considered to be representation of Hari-Hara (Pl. 107). In course of this change, the *vṛṣabha* was removed to the northern side, the *vāhana staṁbha* in front of the *bhoga-maṇḍapa* was surmounted with Garuḍa and Nandī. The Śaivite *āyudha* of the temple was replaced by a new emblem combining *cakra* of Viṣṇu and *pināka*-bow of Śiva. In the new system of worship, Vaiṣṇava images, including Jagannātha, had their due place in the main temple complex and shrines erected in the compound of the Liṅgarāja.

THE PROCEDURE OF WORSHIP BY THE PILGRIMS

The Liṅgarāja temple is visited by pilgrims throughout the year. On special occasions, such as *Śivarātri* and other festivals, the devotees gather in large numbers. Puri, being an important centre of pilgrimage, is visited by people from all parts of India and many of them also come to Bhubaneswar to have a *darśana* of Lord Liṅgarāja. It is believed that full merit of *tīrtha yātrā* is obtained by making Liṅgarāja as a *sākṣī* (witness) for the visit. The presence of innumerable *liṅgas* and temples in Bhubaneswar is an important consideration for visiting this holy *kṣetra* and its foremost temple, the Liṅgarāja temple. The *sanātana liṅga*, called Tribhuvaneśvara located in Ekāmra in Utkal Deśa, according to *Śiva Purāṇa (Uttara Khaṇḍa),* is the root of all the *Jyotirliṅgas* of India.[22] It has been called Liṅgarāja, being the Lord of twelve *Jyotirlingas*. The text describes the greatness of Liṅgarāja Tribhuvaneśvara.[23]

The *Sthaḷa Māhātmyas* such as *Ekāmra Purāṇa,*[24] *Ekāmra Candrikā,*[25] *Svarnāḍri Mahodaya,*[26] etc. recommend the procedure to be followed by the pilgrims for visiting the Liṅgarāja temple. The pilgrims are advised to take bath in the Bindutīrtha and being purified, visit Puruṣottama (Ananta Vāsudeva), Devī Pādaharā and Tīrtheśvara; thereafter, proceed to the temple of Tribhuvaneśvara through the *Siṁhadvāra.* The texts refer to the order of visit to the deities inside the Liṅgarāja temple and mention the prayer to be recited by them. The order prescribed in the *Svarṇādri Mahodaya, Śiva Purāṇa (Uttara Khaṇḍa)* and *Ekāmra Candrikā* includes visit to the following divinities:

1. Vināyaka
2. Gopālinī

Fig. 17. Bhubaneswar: The Temple City of Śiva (W.W. Hunter, 1872).

3. Kumāra
4. Vṛṣabha
5. Ganacaṇḍa
6. Kalpataru
7. Sāvitrī
8. Tribhuvaneśa

The *Ekāmra Purāṇa*,[27] however, mentions the same divinities under the names such as Kṛttivāsa, Gopālinī, Ganacaṇḍa, Kumāra, Vināyaka, Vṛṣabha, Kalpataru and Sāvitrī. The following procedure and prayers are quoted from the *Śiva Purāṇa (Uttara Khaṇḍa)*.[28]

On entering the temple the devotees should first offer worship to Vināyaka and utter the following prayer:

> Obeisance to Vighneśvara, the bestower of
> all *siddhis*, please favour me to approach
> Bhuvaneśa without any obstacle.[29]

Thereafter, proceeding to Gopālinī, the devotee should recite the following:

> Salutations to you oh Gopālinī,
> the destroyer of Kīrtti and Vāsa,
> Oh Bhubaneśvarī, grant me off-spring,
> prosperity, well-being and fame.[30]

Then god Kumāra is addressed with the following prayer:

> Salutations to you oh the destroyer of the
> Krauñca mountain, the delighter of Pārvatī
> salutation to the leader of the divine army,
> grant me to attain heaven.[31]

After visiting Kumāra, one should proceed towards *Vṛṣabha*, the mount of Śiva and utter the following mantra:

> Salutation to Paramānanda, the giver of
> merit of visiting all *tīrthas*, obeisance to you,
> the form of sacrifice, please grant me
> devotion to Śiva.[32]

Then the devotee proceeds to Ganacaṇḍa and recites the following verse:

> Salutation to Caṇḍarudra, the delighter of
> the gods. Please grant me strength, virility,
> brilliance and fortitude.[33]

Then one should proceed to Kalpataru, the wish-fulfilling tree, and after making three circumambulations recite the following mantras:

> Salutation to Kalpavṛkṣa, the granter of
> imagination and success, meditated upon by
> Brahmā, Viṣṇu and Śiva, fulfil my desires.[34]

Then the devotee proceeds to the south-west direction of the Lord Liṅgarāja and offers prayer to Sāvitrī, thus:

> Salutation to Vedamātā, the mother of
> Vedas, who assumes the form of Sāvitrī.
> Oh Sarvavibhāvinī, source of all creation
> grant me divine wisdom, and intelligence.[35]

Finally, the devotee moves to Tribhuvaneśa *liṅga* and utters the following *mantra*:

> Salutation to Tribhuvaneśa, Salutation to
> Kṛttivāsa, Oh Lord grant me liberation the
> result of your *darśana*.[36]
>
> Oh Śaṅkara, whatever I have done through
> the visit of your eight manifestations, kindly
> grant me the entire result through your favour.[37]

The devotee should bow down on the ground and feel satisfied at the grace of the Lord.

The *darśana vidhi* mentioned above is not followed completely by the pilgrims at present. After visiting the temple of Gaṇeśa, the pilgrims ascend the steps and proceed to the *jagamohana* through its southern entrance and have a *darśana* of Liṅgarāja from the *jagamohana* and whenever access is allowed to the *sanctum sanctorum,* they worship Liṅgarāja with *puṣpa, gandha, dhūpa, dīpa* and *naivedya.* Sometimes, the pilgrim may choose to offer *puṣpa* and *dīpa* of his own without the help of any temple priest. When he wants to offer *pūjā* or *naivedya,* he has to take the help of a priest. When the pilgrims are not allowed to the *garbhagṛha,* the priest is allowed to go there and therefore, he can offer *pūjā* for the pilgrim. He receives an amount as his *dakṣinā* for his services. While worshipping for the devotee the priest utters the name and *gotra* of the *yajamāna.* The *bhoga* offered to Liṅgarāja is considered as *prasāda.* The *bhoga* consists of coconut, banana, *korā* (sweetmeat of coconut) and *khai* (puffed sugar coated rice). The devotees generally offer milk, coconut water, holy water and the flowers, such as *caṁpaka, nāgeśvara,* lotus, *dhatturā, arka,* etc. on the Śivaliṅga with the help of the priests. They are allowed to make *ardha-pradakṣiṇa* of the *liṅga pīṭha.* The individual devotee repeats the *mantras* uttered by the priests. Often, in the *mantras,* Liṅgarāja is spoken of as Hari-Hara. After coming out from the temple, the devotees make a *pradakṣiṇa* of the temple by visiting the *pārśva-devatās,* such as Gaṇeśa, Kārttikeya and Pārvatī and other minor shrines. It is said that by circumambulating only once the sin of *brahmahatyā* is destroyed; two circumambulations assure kingdom and the third one gives glory of Indra. The *Ekāmra Purāṇa* mentions that after taking bath in the Bindutīrtha, the devotee has to make three *pradakṣiṇas* of the Liṅgarāja.[38] The number of taking baths and *pradakṣiṇas* progressively increases as per the procedure prescribed by the *Ekāmra Candrikā*.[39] The number of *pradakṣiṇas* and baths progressively increases up to eight times. Facing east, south-east, south, south-west, west, northwest, north, and north-east, the devotee has to utter *mantras* in honour of the deity.[40] The worship of Bhubaneśa for eight times, probably suggests the eight forms of Rudra. The eight forms are (i) *Śarva* (earth),

(ii) *Bhava* (water), *(iii) Rudra* (fire), (iv) *Ugra* (wind), (v) Bhīma (ether), (vi) Paśupati (soul), (vii) Īśāna (sun), and (viii) Mahādeva (moon).[41] The eight forms of Bhubaneśa are the same as the eight forms of Śiva. The visit to Pārvatī temple has now become a regular feature though it is not included in the *darśana vidhi* mentioned earlier. Over the centuries, several minor shrines have been erected in the courtyard. Some of these have lost importance while others have gained importance. The most frequented shrines are those situated near the ritual *path* meant for the circumambulation of the temples.

The worship of Liṅgarāja involves the visit to other *liṅgas* in the Ekāmra Kṣetra. The *Ekāmra Purāṇa* prescribes the performance of the *chāyā yātrās* on auspicious *tithis* such as *pūrṇimā, amāvasyā, ekādaśī, dvādaśī, caturdaśī* and *saṁkrānti.* The performance of *chāyā yātrā* on *vaiśākha pūrṇimā* is highly meritorious. The rituals involve bath in the Bindusara, worship of Liṅgarāja and visit to various *liṅgas* in the Ekāmra Kṣetra.[42]

In recent years, to cater to the needs of the pilgrims, shrines in honour of Santoṣīmā, Tāriṇī, etc. have come up and worship of Śanigraha has also become popular inside the Liṅgarāja compound.

The worship of Liṅgarāja has some special features. Though it is basically a centre of Śaivism, it has incorporated, over the centuries, several features of Vaiṣṇavism. There is a view that a Vaiṣṇava should not enter a Śiva temple even if chased by an elephant, but in case of Liṅgarāja temple, there is no sectarian difference between Śaivism and Vaiṣṇavism. The highest synthesis of Śaivism and Vaiṣṇavism on a philosophical level as well as in iconography, rituals and festivals are to be found in this temple. As a place of Śaivite worship, Liṅgarāja is not affiliated to any particular Śaiva sect. The presiding *liṅga* in the temple, called Liṅgarāja, is regarded as the highest *liṅga* and it is identical with Brahmana, the Supreme Being. There is also some difference in the nature of the *bhoga* offered to Jagannātha and Liṅgarāja, where *korā* and *khai* are the popular items of the *bhoga.* Another important feature of daily routine is the ceremonial dressing of the *liṅga*, called *veśa* in local terminology. On special occasions, there are characteristic *veśas* appropriate to the occasions.

The main emphasis in the worship is placed on devotion. It is mentioned in the *Śiva Purāṇa* that, "a person without devotion is not liberated even after doing everything. But one with devotion is liberated even without doing anything".[43] Devotion is a boat that saves one from the ocean of sins.[44]

Those who worship Lord Śiva are excellent and blessed. They alone attain salvation and are never subjected to misery. They can get good fortune, strength, wealth, charming houses in this life and after death, they would attain salvation.[45] A devotee should not take meal without worshipping Śiva. If he takes food, there is no attainment of merit for him.

DAILY CEREMONIES

The *sanctum sanctorum* of Liṅgarāja temple has a Śivaliṅga as the object of worship. In later period this was considered to be Hari-Hara. Besides the phallic emblem, Liṅgarāja is represented through his metalic *utsava vigraha* housed in a separate shrine (No. 30), just near the southern entrance of the *jagamohana.* The *pūjā* of Lord Liṅgarāja is performed, among others, by a group of *sevakas*

Pl. III. Car Festival of Liṅgarāja.

called *Baḍu.* In earlier times the *pūjā* of Tribhuvaneśvara is said to have been performed by the *Śavaras.* Later on, the temple had special functionaries and the services were organised on the basis of caste groups, locally called *Niyoga.* The temple functionaries were traditionally divided into thirty-six *Niyogas* known as *chatiśā niyoga* or thirty-six classes of *sevakas* serving the deity.

The daily ceremonies of Lord Liṅgarāja start early in the morning and continue till late evening. The temple gates are thrown open early in the morning between 5.30 a.m. and 6 a.m. The door is opened by the functionary called *Pharaka* who has the key. The opening takes place in presence of a representative of *Pañcāyat* and the *Pāḷiā Baḍu.* The *sevaka,* i.e., the *Pāḷiā Baḍu* enters the temple with a *kalaśa* of water and sprinkles the water on all the Śivaliṅgas inside the temple. Then the *sanctum* door is opened and a servent called *Akhanda* now performs the *maṅgala ālatī* or auspicious waving of light in honour of Lord Liṅgarāja. The deity wakes up from his sleep; this ceremoney is called *Pahaḍa Bhaṅgā.* Thereafter, the *Pāḷiā Baḍu* removes the *bīlva* leaves, flowers, etc. placed on the *liṅga* in the previous night. The ceremony of the washing of teeth is performed with a twig and after being bathed, the Lord is offered flowers and *bīlva* leaf, etc. Then Lord Liṅgarāja is ready for public *darśana.* This gathering of devotees wanting to have a view of the Lord is called *sāhāṇa melā.* Generally it continues from 7.30 a.m. to 12 noon. On special occasions, however, the *sanctum* remains open for a much longer period. After *sāhāṇa melā,* a purificatory ceremony or *mahāsnāna* takes place. The *Pāḷiā Baḍu* bathes the deity and washes the *liṅga pīṭha* with water. Then, *Pañcāmṛta,* consisting of milk, honey, curd, butter and *guḍa* (jaggery), is poured on the *liṅga* for purification. Thereafter, the *liṅga* is dressed and decorated with ornaments, flowers, etc.

Lord Liṅgarāja is offered *bhoga* eight times daily and this includes five *avakāśa*s and three *dhūpa*s. These comprise the followings:

1) *Bāla dhūpa* or *Vāla Ballava*
2) *Sakāḷa dhūpa*
3) *Bhoga-maṇḍapa dhūpa* or *Chatrabhoga*
4) *Vīrakiśore Ballava*
5) *Dvipahara dhūpa* or *Madhyāhna dhūpa*
6) *Ṭerāphiṭā*
7) *Sandhyā dhūpa*
8) *Baḍa siṅghāra*

The first food offering or breakfast of the Lord is called *Vāla Ballava* or *Bāla dhūpa.* The offering includes items such as *korā, khai, curd,* etc. This offering is conducted by the *Brāhmaṇa sevaka,* called *Panti Baḍu.* After this *dhūpa* the *sanctum* is cleaned with water by the *Pāḷiā Baḍu.* This is preceded by Sūrya *pūjā* in the minor shrine of the Sun god in the south-east corner. The *dvārapāla pūjā* is also a part of the daily ritual.

The first important *bhoga* called *Sakāla dhūpa* or the morning meal is offered to the Lord in the *sanctum.* The *bhoga* consists of rice, *khecuḍi,* green leafy vegetables, *puli, haṁsakeli, eṇḍuri* (cake), *kānti* and other items. The *Sakāl dhūpa* is performed with the co-operation of various *sevakas,* such as *Paṇḍā, Patrī, Hadapa Nāyak, Bhitar Khuṅṭiā, Panti Baḍu, Garā Baḍu,* etc. The *Panti Baḍu* decorates the floor with powdered rice; *Bhitara Khuṅṭiā* stands as the guard at the gate; *Haḍapa Nāyak* provides water and arecanut; *Garā Baḍu* provides the wooden seat, water and flowers; *Patrī* places the required sixteen *upacāras* at the disposal of the *Paṇḍā Brāhmaṇa,* who conducts the actual offering. During the offering ceremony various musical instruments are played by the *sevakas,* such as *ghaṇṭuā, kāhālia* and others. Two *sevaka*s hold white umbrella and black umbrella in honour of the deity near the *sanctum* door.

After the *Sakāla dhūpa* is over, there comes the *Ālati* ceremony (ceremony of waving light). The *Ālati* ceremony of Liṅgarāja is of various types, such as *karpūra ālati, piṭhau ālati, patri ālati*, etc. The ceremonial waving of light is conducted in a rhythmic motion in front of the deity. The objects used for this purpose are camphor, clarified butter and rice paste fixed with lighted sticks. Sometimes the seven lighted wicks are used in the *Ālati.*

There is another *bhoga* known as *Chatrabhoga* which is offered in the *bhoga-maṇḍapa.* This *bhoga,* meant for sale among the pilgrims, includes huge quantity of food items, such as rice, dal, curry, etc. After this *bhoga* is over, the *sanctum* is purified and is kept open for the devotees.

There is a view that the food offering to Śivaliṅga is not to be accepted, but being regarded as Hari-Hara, offering to Liṅgarāja is accepted by the gods, *asuras* and men irrespective of sectarian differences among the Śaivas and Vaiṣṇavas. It has been proclaimed that offering to a *liṅga* is not acceptable except the offering to Tribhuvaneśvara.[46]

There is another offering to the Lord before the mid-day meal which is known as *Vīrakishore Ballava dhūpa.* The *Paṇḍā, Patrī, Garā Baḍu* and *Brāhmaṇas* should be present at the time of offering. The food comprises sweetmeat preparations, such as *kākarā, tripuri,* etc.

The mid-day meal called *Dvipahara dhūpa* or *Madhyānha dhūpa* is offered in earthen pots to the deity. The practice was in vogue by the 13th century. Inscription of Anaṅgabhīmadeva III (AD 1211-1238) refers to offering of earthen pots of cooked food daily to the deity.[47] The earthen pot was called *Āṭikā,* which indicates that *bhoga* was offered to the deity in the earthen pots. Yet another inscription of the 13th century refers to *Nirmālya* prepared from *taṇḍula* or rice.[48] By the 13th century land endowments have been made for the food offering *(naivedya)* to the deity Kṛttivāsa.[49] The offering consists of cooked food, such as rice, dal, curry, etc. The cooking is done in the kitchen complex of the temple. After offering to the Lord a portion of the *bhoga* is presented to goddess Pārvatī in her temple.

After the mid-day meal, the *mahāsnāna* takes place, the door is closed and the deity takes rest (*pahaḍa*). After this, the *ṭerāphiṭā* offering consisting of cake, etc. is served to the deity and the temple is once again opened for pilgrims. The door is then closed again for the mid-day rest of the Lord.

At about 7 p.m. the temple door is thrown open for the performance of evening rituals, known as *Sandhyā Ālati.* During this time the *sanctum* door is opened for public view of the Lord. This time another light-meal offering, called *Sāhāṇa dhūpa,* is offered by the *sevaka*s. The second food offering, called *Sandhyā dhūpa,* is conducted at around 8.30 p.m. In the *Sandhyā dhūpa* offering several items, such as *laḍu, khajā, āriṣā pīṭhā, kharjūra,* etc. are offered to the Lord Liṅgarāja. After this, public *darśana* is arranged for the devotees for a brief period.

The *Baḍasinghāra* ceremony is conducted before the midnight. The *Baḍasinghāra* offering includes items such as *dahipakhāl* (rice mixed with curd), *bhajā, sākara, khaṭā,* etc. The ritual consists of the worship of the metal image of Pañcavaktra Mahādeva and offering of *Puṣpāñjali* (offering of flowers) in his honour. After this final ceremony is over, the temple doors are closed around midnight.

The cycle of daily rites, as regards the local terminology and timings, are quite similar to those of the Jagannātha temple at Puri.

FESTIVALS

The festivals of Lord Liṅgarāja are held throughout the year. A festival is called *yātrā,* meaning 'journey.' The *Nibandhakāras* of Orissa have mentioned fourteen festivals or *caturdaśa yātrā.* The *Kālasāra*[50] of Gadādhara Rājaguru speaks of the major fourteen festivals with their timing and rituals. The *Sthala Māhātmyas* such as the *Ekāmra Purāṇa,*[51] the *Svarṇādri Mahodaya,*[52] and the *Ekāmra Candrikā*[53] provide details about the observance of such festivals. The *Kapila Saṁhitā*[54] refers to only *Sapta Yātrā* (seven festivals) such as (1) *Prathamāṣṭamī,* (2) *Māgha Saptamī,* (3) *Yātrā* on the occasion of Sunday falling on the bright fortnight of *Phālguna,* (4) *Ratha Yātrā,* (5) *Caitra Śukla Caturdaśī,* when Madana worshipped Śiva, (6) *Āśāḍha Śukla Aṣṭamī,* when Śiva undertakes journey to Paraśurāmesvara, and (7) *Kārtika Śukla Dvitīyā,* journey to Yameśvara. Out of fourteen *Yātrās,* Liṅgarāja proceeds to different Śiva temples in the Ekāmra Kṣetra and is worshipped with other *liṅgas* as per the prescribed rites. Therefore, the term *yātrā* applied to the festivals of Liṅgarāja seems appropriate. The other seven *yātrās* are observed in the temple, but the term *yātrā* is also applied to them. The fourteen major festivals beginning with *Prathamāṣṭamī* are as follows:

Prathamāṣṭamī	*Mārgaśīrṣa*	November/December
Pravaraṇa ṣaṣṭhī	*Mārgaśīrṣa*	November/December
Puṣyābhiṣeka	*Pauṣa*	December/January
Ghṛtakaṁbala	*Māgha*	January/February
Māgha saptamī	*Māgha*	January/February
Śivarātrī	*Phālguna*	February/March
Ratha yātrā	*Caitra*	March/April
Damanabhañjikā	*Caitra*	March/April
Candana yātrā	*Vaiśākha*	April/May
Parasurāmāṣṭamī	*Āṣāḍha*	June/July
Śayana caturdaśī	*Āṣāḍha*	June/July
Pavitrāropaṇa	*Śravana*	July/August
Yama dvitīyā	*Kārttika*	October/November
Utthāpana yātrā	*Kārttika*	October/November

1. Prathamāṣṭamī

This festival is celebrated on the *Kṛṣṇāṣṭamī* of *Mārgasīrṣa.*[55] On this occasion the *calanti pratimā* of Lord Liṅgarāja, called Candraśekhara, is taken out from the temple in a procession to the

Varuṇeśvara temple. The ritual there consists of the ceremonial bathing of the image in the holy water of the *Pāpanāśinī Kuṇḍa.* New clothes are offered to the deity during worship and thereafter, the deity returns to the Liṅgarāja temple. In local traditions, it is believed that Liṅgarāja goes to his maternal uncle for the ceremony of *Prathamāṣṭamī.*

2. *Pravaraṇa Ṣaṣṭhī*

The *Pravaraṇa ṣaṣṭhī* or *Pravaraṇa utsava* is held on the sixth day of the bright half of the *Mārgaśīrṣa.*[56] Locally this festival is known as *Oḍhana ṣaṣṭhī.* With the advent of the winter, Lord Liṅgarāja has to be covered with new garments for which this is called *Pravaraṇa utsava.* The new garment is purified on the previous day in a ceremony called *adhivāsa.* It is offered to the deity on the sixth day of the bright half of the *Mārgaśīrṣa* and it is used by him as *Pravaraṇa* till the *Śivarātri.*

3. *Puṣyābhiṣeka*

This festival is performed on the full moon day in the month of *Pauṣa,* when it falls with the *Puṣyā nakṣatra.*[57] This day is considered to be auspicious, being the birth day of Lord Liṅgarāja. On the previous night the *adhivāsa* is performed with the bringing of one hundred and eight pitchers filled with water from the Bindusarovara. On the *Pūrṇimā* day, the Lord is bathed with that sacred water and offered worship with *bīlva* leaf, mustard flowers along with offering of *bhoga, dhūpa* and *dīpa.* The ceremony takes place in a special *maṇḍapa,* locally called *Beheraṇa Maṇḍapa. Pūṣyābhiṣeka* is also performed in the Jagannātha temple at Puri.

4. *Ghṛtakaṁbala Ceremony*

This festival is celebrated on *the Makara Saṅkrānti.* On the *caturdaśī tithi,* the *utsava vigraha* of the Lord is taken to the *Makara maṇḍapa.* There, the *ghṛta* prepared out of milk and the fur-blanket, usually brought from Nepal, are offered to the deity, for which this ceremony is called, *Ghṛtakaṁbala.*[58] On this occasion *makara* rice is also offered to the deity. The taking of *makara* rice is also called, *navānna bhakṣaṇa* or *Nuākhiā,* as it involves the eating of the rice of newly harvested paddy.

5. *Māgha Saptamī*

This festival is celebrated on the seventh day of the bright half of the month of *Māgha* and hence, it is known as *Māgha Saptamī.*[59] The day is specially sacred to the Sun god. On this day, the representative of Liṅgarāja is taken out in a procession to the Bhāskareśvara temple, located in Bhubaneswar. Bhāskareśvara, the Śivaliṅga, is named after Bhāskara, the Sun god. After joint worship of both Śiva and Sūrya, the deity returns to the Liṅgarāja temple. *Māgha Saptamī* is also known as *Ratha Saptamī,* as on this day the Sun god got his chariot. The chariot of Lord Liṅgarāja is constructed as per the specification of the Bhāskareśvara temple.

6. *Śivarātrī*

The most important festival of the temple is *Śivarātrī. Śivarātrī* or Śiva's night, is a popular fast and festival. In tantric literature, it is believed to be a *Kāḷarātrī.* It is considered to be a sacred night. It is held on the fourteenth day of the dark half in the month of *Phālguna.*[60] According to the *Śiva Purāṇa,* following a different system of calculation of the month, the *Śivarātrī* falls in the dark half of the month of *Māgha.*[61] The glory of *Śivarātrī* is described in the *Koṭirudra Saṁhitā* of the *Śiva*

Pl. IV. Liṅgarāja: Female figure.

Purāṇa.[62] At the Liṅgarāja temple, devotees in large number come to the temple from early morning and spend the day in prayer and other festivities. According to the *Ekāmra Purāṇa,* it is highly meritorious to perform the *Mahāsnāna* of Tribhuvaneśa with milk, curd, honey, etc.[63] A special feature of the *Śivarātrī* is the placing of a *Mahādīpa* on the top of the temple in the night. On every *caturdaśi* night *Mahādīpa* is also placed on the temple, but this rite on *Śivarātrī* is specially meritorious.

7. Ratha Yātrā

Like *Śivarātrī, Rath Yātrā* is considered to be an important festival in the Liṅgarāja temple. It is celebrated in the month of *Caitra* on *Śuklāṣṭamī*[64] (eighth day of the bright fortnight). The *Ekāmra Purāṇa* describes this festival in two chapters.[65] The same is also repeated in later texts such as *Svarṇādri Mahodaya*[66] and *Ekāmra Candrikā.*[67] The *Kapila Saṁhitā*[68] also includes this festival of *Ratha Yātrā* or *Aśoka Yātrā* as one of the seven *yātrās.* The festival was so popular that it finds mention in the *Tirthacintāmaṇi* of Vācaspati Miśra, *Kālasāra* of Gadādhara, *Kālanirṇaya* of Raghunātha, etc. It was an important festival of Lord Liṅgarāja and it is variously known in the texts as *Ratha Yātrā, Aśoka Ratha Yātrā* and *Aśoka Yātrā,* as it was held on the *Aśokāṣṭamī* day. On this day, the *utsava vigraha* of Liṅgarāja, the Śivaliṅga, which is believed to have been consecrated by Rāmacandra, along with Gopālinī (Pārvatī), Kumāra and Nandikeśvara including the image of Govinda are taken out in a chariot from the Liṅgarāja temple to Rāmeśvara[69].

The chariot is called *Devadalan*[70] like the chariot of Subhadrā at Puri. According to *Śiva Purāṇa,* the cosmic chariot of Śiva was built by Viśvakarmā.[71] It was golden in colour and was known as *Rukma Ratha* (made of gold). Locally the chariot of Lord Liṅgarāja is called *Rukuṇā Ratha,* a term derived from *Rukma Ratha.*[72] The *Śiva Purāṇa* has mentioned symbolically that the chariot's right wheel was Sun god and the left wheel was the Moon.[73] The right wheel had twelve spokes. The twelve Ādityas presided over there. The left wheel had sixteen spokes, symbolic of the sixteen digits of the Moon.[74] The chariot of Lord Liṅgarāja seems to have followed the legend of the burning of Tripurā.[75] The local people believe that the *Rukuṇā Ratha* is *aṇaleuṭā* and it does not retreat or take an about-turn during the return journey. This is because of the fact that the chariot has four portals on the four sides and, therefore, on the return journey the chariot has no necessity to make a turn. The four wooden horses represent the four Vedas[76] and Brahmā serves as the charioteer.[77] The chariot of Liṅgarāja has four wheels, the wheels of the right side represent the Sun god and the wheels of the left side represent the Moon.[78] According to *Śiva Purāṇa,* the chariot festival for the goddess Ambikā is held on the third day of the bright half of *Āṣāḍha*[79] (Pl. 147).

The chariot festival lasts for five days. The chariot is drawn by the devotees from the Liṅgarāja to Rameśvara and it makes return journey after five days. *Ratha Yātrā* is considered to be the very special among the fourteen festivals *(yātrās)* of Lord Tribhuvaneśvara and beholding the Lord on the chariot is considered to be highly meritorious. The *Ekāmra Purāṇa* prescribes propitiatory rites in the event of the breaking of different parts of the chariot, such as *śira, kalaśa, cakra, sārathi, dhvaja,* etc. Such incidents are not good for the king and the state.[80]

8. Damanabhañjikā

The festival of *Damanabhañjikā* is observed on the fourteenth day of the bright fortnight of *Caitra.*[81] The venue of the celebration is in front of the Tīrtheśvara temple. On this day the *Utsava Vigraha* of the Lord is taken to that place in a procession. There the image is presented with a branch of the *Damanaka* plant along with a garland of *Damanaka* flowers.[82] When the representative of the Lord is not able to join this festival, in his place the metal image of *Pañcavaktra Mahādeva* attends the festival of *Damanabhañjikā*.[83]

9. *Candana Yātrā*

The *Candana Yātrā* is held for twenty-one days from the *Akṣaya Tṛtiyā*, i.e., the third day of the bright fortnight in the month of *Vaiśākha*.[84] Everyday the proxy image of Lord is taken to the Bindusara, where the Lord enjoys the boating festival. The Lord is carried in a boat to a *maṇḍapa* inside the Bindusara. *Candana Yātrā* is equally an important festival of the Jagannātha temple at Puri. The festival is also observed in important Vaiṣṇava temples of Orissa. In the Ekāmra Kṣetra, the proxy image of Liṅgarāja is accompanied, among others, by the image of Kapileśvara.

10. *Parasurāmāṣṭamī*

This festival is conducted on the eighth day of the bright fortnight of *Āṣāḍha*.[85] On this day the *Utsava Vigraha* of Liṅgarāja is carried to the Paraśurāmeśvara temple and worshipped there. According to a legend, this *yātrā* had its origin in the assurance of Śiva to Paraśurāma to visit his place. Paraśurāma is assigned by Śiva to be the protector of the *kṣetra* and there is a temple in the Ekāmra Kṣetra, known as Paraśurāmeśvara temple.

11. *Śayana Caturdaśī*

It is believed that Śiva goes to sleep on the fourteenth day of bright fortnight of *Āṣāḍha* and hence this festival is called *Śayana Caturdaśī*.[86] An important feature of this festival is the placing of metal images of Śiva and Umā on a couch.

12. *Pavitrāropaṇa*

While Viṣṇu's *Pavitrāropaṇa* is held on the twelfth day of the bright fortnight of *Śrāvaṇa*, this auspicious rite of Liṅgarāja is held on the fourteenth day of the bright fortnight of *Śrāvaṇa*.[87] On this day sacred thread made of Kuśā grass and cotton is presented to Lord Liṅgarāja.

13. *Yama Dvitīyā*

The festival of *Yama Dvitīyā* is celebrated on the second day of the bright half of the month of *Kārttika*.[88] The venue of the celebration is the Yameśvara temple located in the Ekāmra Kṣetra. The proxy image of Lord Liṅgarāja is taken there and is worshipped in front of the Yameśvara *liṅga*. On the return journey Liṅgarāja spends some time in the Bhāratī Maṭha, which is locally believed to be the house of his sister Bhāratī Devī.[89]

14. *Utthāpana Caturdaśī*

Utthāpana Caturdaśi or *Utthāna Yātrā* is held on the fourteenth day of the bright half of *Kārttika*.[90] It is believed that, Śiva goes to bed on the fourteenth day of the bright fortnight of *Āṣāḍha* and rises up from the bed on the fourteenth day of the bright half of *Kārttika*. It is a significant day for worship as the Lord wakes up from slumber of four months.

Besides the fourteen *yātrās* more than seven minor festivals *(upa yātrās)* are also observed in the Liṅgarāja temple. These include festivals such as *Sarasvatī Pūjā (Māgha), Bhaumī Ekādaśī (Māgha),*

Kapila Yātrā (Phālguna), Dola Pūrṇimā (Phālguna), Śītalā saṣṭhī (Jyeṣṭha), Janmāṣṭamī (Bhādrav), Durgāṣṭamī (Āśvina), etc.[91] Some of the festivals are Śaivite in character, while the festivals such as *Janmāṣṭamī, Dola Pūrṇimā* are associated with Viṣṇu. The festivals seem to have multiplied over the centuries and the concept of Hari-Hara helped the admixture of Śaivite and Vaiṣṇavite festivals. During the month of *Kārttika*, Liṅgarāja is adorned with a crown to assume the form of *Dāmodara* or Viṣṇu. It is called *Dāmodara Veśa* of Liṅgarāja. It is observed when the *Sakāla dhūpa* and the *Sāhāṇa dhūpa* are served to the deity.[92] The *Śiva Purāṇa* mentions the *Rāsakrīḍā* of Śiva in the Binduhrada along with eight *sakhīs* of Pārvatī.[93] This is a clear indication of the influence of the *Rāsakrīḍa* of Kṛṣṇa and Rādhā held on the full moon day of *Kārttika.*

NOTES AND REFERENCES

1. *Ekāmra Purāṇa*, 42.8.
2. *Śiva Purāṇa (Uttara Khaṇḍa)*, 30.57.
3. *Svarṇādri Mahodaya*, 25.
4. *Ibid.*, 25.29.
5. *Śiva Purāṇa (Uttara Khaṇḍa)*, 30.16.
6. *Śiva Purāṇa, Śatarudra Saṁhitā*, 41.39.
7. *Śiva Purāṇa, Rudra Saṁhitā, (Yuda Khaṇḍa)*, 57.63.
8. *Ekāmra Purāṇa, Kīrttivāsa Upāksyāna*, 34.36.
9. *Ibid.*, 36.38-40.
10. *Ibid.*, 36.65.
11. *Śiva Purāṇa (Uttara Khaṇḍa)*, Chs. 26-27.
12. *Sāralā Mahābhārata, Vanaparva* (Oriya), pp. 80-89.
13. *Ibid.*, p. 89.
14. S. Tripathy, "Ekāmra-Bhubaneśvara", *OHRJ*, Vol. XXXIII, No. 1 & 2, 1987, pp. 147-148.
15. *Ekāmra Candrikā*, 2.6.
16. *Ibid.*, 2.11-12.
17. *Ibid.*, 2.24.
18. R.C. Hazra, "The Ekāmra Purāṇa: A Work of Orissa", *Poona Orientalist*, Vol. XVI, Nos. 1-4, pp. 70-76.
19. *Śiva Purāṇa, Vidyeśvara Saṁhitā*, 11.25-29.
20. *Ibid., Vāyavīya Saṁhitā*, 24.27.
21. *Ibid.*, 24.28.
22. *Śiva Purāṇa (Uttara Khaṇḍa)*, 3.62.
23. *Ibid.*, Ch. 3.
24. *Ekāmra Purāṇa*, Ch. 55.
25. *Ekāmra Candrikā*, Chs. 2-3.
26. *Svarṇādri Mahodaya*, Ch. 4.
27. *Ekāmra Purāṇa*, 55.13-14.
28. *Śiva Purāṇa (Uttara Khaṇḍa)*, 30.57-74.
29. *Ibid.*, 58-60.
30. *Ibid.*, 61.
31. *Ibid.*, 63.

32. *Ibid.*, 65.
33. *Ibid.*, 67.
34. *Ibid.*, 69.
35. *Ibid.*, 71.
36. *Ibid.*, 73.
37. *Ibid.*, 74.
38. *Ekāmra Purāṇa*, 63.60.
39. *Ekāmra Candrikā*, 13.4-20.
40. *Ibid.*
41. *Śiva Purāṇa*, *Śatarudra Saṁhitā*, 2.3.
42. *Ekāmra Purāṇa*, 64; See also *Ekāmra Candrikā*, Ch. 14.
43. *Śiva Purāṇa*, *Vayavihga Saṁhitā*, 25.56.
44. *Ibid.*, 25.62.
45. *Ibid.*, 26.16-19.
46. *Śiva Purāṇa (Uttara Khaṇḍa)*, 3.69.
47. *Epigraphia Indica*, Vol. VI, pp. 73 ff.
48. *Ibid.*, Vol. XXIX, pp. 47-48.
49. See Appendix-B.
50. *Kālāsara* of Gadadhara Rajaguru, 9, 190.
51. *Ekāmra Purāṇa*, 66-69.
52. *Svarṇādri Mahodaya*, Chs. 20-24.
53. *Ekāmra Candrikā*, Chs. 10-13.
54. *Kapila Saṁhitā*, 19.2-30.
55. *Ekāmra Purāṇa*, 66.2-7. See also *Ekāmra Candrikā*, 10.15-23; *Kapila Saṁhitā*, 19.2-6.
56. *Ibid.*, 66.8-14; *Ekāmra Candrikā*, 10.24-30.
57. *Ibid.*, 66.15-25. See also *Ekāmra Candrikā*, 10.31, 55.
58. *Ibid.*, 66.26, 33, See also *Ekāmra Candrikā*, 10.56, 79.
59. *Ibid.*, 66.34-38; See also *Ekāmra Candrikā*, 10.80, 90; *Kapila Saṁhitā*, 19.7-11.
60. *Ibid.*, 66.39-48; See also *Ekāmra Candrikā*, 11.1-21.
61. *Śiva Purāṇa*, *Koṭirudra Saṁhitā*, 38.24.
62. *Ibid.*, Chs. 38-40.
63. *Ekāmra Purāṇa*, 66.41-42.
64. Pandit Mangobinda Mahasupakar, *Bhubaneswar Aitihya*, p. 138; See also *Kapila Saṁhitā*, 19.20-22.
65. *Ekāmra Purāṇa*, Chs. 67-68.
66. *Svarṇādri Mahodaya*, Ch. 21.
67. *Ekāmra Candrikā*, 11.22-116.
68. *Kapila Saṁhitā*, 19.20-22.
69. U.N. Dhal, "Ratha Yātrā in Ekāmra Kṣetra", *Culture Indica*, p. 39.
70. *Ekāmra Purāṇa*, 67.13; See also *Ekāmra Candrikā*, 11.31.
71. *Śiva Purāṇa*, *Rudra Saṁhitā*, Section-V, 8.5.
72. U.N. Dhal, *op. cit.*, p. 40.
73. *Śiva Purāṇa*, *Rudra Saṁhitā*, Section-V, 8.6.

74. *Ibid.*, 8.7-8.
75. *Ibid.*, Ch. 10.
76. *Ibid.*, 8.27; See also *Ekāmra Purāṇa*, 67.37.
77. *Ibid.*, 8.24; See also *Ekāmra Purāṇa*, 67.42; *Ekāmra Candrikā*, 11.27.
78. *Ekāmra Purāṇa*, 67.34; See also *Ekāmra Candrikā*, 11.46.
79. *Śiva Purāṇa, Umā Saṁhitā*, 51.63.
80. *Ekāmra Purāṇa*, 68.34, 44.
81. *Ibid.*, 69.4-20; See also *Ekāmra Candrikā*, 11.117-132.
82. U.N. Dhal, "A Note on the Sacred Rituals at Ekāmra Kṣetra (Bhubaneswar)", p. 4.
83. Pandit Mangobinda Mahasupakar, *op. cit.*, p. 138.
84. *Ekāmra Purāṇa*, 69.21-27; See also *Ekāmra Candrikā*, 11.133-141.
85. *Ibid.*, 69.28-30; See also *Ekāmra Candrikā*, 11.142-159; *Kapila Saṁhitā*, 19.26-27.
86. *Ibid.*, 69.31-42; See also *Ekāmra Candrikā*, 12.1-20.
87. *Ibid.*, 69.43-74; See also *Ekāmra Candrikā*, 12.21-57.
88. *Ibid.*, 69.75-78; See also *Ekāmra Candrikā*, 12.58-72; *Kapila Saṁhitā*, 19.28.
89. Pandit Mangobinda Mahasupakar, *op. cit.*, p. 139.
90. *Ekāmra Purāṇa*, 69.79-82; See also *Ekāmra Candrikā*, 12.73-85.
91. M. Mahāpātra, *Traditional Structure and Change in an Orissan Temple*, pp. 78-85.
92. N.K. Bose, N. Patnaik and A.K. Roy, "Organization of Services in the Temple of Liṅgarāja in Bhubaneswar," *Journal of the Asiatic Society Letters*, Vol. XXIV, p. 92.
93. *Śiva Purāṇa (Uttar Khaṇḍa)*, Ch. 10.

VII

Functionaries and Management

The builders of the temples also made arrangements for the organisation of services and the management of the temples. The officers and a number of other functionaries were instituted to perform various functions. In medieval period, the presiding deity of the temple was considered as a king and the paraphernalia of a royal court was repeated in the temple. The temple inscriptions of the Gaṅgas and the Sūryavaṁśī Gajapatis throw light on various temple functionaries. In important temples, such as the Liṅgarāja and Jagannātha, there were elaborate arrangements for the organisation of services. An Oriya inscription of the ruined Konarak temple mentions temple functionaries, such as *Bhaṇḍāra Adhikārī, Koṣṭhakaraṇa*, etc.

The service groups of the Liṅgarāja temple are divided into four *varṇas.* They can also be divided into two groups, *Bhitara sevaka* and *Bāhāra sevaka,* performing their duties inside and outside of the temple respectively. In the Liṅgarāja temple the untouchable classes, who fall outside the *varṇa* system, were not allowed into the temple. The *Śūdra sevaka*, however, had an important role to play and they even enjoyed the right to supply water for use in the kitchen.

The *Brāhmaṇa sevakas,* according to traditions, originally came from South India and were known as *Kamā Brāhmaṇas.* In course of time, however, their number decreased and the kings of Orissa brought *Brāhmaṇas* from Kanauj. Subsequently, the *Brāhmaṇa sevakas* of the Liṅgarāja temple were divided into two *bāḍas* or sections on the basis of their lineage and these two *bāḍas* are now known as *Uttara bāḍa* and *Dakṣiṇa bāḍa*. The *Uttara bāḍa sevakas* include *Mahāpātra, Paṇḍā, Mahāsuāra, Garābaḍu, Pati* and *Sangitra*, etc. The *Dakṣiṇa bāḍa Brāhmaṇas* comprise *Mahāpātra, Padhiāri* and *Samantrā*. The *Mahāpātras,* belonging to the *Uttara bāḍa,* are again subdivided into *Rājavaṁśīya Mahāpātras* and ordinary *Mahāpātras*. The *Paṇḍā sevakas* are entrusted with various services as per their classifications, such as *Akhaṇḍa, Bhitar Khuṇṭiā, Cāngaḍā, Carcāyita, Dhopakhāḷa, Garā Baḍu, Haḍapa Nāyak, Mahāsuāra, Mekāpa, Pañcuāti, Paṇḍā, Panti Baḍu, Pārvatī, Patrī, Paśupālaka, Puṣpāñjali, Trāsa*, etc.[1] The *Paṇḍā Brāhmaṇas* or the *Brāhmaṇa sevakas* perform the special rites during festivals, such as *Paṇā Saṁkrānti, Makara Saṁkrānti, Dola* festival, etc. The *Paṇḍā Brāhmaṇas* belonged to the *Sāma* or *Yajur Veda.*

BAḌU SEVAKA

The origin of the *Baḍu* class is obscure. Some scholars believe that *Baḍu* is derived from *Baṭu* and they belong to a *Brāhmaṇa* class. The surname *Baḍu* is held by both *Brāhmaṇa* and *Śūdra* functionaries of the temple. The suggestion of R.D. Banerjee[2] that, "they were reconverted Buddhists" is hardly convincing. K.C. Panigrahi[3] identified them with a "group of non-brahmin priests like the *Daitāpatis* in the Jagannātha temple at Puri". The persons belonging to this group have surnames such as *Baḍu, Sāmantrā, Mahāpātra, Makadam* and *Singhāri*. The *Baḍus* perform various services in the temple. They also help the pilgrims who visit the temple. Depending on their specific functions the *Baḍus* are known as *Pālia Baḍu, Pochā, Pahaḍa, Pharaka, Khaṭaśeja*, etc.

PAÑCUĀTI

The term is derived from *Pañcāyat* and it represents a committee of five, which coordinates the activities of the different service groups. The committee is drawn from both *Paṇḍā Brāhmaṇas* and the *Baḍu* class. When there is any dispute among the service groups, this is settled at the level of this committee. On specific occasions representatives of this committee are to remain present.

In the management of the temple, five *sevakas* play a dominant role. These are *Pañcāyat, Sāmantrā, Makadam, Parichā* and *Parakarana. Parichā* is the leading functionary who supervises the daily rituals and ceremonies. The *Makadam* is connected with the services of the goddess Bhubaneśvarī. In addition, he is entrusted with the lock and key of the ornament box of the temple.

Traditionally a group of thirty-six persons render service to the deity and they belong to thirty-six *Jātis* or *Niyoga*. The *Chatiśā niyoga* or thirty-six classes of *sevakas,* serving in the temple comprise the following:

PĀLIĀ BAḌU

The *Pāliā Baḍus* are a class of *sevakas* who enjoy the right to offer flowers and *bīlva* leaf to the deity Liṅgarāja. They pour oblation of water on the *liṅga* on behalf of the pilgrims. They have the right to dress the Lord. The *Pāliā Baḍu* comes into intimate contact with the deity, being his *aṅgasevaka*. They perform their duties on the basis of their *pāli* or the day, specifically assigned to each *Baḍu*.

The same *Baḍu* does not perform the duty everyday. He has to wait for his *pāli* or turn. The *Baḍu,* whose turn is to serve on a particular day, is called *Pāliā Baḍu.*

PHARAKĀ

Pharakā serves as the guard or the watchman of the temple. After all the daily ceremonies are over, the temple door is closed by the *Pharakā.* In the early morning, the door is also opened by the *Pharakā* in presence of the Superintendent or other temple functionaries. Being in charge of watch and ward of the temple in the night, he has to stay inside the temple.

KHAṬAŚEJA

The *Khaṭaśeja sevaka* of the *Baḍu* class has the duty to arrange the bed of the deity during *Baḍasiṅghāra nīti,* after which the Lord goes to sleep.

POCHĀ

The *Pochā sevaka* also belongs to the *Baḍu* class and he has the duty to clean the floor of the *sanctum sanctorum* after the performance of the *nītikānti* or the ceremonies.

PAHAḌA

The *Pahaḍa sevaka* has to screen the *sanctum* during the *Pahaḍa* or food offering of the deity. For example, when the food is offered to deity a screen is placed so that the deity is not disturbed while taking his meals. The *Pahaḍa sevaka* also belongs to the *Baḍu* class.

PŪJĀ PAṆḌĀ

They are a class of *Brāhmaṇas* connected with the *pūjā* (worship) of Liṅgarāja and hence, they are called *Pūjā paṇḍās* or simply *Paṇḍās.* They offer various services in the temple, such as worship of the Liṅgarāja with sacred *mantras* and offering of food. In the kitchen of the temple, they perform *homa* before the food is cooked for the Lord. Being the *Brāhmaṇa* priests of the Lord, they enjoy superior status. According to local traditions, in former days, they were brought from Kanauj to perform sacred rites and according to another tradition, when their number dwindled, they were again brought from Sākhigopāl in Puri district. The *Pūjā paṇḍās* or the *Paṇḍā sevakas* are divided into two groups, such as *Nārada Paṇḍā* and *Vāsudeva Paṇḍā.* The *Pūjā paṇḍas* have an important role in the *Ratha Yātrā,* being assigned with the duty to sprinkle the holy water, when the deputies of Liṅgarāja make *Pradakṣiṇa* around the chariot.

PATRĪ

This functionary assists the *Pūjā paṇḍā* in conducting sacred rites. They bring all *pūjā* articles, such as *dhūpa, dīpa, puṣpa,* etc. and help the *Pūjā paṇḍā* with required *upacāras* during the performance of *pūjā* rites. They are said to be divided into two principal groups, i.e., *Uttara bāḍa* and *Dakṣiṇa bāḍa.* Their help is considered essential for conducting sacred rites of the temple.

PANTI BAḌU

The *Panti Baḍu sevaka* has the duty to decorate the floor of the *sanctum* with *maṇḍala* designs with rice powder before the *Pūjā paṇḍā* performs the actual rites. Being from a class of *Brāhmaṇa,* he can also offer dry food to the deity, but not cooked food. He also arranges the food offering in their proper position. He keeps watch on the *bhoga* and after offering of the *bhoga* he distributes it among the *sevakas.* Like the *Patrīs,* they were divided into *Uttara bāḍa* and *Dakṣiṇa bāḍa.*

GARĀ BAḌU

These functionaries bring waterful brass-vessel called *garā* or *gaḍu* to the place of the *pūjā* in front of the deity. It is said that the word *Garā Baḍu* was a corrupt form of *Gargabaṭu.* He places the wooden seat for the *Pūjā paṇḍā* and assists him to wash his hand in water. When the *Pūjā paṇḍā* is ready to offer food, he summons the *Mahāsuāra* or the principal cook to send the cooked food.

HAḌAPA NĀYAK

These functionaries belong to the *Mahāsuāra* class. They are in charge of the preparation of *Tāmbūḷa* for the deity. During *bhoga* offering they supply water and betel-nut, etc. to the *Pūjā paṇḍā.*

BHITAR KHUNṬIĀ

These functionaries prevent the outsiders to enter the temple during the *bhoga* offering. They open and close the door as per requirement and control the people by hurling cane sticks.

DHOPAKHĀḶA

The duty of these functionaries is to clean the kitchen by washing it with water mixed with cowdung. This is performed meticulously to purify the kitchen before the cooking takes place.

CĀṄGAḌĀ

These functionaries are in charge of the clothes meant for the deity. They send the used clothes to the washerman and receive them back after cleaning. They place the clothes in a *Cāṇgaḍā* (basket) for the use of the deity.

CHATĀ

These functionaries hold the *Chatā* or *Chatra* of the deity. These parasols or *Chatās* are of two types, i.e., white and black. Traditionally *Chatra* is a symbol of royalty. When the *yātrās* or festivals are held, the *Chatā sevakas* carry the parasol. When *bhoga* is offered to the deity, the *Chatā sevaka* also holds the parasol in front of the deity. Usually the *Chatā sevakas* of the *Uttara bāḍa* hold the white parasol and such *sevakas* of the *Dakṣiṇa bāḍa* carry the black parasol. This *sevā* is named after *Chatā* or parasol and those who perform this specific duty are known as *Chatā sevakas.*

TRĀSA

The *Trāsa* is a cone-shaped insignia made of cloth embossed with *ardhacandra bindu* or crescent moon with a dot upon it. The *Trāsa* is used during *bhoga* offerings and the *yātrās.*

PAŚUPĀḶAKA

These functionaries are called *Paśupāḷaka* for being connected with Paśupati Śiva. Liṅgarāja being a phallic emblem is represented by his *Vije Pratimās* or *Utsava Vighrahas,* usually metal images. These are kept in the *Dakṣiṇaghara* or the chamber near the southern entrance of the *jagamohana.* The *sevakas* belonging to the *Paśupāḷaka seva* are kept in charge of these images. Besides, they perform other duties also connected with daily ceremonies.

PUṢPĀÑJALI

Puṣpāñjali sevā is the last *nīti* or routine ceremony of the temple. When all the rites are over and after the *Baḍasiṅghāra dhūpa,* the bed is arranged for the Lord. The deputy of the Liṅgarāja, i.e., the *Pañcavaktra Mahādeva* is placed on a wooden *daṁbaru,* then *Puṣpāñjali* is offered in honour of the Lord. This *sevā* is usually performed by *Pūjāpaṇḍās* and *Patrī sevakas.*

MAHĀSUĀRA

The term *Mahāsuāra,* derived from *Mahāsūpakāra,* denotes functionaries entrusted with the cooking of food for the deity. No other *sevāyata* has the right to prepare *bhoga.* As already noted, Liṅgarāja is offered food eight times daily, which include cooked rice, dal, curry, etc. and dry food such as sweetmeats and other items. *Mahāsuāra* belongs to the *Brāhmaṇa* class. They are divided into two groups, such as *Nāyak Mahāsuāras* and *Sunāthāli Mahāsuāras.*

PĀRVATĪ

These functionaries are exclusively attached for the service of goddess Pārvatī, hence such *sevakas* are also called *Pārvatī.* These *sevakas* decorate the goddess with dress, vermilion, flowers and ornaments. They are also entrusted with the duty of presenting the consecrated *bhoga* of Lord Liṅgarāja to goddess Pārvatī after *Sakāḷa dhūpa, Dvipahara dhūpa* and *Sandhyā dhūpa.* An inscription of the 13th century, engraved in the *pīṭha* of Pārvatī temple, records daily offering of two earthen pots of cakes to goddess Umādevī (Pārvatī) by one Bhīma Bahika through Yaśodhar Mahārāṇā.[4]

GOPĀLUNĪ (GOPĀLINĪ)

Just as Pārvatī has a group of *sevakas,* goddess Gopālinī (Bhuvaneśvarī) has also exclusive *sevakas.* They are entrusted with the performance of the daily ceremonies of the goddess. They bathe the goddess and decorate her with ornaments, flowers, etc.

MEKĀPA

These functionaries serve as the store-keepers of the ornaments, jewellery and clothes of Lord Liṅgarāja. The *Mekāpa* hands over the items required for the daily rites to the *Cāṅgaḍā sevaka,* who in turn, passes over the items to *Pāliā baḍu* for dressing the deity. The *Mekāpa* belongs to the category of *Brāhmaṇa sevaka,* but he has no right to enter the *sanctum* during the time of *bhoga* offering to the deity.

CARCĀYITA

This group of *sevakas* are entrusted with the responsibility of supervising the performance of daily ceremonies and festivals of the temple. The *Carcāyita* has the power to make alternate arrangements during the absence of a *sevaka* and he can also recommend action against a *sevaka* guilty of negligence of duty. At present this *sevā* is performed on rotation by *Baḍu sevaka, Brāhmaṇa sevaka* and *Pūjā paṇḍā.*

AKHAṆḌA

The *Akhaṇḍa sevaka* has the duty to tend the *dīpa* within the temple when *pūjā* is conducted. The traditional lamp of the temple being lit with oil, *Akhaṇḍa* has to attend the lamp by pouring additional oil as per requirement, to ensure continuity of light. He is, however, not allowed to come close to the deity during the offering of *bhoga.*

KOṬHA BIṢOYĪ

These functionaries are also called *Parva yātrā Biṣoyī.* They supply all articles to the kitchen required for the cooking of food for the Lord. They are *Brāhmaṇa sevakas* and on occasions, such as *Ratha yātrā, Dola yātrā, Candana yātrā,* etc. they supply dry food offerings for the deity.

GUḌIĀ BIṢOYĪ

This *sevaka* discharges the function of a confectioner for the temple. The word *Guḍiā* is derived from *Guḍa* (molasses), out of which various sweetmeats are prepared. The popular sweetmeat called *Korā* is prepared from coconut and sugar, while *Khai* is prepared out of puffed rice, molasses and coconut crunch. They also prepare *muān* during festive occasions with puffed rice and sugar, which are of conical shapes.

MASĀLĀ

The *Masālā sevaka* supplies the articles used for making *Pān* (betel-leaf) for the deity. He supplies various kinds of spices used in the temple and for the preparation of betel-leaf. The articles include *Jīrā* (cumin seed), *Hengu* (asafoetida), *Alaica* (cardamom), *Tejpatra* (bay-leaf), *Pān* (betel-leaf), *Marica* (black pepper), etc. He is a functionary from the *Vaiśya* class. In addition to payment for supply of such articles, he has been given rent-free land.

ROṢA PĀIKA

He is a servant of *Śūdra* caste attached to the kitchen of the temple. He supplies water, sweeps the courtyard of the kitchen, washes utensils used for cooking and performs such other works connected with the kitchen.

GHAṆṬUĀ

The *Ghaṇṭuā* or the *Ghaṇṭā sevaka* plays the gong or *ghaṇṭā* during the ceremonial offerings of the *bhoga* to the deity. This *sevaka* belongs to the *Śūdra* caste.

SAMARTHĀ

This class of temple servants are engaged in various works, such as grinding of rice and pulses, supply of water for cooking, etc. The *Samarthā* has the special responsibility of hoisting the flag on the top of the temple and carrying the *Mahādīpa*. The *Samarthā* is from a *Śūdra* caste like the *Roṣapāika* and *Ghaṇṭuā.*

MĀDALĀ

The word *Mādalā* is derived from *Mardala,* which means a traditional percussion musical instrument. This *sevaka* beats the drum during the time of worship of the deity.

JYOTIṢA

This functionary consults the *Pāñji* (almanac) and indicates the auspicious time for observance of rituals and festivals. He is expected to be well-versed in astrological and astronomical calculations. During the beginning of the new year in the month of *Caitra,* the *Jyotiṣika* makes a forecast of events, likely to occur during the ensuing year. The royal families in Orissa usually employ astrologers in their courts. In the same manner, Liṅgarāja being regarded as a king, employs an astrologer in the temple services.

TELEṄGĀ

This *sevaka* plays on the *Teleṅgī vādya* (musical instrument of Telugu speaking area) during food offering. According to traditions this practice originated during the medieval times, when Orissa was a bi-lingual kingdom and extended over parts of Andhra Pradesh. *Telengī vādyas* are still popular in some parts of Orissa, but in the temple of Liṅgarāja it has been discontinued.

KĀHĀLIĀ

The *Kāhāliā* blows the musical instrument called *Kāhali* (trumpet) during the *dhūpa* offering of Liṅgarāja. The sound of the trumpet signifies the food offering to the deity.

RAJAKA

The *Rajaka,* locally called '*Dhobā*', serves as the washerman of the temple. The used clothes of Liṅgarāja are taken to a tank and washed there. In the process of washing, the clothes are not boiled and chemicals are not used to make the clothes clean. The sun-dried clothes are handed over to the *Cāṅgaḍā sevaka* for use in the temple.

MAŚĀLCĪ

The *Maśālcī bārika* or barber has the duty to hold *Maśāla* or the traditional torch in the *jagamohana* during the night. Particularly, during the procession of the deity at night, the torch-bearer accompanies the deity.

KUṀBHĀRA

The *Kuṁbhāra* or the potter supplies earthen pots for use in the temple. The inscription of the Pārvatī temple[5] refers to earthen pots filled with cakes *(Piṣṭaka Āṭikā)* which indicates that earthen pots were used in the temple for which there could have been potters to supply the same. With the increase of the demand for earthen pots, the temple authorities have to purchase these from outside potters.

Although traditionally the number of service group is thirty-six, in course of time the number has increased with new additions, as the following:

GAUḌA

Milkman for supplying milk to the temple.

BĀURI

He belongs to the untouchable class and until recent times he was not allowed to enter the temple. During *Ratha yātrā,* he has to sweep the road on which the chariot proceeds. They cut trees to provide timber for the construction of chariot. Stone cutting is also done by them.

CAPARĀSĪ

He is entrusted with the work of guarding the entrance to the temple and to monitor the smooth flow of pilgrims.

KEUṬA

He belongs to the fishermen (*kaivartta*) class. He rows the boat of the Lord along with his associates during the *Candana* festival.

PRADHĀNA

They supply firewood to the kitchen of the temple. They also render assistance during the construction of the chariot.

BAḌHEĪ

The *Baḍheī* or the carpenter constructs the chariot. He also makes the boats required for the *Candana* festival.

KAMĀRA

He is the ironsmith of the temple. He has the duty to prepare all types of iron implements required in the temple.

TELĪ

The *Teli sevaka* is the traditional oil supplier to the temple for various purposes including the oil required for the *maśāla* and *triśākha,* the latter being a light consisting of three *śākhās* or three branches.

VIMĀNA-ĀPAṬIĀ

They carry the *Vimāna* of the Lord during ceremonial processions and festivals. While carrying palanquin on their shoulders, they are known as *Palanki Āpaṭiā* or palanquin bearers.

PARKARAṆA

They mantain the records of the temple and serve as the scribe for the various *sevā* groups. The *Parakaraṇa* maintains a list of *sevakas* and the *sevakas* concerned are notified to attend to their duties on a particular day. All the records of the temple are kept in their charge.

BHOI BEHERĀ

They help in the construction of the chariot by cutting timbers. They also pull the chariots. They clean the boats on the eve of the *Candana* festival and perform various work of unskilled nature.

DARJĪ

He belongs to the tailor class and prepares flags, the cloth covering the chariot, canopies of the *maṇḍapas,* umbrellas, etc.

RAṄGANĪ

They belong to the *citrakāra* (painter) class and they paint the chariots and boats.

KALAŚĪ

During the *Ratha yātrā,* the *Kalaśī* controls the movement of the chariot and gives direction as to stop the chariot or to draw the chariot forward.

NIṢAṄKA

They belong to the *Pāika* or the traditional *militia* class. The word *Pāika* seems to have been derived from the *Pādātikah* or the foot soldier. They provide protection to the chariot during the *Ratha yātrā.* They were considered to be fearless for which they are called *Niṣaṅka.*

The functionaries of the temple receive certain emoluments and amenities for their services. Sometimes they are granted rent-free land. They are entitled to receive *khei* or share of the food offerings for their *khaṭani* or work. Some functionaries get *dakṣiṇā* from the *Yajamāna*-pilgrims for conducting *pūjā* on their behalf. Sometimes the *sevakas* are paid in cash for their specific work. For example, *Kāhāliā, Telengā, Dhobā* and others get a fixed amount per month.

The smooth conduct of rituals and festivals largely depends upon the cooperation and the collective efforts of the *sevakas.* Sometimes dislocation takes place in the daily *nītis* and *dhūpas* due to lack of co-ordination and friction among the *sevakas.*

In the early phase, when the deity was worshipped in the Ekāmravana, or when the temple was of modest dimension, there could have been a few functionaries. With the construction of a great temple in the 11th century and subsequent addition of the *nāṭa-mandira* and *bhoga-maṇḍapa,* there was corresponding increase in the employment of functionaries. The resources of the temple increased due to donations and land grants during the Gaṅga period. Anaṅgabhīmadeva III is said to have made elaborate agrrangements for performance of rituals and festivals through land endowments. The inscriptions of the Gaṅga period found in Orissa and Andhra Pradesh throw light on the functionaries and management of temples. The offices are usually held on hereditary basis. The functionaries can be divided into three principal categories, (1) religious functionaries connected with ritual and ceremonies, (2) administrative functionaries, who perform supervisory and administrative functions, and (3) other functionaries connected with the temple, such as torch-bearers, goldsmiths, carpenters, dancers, musicians, etc. The functionaries, such as *Caparāsī, Makadama,* etc. are modern creations. The *pañcāyat* or the committee of five in the Liṅgarāja temple is an important feature of the management of the temple.

An inscription of the Brahmeśvara temple refers to the *Devadāsīs* in that temple. The *Devadāsī* system existed in the Liṅgarāja temple, which is evident from the construction of the *nāṭa-mandira* though such *sevā* no longer exists now. The organisation of services at Liṅgarāja follows the traditional pattern as at the Jagannātha temple. In 1805 Charles Grome[6] had prepared an elaborate report on the establishment of the Jagannātha temple. No such document, however, is available on the functionaries of the Liṅgarāja temple.

In 1958, Nirmal Kumar Bose, Nityananda Patnaik and Ajit Kishore Ray attempted a systematic documentation of the organisation of services in the Liṅgarāja temple, Bhubaneswar.[7] Their research covered various aspects of the temple, such as daily services, annual celebrations, service groups, their castes, distribution of services and emoluments based on direct observation and some official records. The Harvard-Bhubaneswar Project was initiated in 1961 to study rapid urbanization and the resulting sociological changes in Bhubaneswar. This study demonstrated the changes and adaptations that had occured in the temple town. In 1981 Manamohana Mahapatra[8] who was earlier associated with the Harvard-Bhubaneswar Project, published his study on important changes in the lifestyle of the temple functionaries, especially after the establishment of the new capital at Bhubaneswar. He has tried to show how the younger generation of the service groups have switched over to other professions for which ample opportunities are available with growing urbanisation. In spite of new changes the continuity can also be noticed with the use of surnames such as *Mahāpātra, Parichā, Makadam, Sāmantrā, Pūjā paṇḍā, Rājaguru,* and others.

MANAGEMENT OF THE TEMPLE

Traditionally, the management of the temple was under the direct control of the ruler, but the conduct and management of its affairs were vested in the hands of the *Parichā* (Superintendent) and other principal functionaries. Inscriptions of the Eastern Gaṅgas and the Sūryavaṁśī rulers throw light on the system of management of the temples and organization of their services.[9] The system apparently continued under the Mughal rule, when the Rājā of Khurdā supervised the affairs of the Liṅgarāja temple. Khurdā, however, came under the possession of the British from 1805 and the Rājā of Khurdā was kept as a prisoner at Midnapur. In 1809, the Rājā of Khurdā became the Superintendent of the Jagannāth temple. The Liṅgarāja temple came under the jurisdiction of the Board of Revenue in 1810. It was not possible, however, on the part of the

Christian authorities to supervise the internal affairs of a Hindu temple. Therefore, a 'Local Agent' was appointed to look after the internal management through the traditional *pañcāyat* of the temple.

In 1863, consequent upon the mismanagement of the temple, "the District Judge took charge of it under the Civil Procedure Code and placed the Superintendence in the hands of a committee".[10] In 1926, the post of a Superintendent was created and he was made responsible to the committee for the administration of the temple. In 1936, the office of the Superintendent was designated as Manager.

After the creation of the new province, "the Orissa Hindu Religious Endowment Act" came into force on August 31, 1939 and it was further amended in 1954. The Act, among others, provided for a Commissioner of Endowments for the administration of all religious endowments in the state. The Liṅgarāja temple also came under his direct control. Later on in 1952 for the effective management of the temple, a 'Scheme' was framed under the general provisions of the Orissa Hindu Religious Endowments Act IV of 1939 and the temple was administered, according to this 'Scheme'. The 'Scheme' provided that "the Liṅgarāja temple with its Endowments shall be administered by a Board of Trustees not exceeding five in number to be appointed by the Commissioner who shall hold office for such a period not exceeding five years as may be fixed by him". Subject to the control of the Board of Trustees, the Executive Officer is to "manage the properties and affairs of the temple and arrange for the conduct of the daily worship, ceremonies and festivals of the temple according to the usage". The Executive Officer is responsible, among others, for the custody of all records and properties including cash and valuables of the Temple.

The temple is now under the management of a Trust Board. The Executive Officer, who is on deputation from the Office of the Endowment Commissioner, Orissa, is the *ex-officio* Secretary of the Trust Board.[11]

NOTES AND REFERENCES

1. N.K. Bose *et al.*, "Organization of Services in the Temple of Liṅgarāja in Bhubaneswar", p. 93.
2. R.D. Banerjee, *History of Orissa*, p. 36.
3. K.C. Panigrahi, *Archaeological Remains at Bhubaneswar.*
4. B.V. Nath, "The Pārvatī Temple Inscription at Bhubaneswar", *OHRJ*, Vol. III, No. 3, December 1954, p. 149.
5. *Ibid.*
6. K.S. Behera and others (eds.), *Charles Grome's Report on the Jagannatha Temple, 1805,* Orissa State Archives, Bhubaneswar, 2002.
7. N.K. Bose *et al.*, *op. cit.*, pp. 85-129.
8. M.M. Mahapatra, *Traditional Structure and Change in an Orissan Temple,* Calcutta, 1981.
9. C.V.R. Rao, *Administration and Society in Medieval Andhra (AD 1038-1538) Under the Later Eastern Gangas and the Sūrya Vaṁśi Gajapatis,* Nellore, 1976.
10. L.S.S. O'Malley, *Puri: A Gazetteer,* p. 240.
11. N. Senapati (ed.), *Orissa District Gazetteers, Puri,* p. 731.

VIII

Conservation of the Temple

The tradition of construction and conservation of temples in Orissa has been a continuous process. As early as the 1st century BC Khāravela, the greatest king of ancient Kaliṅga, is said to have renovated all religious structures[1] *(savva devāyatana saṁkāra kāraka)* including secular buildings, such as gateways and walls. This tradition to repair temples continued in Orissa in later period. King Hastivarman of the Eastern Gaṅga family of Kaliṅga (6th-7th centuries AD) made provision for the repair of temple of Viṣṇu *(khaṇḍa sphuṭita saṁskarāya)*. The *Linga Purāṇa*[2] mentions that "If anyone repairs or rebuilds the old, dilapidated, fallen or broken temples and reconstructs them with doors, etc. or if he repairs the mansion, platform, rampart or the ornamental gateway he derives more benefit than even the original maker." *Pratiṣṭhā Lakṣaṇasāra Samuccaya*[3] refers to the process of *Jīrṇoddhāra*. The *Ekāmra Purāṇa*[4] preserves the tradition that the Liṅgarāja temple was rebuilt thirteen times and the Brahmeśvara was rebuilt eleven times. Built in the 11th century the existing temple of Liṅgarāja was repaired on several occasions. The Liṅgarāja temple inscription of Anaṅgabhīma III (AD 1206-1238) records the arrangement made for the periodical repair of the *maṇḍapa* of this temple.[5] Five *vāṭikās* of land were given to a potter for repairing the roof of the *maṇḍapa* every 12 years. Two *vāṭikās* of land were given to a *cūrṇakāra* (lime maker) for white-washing the *maṇḍapa* once in a year. One *vāṭikā* of land was given to a sweeper for sweeping the *maṇḍapa* three times a day. Repair to the *maṇḍapa* was carried out by Govinda Senapati.[6] It appears that permanent land endowments were made to ensure the repair of the temple.

The history of conservation of the temple during the succeeding Sūryavaṁśī dynasty is not known precisely.

In 1803 Orissa came under the supremacy of the British. The government, however, did not take steps for repairing the temples of Bhubaneswar. This is evident from the accounts of Andrew Stirling and the drawing published by him in the *Asiatic Researches*[7] (1825). William F.B. Lourie, who visited Bhubaneswar around the mid 19th century, records, "Bhubaneswar enjoys no support from government in any way, and we question very much whether it now receives any from the Rajah of Khurdah, although it did formely the present Rajah's ancestors having granted some of the lands and endowments attached to it"[8] (Pl. 148).

The first initiative for the conservation of the temples of Bhubaneswar came from the enlightened people of Cuttack. In 1884, a public meeting was held in the premises of Cuttack Printing Company for the conservation of Bhubaneswar temples. Śrī Biharilal Gupta, District Judge, Cuttack was the President of this meeting and Babu Hariballava Vasu gave a short speech regarding the necessity of preserving Bhubaneswar temples. He said that nearly 1.5 lakhs will be required and the expenditure cannot be met from the temple's fund. Therefore, he suggested for a formation of a Temple Conservation Committee. The proposal was accepted. Choudhury Krutibash Dash and Rājā of Athagarh were chosen as Presidents, Priyanath Chatterji and Rash Bihari Nayak became the Secretaries of the Committee. It was decided to have its branches in different places to collect donations and the government was to be moved for the sanction of funds through the District Judge of Cuttack. The President pointed out that at one time there were ten thousand temples at Bhubaneswar under worship and lighting of evening lamps must have presented a grand spectacle. In course of time, however, many temples collapsed, and many others, being broken, became the den of bats. The remaining one unless urgently repaired could not survive for long. Its artistic qualities are not in anyway inferior to the best artistic works of Europe. If such artistic works perish because of the lack of conservation, it will be considered not only a serious concern but also a grave sin. He pointed out that the conservation of the temples should have been taken place much earlier as there has been long neglect, and he hoped the endeavours to be successful and expected cooperation in this matter from all.[9]

A notice dated December 14, 1893 was published in the *Utkala Dīpikā,* the leading Oriya journal of Orissa, to draw public sympathy and help towards preservation of the Bhubaneswar temples. A meeting was also proposed to be organized on January 7, 1894 under the Chairmanship of Biharilal Gupta, District Judge, Cuttack.[10]

Lord Curzon's proposed visit to Orissa raised hope for the preservation of ancient art of Orissa. An enlightened Oriya in a letter dated October 29, 1900[11] addressed to the Editor of *Utkala Dīpikā,* drew attention to the proposed visit of Lord Curzon to Orissa in December 1900. In view of Lord Curzon's interest in antiquarian studies, it was expected that Curzon would certainly visit the ancient monuments of Orissa and take interest in their preservation. It was the first visit of a Governor General to Orissa. Meanwhile, the Public Works Department had undertaken conservation of major temples of Bhubaneswar under the supervision of M.H. Arnott.

Lord Curzon visited the historic city of Puri in December 1900 and came to Bhubaneswar by train. He visited the Bhubaneswar temple in a horse-drawn carriage. The priests of the great temple presented an address of welcome in which they mentioned about Curzon's interest for

Fig. 18. Great Pagoda at Bhubaneswar and other adjoining temples (Andrew Sterling, Asiatic Researches, Vol. XV, 1825).

preservation of monuments. Lord Curzon showed great interest in the Liṅgarāja temple. While watching the temple, he reviewed the on-going work of conservation undertaken by M.H. Arnott and instructed him how the progress to be made for completion of the work. Incidentally, he told Priyanath Chatterjee of the Temple Committee, "you are telling that this Hindu temple is very beautiful and its construction technique is so wonderful that all should see it. You also expect that, I should provide funds from the government for protection and preservation of this temple, but you are not allowing me to enter the temple to see it. Is it appropriate to think like that? Priyanath Babu remained silent and he had no answer to give even though Lord Curzon's opinion was reasonable."[12]

The first major attempt to repair the principal temples of Bhubaneswar was undertaken between 1898 and 1903 by M.H. Arnott, Executive Engineer, Bengal Public Works. The programme of repair to the Liṅgarāja temple including the *deula, jagamohana, nāṭa-mandira* and *bhoga-maṇḍapa* was conceived at a total cost of Rs. 2,861.00, half of which was to be contributed by the Temple Committee.

The *kalaśa* of the *deula* had been blown down by severe thunder storm, which occurred in March, 1900 and the stones were lying in the *khapurī* and the *āmlaka.* The *kalaśa* was rebuilt with old and new materials. The steps leading to the *pārśva-devatā* images were displaced. The lintels above the images of Kārttikeya and Pārvatī were cracked and the supports were out of plumb. The outer face of the temple, in the south-west and north-east corner, were damaged by fallen stones. The steps leading to Kārttikeya and Pārvatī were rebuilt. The broken stones in the south-west and north-east of the *bāḍa* of the *deula* were replaced by new ones.

The southern face of the *jagamohana,* above the doorway, was in a bad condition. The southern entrance of the *jagamohana* was composed of two parts: for a distance of 8 feet 3 inches, it is 3 feet 10 inches in width and it then had a width of 7 feet 6 inches for a distance of 5 feet 2 inches. The former width had been lintelled over as it was in a good condition, the latter width was corbelled in both sides, badly cracked and the passage was a source of danger. Therefore, new lintels and supports were erected at the southern entrance and the entire passage was made of uniform width of 3 feet 10 inches. The lintel between the *deula* and the *jagamohana* had cracked. A new lintel was given to the passage between the *jagamohana* and the *deula.* The leaks in the roof and *āmlaka* of the *jagamohana* were closed by plastering the entire *āmlaka* and filling up the stone joints with fine grouting consisting of two thirds of stone lime with one-third of shell-lime, both incorporated with molasses water. Between the *nāṭa-mandira* and the *jagamohana,* there was a chlorite doorway bearing splendid carvings. The lintel of the doorway had severely cracked at many places. The chlorite lintel and its support in the passage between *jagamohana* and *nāṭa-mandira* were removed and sandstones were substituted.

The *bhoga-maṇḍapa* was in a bad condition with broken scroll-work and weathered ornamentation. In order to render the structure watertight, and to prevent further deterioration, the three faces of the *bhoga-maṇḍapa* were thickly plastered so as to fill up inequalities caused by broken stones.[13]

The great temple of Bhagavatī (Pārvatī) within the enclosure of the Liṅgarāja temple, Gaṇeśa and other minor temples within the Liṅgarāja compound had been included in the list of Ancient Monuments in Bengal, located in the Orissa Division.[14]

The Liṅgarāja temple was declared to be a protected monument under the provision of Section 3 of the Ancient Monuments Preservation Act VII of 1904 by Notification No. 578 E, dated the 8th April 1913 of the Government of Bihar and Orissa.

In 1924, the temple required urgent repair and the repair work was undertaken by Sanat Kumar Raichaudhuri, Executive Engineer, Cuttack Division. R.D. Banerjee was deputed by the Archaeological Survey of India to advise the Public Works Department of Bihar and Orissa to undertake the repair. The wooden ceilings of both the *jagamohana* and *sanctum* were removed.

This brought to light, for the first time, the principle of the construction of the main temple with its interior composed of a number of superimposed chambers.[15]

Between 1926-29 renovation of the Liṅgarāja temple and Pārvatī temple were undertaken with funds donated by Rājas, Zamīndārs and money received from Jagannāth temple conservation fund. A marble slab, attached to the inner side of the eastern enclosure wall, records the donation by Mahārāja Brajamohana Deva of Kālāhāndi, Śrī Mahanta Rāmānuja Dās of Emār Maṭha, Puri; Śrī Krushna Singh Mandhātā, Rājā of Nayagarh; Mahārāja Śrī Rajendra Nārāyaṇa Singhdeo of Patna and others.

In 1945, the Central Government in exercise of the powers conferred by Sub-Section (1) of Section 3 of the Ancient Monuments Preservation Act, 1904 (VII of 1904), declared several monuments of Bhubaneswar including the Liṅgarāja to be protected monuments in its Notification F. 4-1(2)/45-F & L, dated the 18th June 1945. In 1958, as a result of the agreement between the trustees of the temple and the Superintendent of the Archaeological Survey of India, Eastern Circle, Calcutta, the Liṅgarāja temple was to be maintained by the Department of Archaeology of Central Government and the trustees were not to undertake any repair to the monument without prior permission of the Superintendent of the Eastern Circle.[16] Since 1958 the repair works were undertaken by the Archaeological Survey of India. In the Liṅgarāja temple, parts of the *deula* and *jagamohana* were made watertight. Similarly, the dislocated *āmlakas* and *kalaśas* of two minor shrines in the enclosure of the temple were re-set and the cracks grouted.[17]

In 1958-59 twelve temples in the compound were thoroughly conserved with re-setting of loose stones, pointing and filling in the crevises. Following the established procedure of the Survey in a few cases the broad mouldings were re-produced without the details of ornamentation.[18]

A minor temple near the kitchen block was dismantled with their stones numbered and entirely re-built in the traditional style. To ensure accuracy of the original design photographs and drawings were made before conservation and after conservation.[19] The Archaeological Survey of India annually attends to the repair, such as re-setting of dislocated stones, finishing of the exterior with recessed pointing, chemical treatment of the surface, rectification of wrong slopes on the ground, etc. Among the short-comings in conservation mention may be made of an erection of a laterite column supporting the *pīḍha* of the *jagamohana* on the northern side, probably done by the Public Works Department. This presents an anachronism and hampers the artistic beauty of the temple. The electrification of the temple done by the Government of Orissa and inaugurated on January 14, 1966 may be considered as an insult to the temple. Lights have been placed on the top of the temple and are out of tune with the artistic outline of the temple. The tubelights sometimes project from the temple. The recent electrification of the temple on 21st October 2001 also shows lack of taste as electrical cables have been drilled through the temple wall and electrical fixtures have been placed too near the base of the temple. This is contrary to the tradition of placing a lamp on the top of the temple in the night of *Śiva Caturdaśī* or *Śivarātrī.*

The urbanization of old town and construction of tall buildings, water towers have affected the visibility of the temple. Once the great tower of the temple was a symbol of the skyline of Bhubaneswar and could be seen from a distance in all sides. In 1822, Andrew Stirling recorded that a traveller could see from Balianta the "lofty massive tower of stone, rising from amidst the thickets, which skirts the adjoining frontier of Khurda".[20] In mid-19th century, Rev. Lourie observed, "the most picturesque view of the great pagoda of Bhobaneser is to be obtained by proceeding two or three miles westward on the road to Khandagiri when, from its vastly superior height, it becomes the only temple observable then it certainly does present a most majestic appearance, towering to the skies like an apotheosis of science, asserting the undisputed right of India to claim a high rank among the scientific nations of antiquity".[21]

The location of an airport at Bhubaneswar during the Second World War, and its development in recent times into an International airport not far from the temple, may affect it as this temple is built without any cement or mortar. The effect of vibration caused by the flying of planes on the temple built of blocks of stones following the simple stacking technique may affect the stability of the temple, which needs serious scientific investigation.

The preservation of the temple is not merely a physical or a structural conservation. Its environment and setting are as important as the archaeological conservation. The hospital complex on the west, the educational institution on the south, the police station on the east, the shopping complex and the lodging houses on the north-east, which are not functionally related to the temple are to be removed.

The Liṅgarāja-Bindusāgara area, which is the principal focus of the Ekāmra Kṣetra, needs serious attention of town planners and conservators. The ritual paths for the procession of the chariot and movable images need to be kept free from encroachments to provide access to different temples for the visit of Lord Liṅgarāja. The sacred tanks used by the devotees require maintenance and upgradation. Long term action plan may be drawn up for the preservation of this great temple and its environs, so that it is handed down to the posterity in all its glory.

NOTES AND REFERENCES

1. B.M. Barua, *Old Brāhmi Inscriptions,* pp. 7-30.
2. *Liṅga Purāṇa,* 77.24-28.
3. *Lakasanasara Samuchaya*, Chapter-20.
4. *Ekāmra Purāṇa,* 63.46.
   एवं ब्रह्मेश्वरे लिङ्गे लिङ्गे त्रिभुवनेश्वरे।
   एकादश च पञ्चाष्टौ प्रसाश्च गतागतः।।
5. *Epigraphia Indica,* Vol. XXIX, pp. 121-133.
6. *Ibid.*
7. A. Stirling, "An Account Geographical Statistical and Historical of Orissa Proper or Cuttack," *Asiatic Researches,* 1825.

8. William F.B. Lourie, *Orissa: The Garden of Superstition and Idolatry,* p. 118.
9. *Utkala Dīpikā,* January 11, 1884, p. 11.
10. *Utkala Dīpikā,* December 23, 1893, p. 391.
11. *Utkala Dīpikā,* November 10, 1900, pp. 340-341.
12. *Utkala Dīpikā,* December 22, 1900, p. 387.
13. *Report with photographs of the repair executed to some of the principal temples at Bhubaneswar and caves in the Khandagiri and Udayagiri Hills, Orissa, India Between* 1898 *and 1903* by M.H. Arnott, published by order of the Government of Bengal, London, 1903. See photograph No. 24, Liṅgarāja in 1892; 30, Liṅgarāja in 1903.
14. List of Ancient Monuments in Bengal, Revised and Corrected up to 31st August 1895, Bengal Secretariat Press, 1896.
15. R.D. Banerjee, *History of Orissa,* Vol. II.
16. See Appendix-F.
17. *Indian Archaeology 1957-58 – A Review,* p. 87.
18. *Indian Archaeology 1958-59 – A Review,* p. 88.
19. Śrī R. Sengupta, "Preservation of Cultural Heritage, National Monuments of Orissa", in *Orissa Review,* Monuments Special, 1976, p. 83.
20. A. Stirling, "Religion, Antiquities, Temples and Civil Architecture", in N.K. Sahu (ed.), *A History of Orissa,* Vol. II, Delhi, 1980, p. 266.
21. William F.B. Laurie, *op. cit.,* pp. 113-114.

IX

Conclusion

Since its erection in the 11th century, the spire of the Liṅgarāja temple has dominated the temple town of Bhubaneswar. One cannot think of Bhubaneswar without the Liṅgarāja. In order to know Bhubaneswar one has to know the Liṅgarāja temple; if one knows the Liṅgarāja, one knows Bhubaneswar. The temple is one of the finest Śiva temples of eastern India. It represents a mature manifestation of the Orissan style of architecture. A proper understanding of this temple depends on understanding of its multi-faceted dimensions. It is not merely an archaeological monument. It is not merely a Śiva temple. It has to be understood in an integral manner taking into account its architecture, sculpture, religion, inscriptions, etc. The Liṅgarāja has to be understood in the manner the architects, priests and the local people, who lived under its shadow, understood it for centuries.

The Liṅgarāja had its early beginning when it was worshipped under a mango tree. Virtually, it is older than its known history and presumably older than the prevailing traditions. Even though the present temple belongs to the 11th century, the sanctity of Ekāmra Kṣetra prior to it and possibility of an earlier temple at the place, cannot be ruled out. The temple was dedicated to Śivaliṅga and was planned as a Śiva temple with Śaivite *pārśva-devatās* and manifestations of Śiva as a part of its decorative programme. In addition to the images of *pārśva-devatās,* such as Gaṇeśa, Kārttikeya and Pārvatī at a higher level on the *gaṇḍi,* there are depictions of Andhakāsura-vadha-mūrtti in the south, Natarāja in the west and Cāmuṇḍā in the north; the placement following the śāstric prescription is similar to the depictions at Khajurāho. On the east, the depiction of seated Lakulīśa indicates its Śaivite connection, but the Liṅgarāja, according to the orthodox texts had no sectarian association. It is conceived as the Brahman, the Supreme Being. In Śiva temples of the earlier phases, the decorative programmes incorporated both Śaivite and Vaiṣṇavite features. At the Liṅgarāja, however, during the Gaṅga period, there was a fine synthesis between Śaivism and Vaiṣṇavism. The Śivaliṅga is regarded as Hari-Hara and the *kṣetra* was designated as *Hariharātmaka kṣetra.* This transformation of a Śiva temple into a temple for Hari and Hara had its influence on its architecture, sculpture, rituals and festivals. The worship also has undergone profound changes. Originally worshipped by the *Śavaras* in the Ekāmravana, in course of centuries it came to assimilate Vedic and Tantric features. In the worship, the *Śūdras, Brāhmaṇas* and others have their due role. At different times various cults, such as Lakulīśa-Pāśupat cult, Yoginī cult, Mātrukā worship, Śaivism and Vaiṣṇavism prevailed at Bhubaneswar. In the premises of the temple Śaiva, Śākta, Viṣṇu, Jagannātha shrines came up indicating the popularity of the *smārtta* form of worship. The worship of Santoṣīmā and Śanigraha represents yet another interesting trend in the form of popular worship. The Liṅgarāja temple with its subsidiary temples and minor shrines in the compound exemplify the currents and cross-currents of religious development of Bhubaneswar.

The architecture of the temple belongs to the developed phase of the Orissan style representing the sanctuary of the *rekhā* order and its *jagamohana* of the *pīḍha* order. In comparison to the earlier phase, the individual elements are well articulated. The sculptural features also belong to the developed phase and served to enhance the beauty and aesthetic appeal of the temple. In the evolution of the Orissan temple style, the temple is a landmark as it represents the climax in art and architecture. It was the first major experiment in building a large temple in Orissa. The Liṅgarāja provided the model for subsequent temples, such as the Jagannātha temple at Puri (12th century) and the Konarak temple (13th century) to follow; while the Konarak is no longer under worship and is in ruins and, the great temple at Puri, until recently, remained hidden under successive coats of plaster, the Liṅgarāja temple is in state of better preservation.

In the context of urbanization and expansion of Bhubaneswar, the conservation of the temple requires serious consideration, not merely for its physical preservation but its environs with the temple-town as a whole. Any project on the conservation of the temple should be based on scientific study of its structure and must include conservation of the environment around the temple and the sacred Bindusāgara tank. The camera in a calm night has captured the radiance of the illuminating temple and its reflection on the water of the Bindusāgara. If, however, high rising buildings come up between the temple and the Bindusāgara, such occurence of reflection may not be possible. The Archaeological Survey of India, the government and the people have the duty to preserve this beautiful temple, one of the finest in India, for the posterity.

APPENDICES

Appendix A: Ekāmra Kṣetra Māhātmya in the Brahma Purāṇa

Appendix B: Liṅgarāja Temple Inscriptions

Appendix C: Chronology of Important Temples at Bhubaneswar

Appendix D: List of Protected and Unprotected Monuments in Bhubaneswar

Appendix E: Genealogy of the Somavaṁśī Dynasty

Appendix F: Agreement between the Trustees of the Liṅgarāja Temple and Superintendent of Archaeology, Archaeological Survey of India, Eastern Circle, Calcutta, on February 10, 1958

APPENDIX A

EKĀMRA KṢETRA MĀHĀTMYA OF THE BRAHMA PURĀṆA

लोमहर्षण उवाच

श्रुत्वैवं वै मुनिश्रेष्ठाः कथां पापप्रणाशिनीम्। रुद्रक्रोधोद्भवां पुण्यां व्यासस्य वदतो द्विजाः ॥१॥

पार्वत्याश्च तथा रोषं क्रोधं शंभोश्च दुःसहम्। उत्पत्तिं वीरभद्रस्य भद्रकाल्याश्च संभवम् ॥२॥

दक्षयज्ञविनाशं च वीर्यं शंभोस्तथाऽद्भुतम्। पुनःप्रसादं देवस्य दक्षस्य सुमहात्मनः ॥३॥

यज्ञभागं च रुद्रस्य दक्षस्य च फलं क्रतोः। हृष्टा बभूवुः संप्रीता विस्मिताश्च पुनः पुनः ॥४॥

पप्रच्छुश्च पुनर्व्यासं कथाशेषं तथा द्विजाः। पृष्टः प्रोवाच तान् व्यासः क्षेत्रमेकाम्रकं पुनः ॥५॥

व्यास उवाच

ब्रह्मप्रोक्तां कथां पुण्यां श्रुत्वा तु ऋषिपुंगवाः। प्रशंशसुस्तदा हृष्टा रोमाञ्चिततनूरुहाः ॥६॥

ऋषय ऊचुः

अहो देवस्य माहात्म्यं त्वया शंभोः प्रकीर्तितम्। दक्षस्य च सुरश्रेष्ठ यज्ञविध्वंसनं तथा ॥७॥

एकाम्रकं क्षेत्रवरं वक्तुमर्हसि सांप्रतम्। श्रोतुमिच्छामहे ब्रह्मन् परं कौतूहलं हि नः ॥८॥

व्यास उवाच

तेषां तद्वचनं श्रुत्वा लोकनाथश्चतुर्मुखः। प्रोवाच शंभोस्तत्क्षेत्रं भूतले दुष्कृतच्छिदम् ॥९॥

ब्रह्मोवाच

शृणुध्वं मुनिशार्दूलाः प्रवक्ष्यामि समासतः। सर्वपापहरं पुण्यं क्षेत्रं परमदुर्लभम् ॥१०॥

लिङ्गकोटिसमायुक्तं वाराणसीसमं शुभम्। एकाम्रकेति विख्यातं तीर्थाष्टकसमन्वितम् ॥११॥

एकाम्रवृक्षस्तत्राऽऽसीत्पुरा कल्पे द्विजोत्तमाः। नाम्ना तस्यैव तत्क्षेत्रमेकाम्रकमिति श्रुतम् ॥१२॥

हृष्टपुष्टजनाकीर्णं नरनारीसमन्वितम्। विद्वांसगणभूयिष्ठं धनधान्यादिसंयुतम् ॥१३॥

गृहगोपुरसंबाधं त्रिकचाद्वारभूषितं । नानावणिक्समाकीर्णं नानारत्नोपशोभितम् ॥१४॥

पुराट्टालकसंयुक्तं रथिभिः समलंकृतम् । राजहंसनिभैः शुभ्रैः प्रासादैरुपशोभितम् ॥१५॥

मार्गगद्वारसंयुक्तं सितप्राकारशोभितम् । रक्षितं शस्त्रसंघैश्च परिखाभिरलंकृतम् ॥१६॥

सितरक्तैस्तथा पीतैः कृष्णश्यामैश्च वर्णकैः। समीरणोद्धताभिश्च पताकाभिरलंकृतम् ॥१७॥

नित्योत्सवप्रमुदितं नानावादित्रनिःस्वनैः । वीणावेणुमृदङ्गैश्च क्षेपणीभिरलंकृतम् ॥१८॥

देवतायतनैर्दिव्यै प्राकारोद्यानमण्डितैः। पूजाविचित्ररचितैः सर्वत्र समलंकृतम् ॥१९॥

स्त्रियः प्रमुदितास्तत्र दृश्यन्ते तनुमध्यमाः । हारैरलंकृतग्रीवाः पद्मपत्रायतेक्षणाः ॥२०॥
पीनोन्नतकुचाः श्यामाः पूर्णचन्द्रनिभाननाः । स्थिरालकाः सुकपोलाः काञ्चीनूपुरनादिताः ॥२१॥
सुकेश्यश्चारुजघनाः कर्णान्तायतलोचनाः । सर्वलक्षणसंपन्नाः सर्वाभरणभूषिताः ॥२२॥
दिव्यवस्त्रधराः शुभ्राः काश्चित्काञ्चनसंनिभाः । हंसवारणगामिन्यः कुचभारावनामिताः ॥२३॥
दिव्यगन्धानुलिप्ताङ्गाः कर्णाभरणभूषिताः । मद्यालसाश्च सुश्रेण्यो नित्यं प्रहसिताननाः ॥२४॥
ईषद्विस्पष्टदशना बिम्बोष्ठा मधुरस्वराः । ताम्बूलरञ्जितमुखा विदग्धाः प्रियदर्शनाः ॥२५॥
सुभगाः प्रियवादिन्यो नित्यं यौवनगर्विताः । दिव्यवस्त्रधराः सर्वाः सदा चारित्रमण्डिताः ॥२६॥
क्रीडन्ति ताः सदा तत्र स्त्रियश्चाप्सरसोपमाः । स्वे स्वे गृहे प्रमुदिता दिवारात्रौ वराननाः ॥२७॥
पुरुषास्तत्र दृश्यन्ते रूपयौवनगर्विताः । सर्वलक्षणसंपन्नाः सुमृष्टमणिकुण्डलाः ॥२८॥
ब्राह्मणाः क्षत्रिया वैश्याः शूद्राश्च मुनिसत्तमाः । स्वधर्मनिरतास्तत्र निवसन्ति सुधार्मिकाः ॥२९॥
अन्याश्च तत्र तिष्ठन्ति वारमुख्याः सुलोचनाः । घृताचीमेनकातुल्यास्तथा समतिलोत्तमाः ॥३०॥
उर्वशीसदृशाश्चैव विप्रचित्तिनिभास्तथा । विश्वाचीसहजन्याभाः प्रम्लोचासदृशास्तथा ॥३१॥
सर्वास्ताः प्रियवादिन्यः सर्वा विहसिताननाः । कलाकौशलसंयुक्ताः सर्वास्ता गुणसंयुताः ॥३२॥
एवं पण्यस्त्रियस्तत्र नृत्यगीतविशारदाः । निवसन्ति मुनिश्रेष्ठा सर्वस्त्रीगुणगर्विताः ॥३३॥
प्रेक्षणालापकुशलाः सुन्दर्यः प्रियदर्शनाः । न रूपहीना दुर्वृत्ता न परद्रोहकारिकाः ॥३४॥
यासां कटाक्षपातेन मोहं गच्छन्ति मानवाः । न तत्र निर्धनाः सन्ति न मूर्खा न परद्विषः ॥३५॥
न रोगिणो न मलिना न कदर्या न मायिनः । न रूपहीना दुर्वृत्ता न परद्रोहकारिणः ॥३६॥
तिष्ठन्ति मानवास्तत्र क्षेत्रे जगति विश्रुते । सर्वत्र सुखसंचारं सर्वसत्त्वसुखावहम् ॥३७॥
नानाजनसमाकीर्णं सर्वसस्यसमन्वितम् । कर्णिकारैश्च पनसैश्चम्पकैर्नागकेसरैः ॥३८॥
पाटलाशोकबकुलैः कपित्थैर्बहुलैर्धवैः । चूतनिम्बकदम्बैश्च तथाऽन्यैः पुष्पजातिभिः ॥३९॥
नीपकैर्धवखदिरैर्लताभिश्च विराजितम् । शालैस्तालैस्तमालैश्च नारिकेलैः शुभाञ्जनैः ॥४०॥
अर्जुनैः सप्तपर्णैश्च कोविदारैः सपिप्पलैः । लकुचैः सरलैर्लोध्रैर्हिन्तालैर्देवदारुभिः ॥४१॥
पलाशैर्मुचुकुन्दैश्च पारिजातैः सकुब्जकैः । कदलीवनखण्डैश्च जम्बूपूगफलैस्तथा ॥४२॥
केतकीकरवीरैश्च अतिमुक्तैश्च किंशुकैः । मन्दारकुन्दपुष्पैश्च तथाऽन्यैः पुष्पजातिभिः ॥४३॥
नानापक्षिरुतैः सेव्यैरुद्यानैर्नन्दनोपमैः । फलभारानतैर्वृक्षैः सर्वर्तुकुसुमोत्करैः ॥४४॥
चकोरैः शतपत्रैश्च भृङ्गराजैश्च कोकिलैः । कलविङ्कैर्मयूरैश्च प्रियपुत्रैः शुकैस्तथा ॥४५॥
जीवंजीवकहारीतैश्चातकैर्वनवेष्टितैः । नानापक्षिगणैश्चान्यैः कूजद्भिर्मधुरस्वरैः ॥४६॥
दीर्घिकाभिस्तडागैश्च 'पुष्करिणीभिश्च वापिभिः । नानाजलाशयैश्चान्यैः पद्मिनीखण्डमण्डितैः ॥४७॥
कुमुदैः पुण्डरीकैश्च तथा नीलोत्पलैः शुभैः । कादम्बैश्चक्रवाकैश्च तथैव जलकुक्कुटैः ॥४८॥
कारण्डवैः प्लवैर्हंसैस्तथाऽन्यैर्जलचारिभिः । एवं नानाविधैर्वृक्षैः पुष्पैर्नानाविधैर्वरैः ॥४९॥
नानाजलाशयैः पुण्यैः शोभितं तत्समन्ततः । आस्ते तत्र स्वयं देवः कृत्तिवासा वृषध्वजः ॥५०॥

हिताय सर्वलोकस्य भुक्तिमुक्तिप्रदः शिवः । पृथिव्यां यानि तीर्थानि सरितश्च सरांसि च ॥५१॥
पुष्करिण्यस्तडागानि वाप्यः कूपाश्च सागराः । तेभ्यः पूर्वं समाहृत्य जलबिन्दून् पृथक्पृथक् ॥५२॥
सर्वलोकहितार्थाय रुद्रः सर्वसुरैः सह । तीर्थं बिन्दुसरो नाम तस्मिन्क्षेत्रे द्विजोत्तमाः ॥५३॥
चकार ऋषिभिः सार्धं तेन बिन्दुसरः स्मृतम् । अष्टम्यां बहुले पक्षे मागशीर्षे द्विजोत्तमाः ॥५४॥
यस्तत्र यात्रां कुरुते विषुवे विजितेन्द्रियः । विधिवद्बिन्दुसरसि स्नात्वा श्रद्धासमन्वितः ॥५५॥
देवानृषीन् मनुष्यांश्च पितॄन् संतर्प्य वाग्यतः । तिलोदकेन विधिना नामगोत्रविधानवित् ॥५६॥
स्नात्वैवं विधिवत्तत्र सोऽश्वमेधफलं लभेत्। ग्रहोपरागे विषुवे संक्रान्त्यामयने तथा ॥५७॥
युगादिषु षडशीत्यां तथाऽन्यत्र शुभे तिथौ । ये तत्र दानं विप्रेभ्यः प्रयच्छन्ति धनादिकम् ॥५८॥
अन्यतीर्थाच्छतगुणं फलं ते प्राप्नुवन्ति वै । पिण्डं ये संप्रयच्छन्ति पितृभ्यः सरसस्तटे ॥५९॥
पितॄणामक्षयां तृप्तिं त कुर्वन्ति न संशयः । ततः शंभोर्गृहं गत्वा वाग्यतः संयतेन्द्रियः ॥६०॥
प्रविश्य पूजयेच्छर्वं कृत्वा तं त्रिःप्रदक्षिणम् । घृतक्षीरादिभिः स्नानं कारयित्वा भवं शुचिः ॥६१॥
चन्दनेन सुगन्धेन विलिप्य कुङ्कुमेन च । ततः संपूजयेद् देवं चन्द्रमौलिमुमापतिम् ॥६२॥
पुष्पैर्नानाविधैर्मेध्यौबिल्वार्ककमलादिभिः । आगमोक्तेन मन्त्रेण वेदोक्तेन च शंकरम् ॥६३॥
अदीक्षितस्तु नाम्नैव मूलमन्त्रेण चार्चयेत् । एवं संपूज्य तं देवं गन्धपुष्पानुरागिभिः ॥६४॥
धूपैर्दीपैश्च नैवेद्यैरुपहारैस्तथा स्तवैः । दण्डवत्प्रणिपातैश्च गीतैर्वाद्यैर्मनोहरैः ॥६५॥
नृत्यजपनमस्कारैर्जयशब्दैः प्रदक्षिणैः । एवं संपूज्य विधिवद्देवदेवमुमापतिम् ॥६६॥
सर्वपापविनिर्मुक्तो रूपयौवनगर्वितः । कुलैकविंशमुद्धृत्य दिव्याभरणभूषितः ॥६७॥
सौवर्णेन विमानेन किङ्किणीजालमालिना । उपगीयमानो गन्धर्वैरप्सरोभिरलंकृतः ॥६८॥
उद्योतयन्दिशः सर्वाः शिवलोकं स गच्छति । भुक्त्वा तत्र सुखं विप्रा मनसः प्रीतिदायकम् ॥६९॥
तल्लोकवासिभिः सार्धं यावदाभूतसंप्लवम् । ततस्तस्मादिहायातः पृथिव्यां पुण्यसंक्षये ॥७०॥
जायते योगिनां गेहे चतुर्वेदी द्विजोत्तमाः । योगं पाशुपतं प्राप्य ततो मोक्षमवाप्नुयात् ॥७१॥
शयनोत्थापने चैव संक्रान्त्यामयने तथा । अशोकाख्यां तथाऽष्टम्यां पवित्रारोपणे तथा ॥७२॥
ये च पश्यन्ति तं देवं कृत्तिवाससमुत्तमम् । विमानेनार्कवर्णेन शिवलोकं व्रजन्ति ते ॥७३॥
सर्वकालेऽपि तं देवं ये पश्यन्ति सुमेधसः । तेऽपि पापविनिर्मुक्ताः शिवलोकं ब्रजन्ति वै ॥७४॥
देवस्य पश्चिमे पूर्वे दक्षिणे चोत्तरे तथा । योजनद्वितयं सार्धं क्षेत्रं तद्भुक्तिमुक्तिदम् ॥७५॥
तस्मिन् क्षेत्रवरे लिङ्गं भास्करेश्वरसंज्ञितम् । पश्यन्ति ये तु तं देवं स्नात्वा कुण्डे महेश्वरम् ॥७६॥
आदित्येनार्चितं पूर्वं देवदेवं त्रिलोचनम् । सर्वपापविनिर्मुक्ता विमानवरमास्थिताः ॥७७॥
उपगीयमाना गन्धर्वैः शिवलोकं व्रजन्ति ते। तिष्ठन्ति तत्र मुदिताः कल्पमेकं द्विजोत्तमाः ॥७८॥
भुक्त्वा तु विपुलान्भोगाञ्छिवलोके मनोरमान् । पुण्यक्षयादिहाऽऽयाता जायन्ते प्रवरे कुले ॥७९॥
अथवा योगिनां गेहे वेदवेदाङ्गपारगाः । उत्पद्यन्ते द्विजवराः सर्वभूतहिते रताः ॥८०॥
मोक्षशात्रार्थकुशलाः सर्वत्र समबुद्धयः । योगं शंभोर्वरं प्राप्य ततो मोक्षं ब्रजन्ति ते ॥८१॥

तस्मिन् क्षेत्रवरे पुण्ये लिङ्गं यद् दृश्यते द्विजाः। पूज्यापूज्यं च सर्वत्र वने रथ्याऽन्तरेऽपि वा ॥८२॥
चतुष्पथे श्मशाने वा यत्र कुत्रच तिष्ठति । दृष्ट्वा तल्लिङ्गमव्यग्रः श्रद्धया सुसमाहितः ॥८३॥
स्नापयित्वा तु तं भक्त्या गन्धैः पुष्पैर्मनोहरैः । धूपैर्दीपैः सनैवेद्यैर्नमस्कारैस्तथा स्तवैः ॥८४॥
दण्डवत्प्रणिपातैश्च नृत्यगीतादिभिस्तथा । संपूज्यैवं विधानेन शिवलोकं व्रजेन्नरः ॥८५॥
नारी वा द्विजशार्दूलाः संपूज्य श्रद्धयाऽन्विता । पूर्वोक्तं फलमाप्नोति नात्र कार्या विचारणा ॥८६॥
कः शक्नोति गुणान् वक्तुं समग्रान् मुनिसत्तमाः । तस्य क्षेत्रवरस्याथ ऋते देवान् महेश्वरात् ॥८७॥
तस्मिन क्षेत्रोत्तमे गत्वा श्रद्धयाऽश्रद्धयाऽपि वा । माधवादिषु मासेषु नरो वा यदिवाऽङ्गना ॥८८॥
यस्मिंस्तस्मिंस्तिथौ विप्राः स्नात्वा बिन्दुसरोऽम्भसि। पश्येद् देवं विरूपाक्षं देवीं च वरदां शिवाम् ॥८९॥
गणं चण्डं कार्तिकेयं गणेशं वृषभं तथा । कल्पद्रुमं च सावित्रीं शिवलोकं स गच्छति ॥९०॥
स्नात्वा च कापिले तीर्थे विधिवत्पापनाशने । प्राप्नोत्यभिमतान् कामाञ्छिवलोकं स गच्छति ॥९२॥
यः स्तम्भं तत्र विधिवत्करोति नियतेन्द्रियः। कुलैकविंशमुद्धृत्य शिवलोकं स गच्छति ॥९२॥
एकाम्रके शिवक्षेत्रे वाराणसीसमे शुभे । स्नानं करोति यस्तत्र मोक्षं स लभते ध्रुवम् ॥९३॥

इति श्रीमहापुराणे आदिब्राह्मे स्वयंभ्वृषिसंवाद एकाम्रक्षेत्रमाहात्म्यवर्णनं नागैकचत्वारिंशेऽध्यायः ।

Appendix B

Liṅgarāja Temple Inscriptions

No. 1. Inscriptions of Anantavarman Coḍagaṅga, Regnal Year 37.

Provenance : On the east inside the third entrance of the Liṅgarāja temple.

Reference : 1. K.C. Panigrahi, *OHRJ*, Vol. I, No. 2 (1952), pp. 1ff.
2. D.C. Sircar, *EI*, Vol. XXX (1953-54), pp. 29-32 and plate.
3. S.N. Rajaguru, *Inscriptions of Orissa* (ed.), Vol. III, Part-II (1961), p. 63.
4. K.N. Mahāpātra, *Bhubaneśvara Abhilekha* (Oriya), (1998), p. 11.

Language : Sanskrit, in prose.

Script : Nāgarī of 12th century AD.

Date : Śaka year 1036 (AD 1114-15), regnal year 37.

TEXT[1]

1. सिद्धम्[2] [।*] सम्वत(त्) ३७[3] शाकाव्दे(ब्दे) ऋतुरामखेन्दुगणि[ते]...
2. शृङ्गारशौर्यशालिना संपूर्णशरत्शशधर[4]करनिकरवि(भ्रत)...
3. प्रव(ब)लमहीपालमहायष(महायश, महौजस)–द्विष(द्)गीयमानवृ(बृ)ह...

---

1. From the facsimile in the *EI*, Vol. XXX. The state of preservation of the letters is not quite satisfactory. A number of letters at the right end of all the lines are completely peeled off. It is sometimes difficult to make out the clear meaning of the contents due to the fragmentary nature of the record.
2. Expressed by a symbol.
3. The numeral for 3 is written as 5 due to the inadvertence of the engraver. Similar symbol for 5 is found in the Mārkaṇḍeśvara temple (Puri) inscription of Coḍagaṅga's 57th regnal year [D.C. Sircar, *EI*, Vol. XXXIII (1959), pp. 181-85 and plate], which has been read by S.C. Sircar as 37 mainly on the basis of the symbol found in the present record. Another similar symbol is found in the Nṛsiṁha temple inscription (Puri) which is also dated the regnal 57 of Anantavarman Coḍaganga along with the Śaka year 1053 (see S.N. Rajaguru, *Inscriptions of the Temples of Puri and Origin of Śrī-Puruṣottama Jagannāth*, Vol. I (1992), pp. 30-32 and plate).
4. Sircar suggests, शरच्छशधर.

4. ज[5]श्रीचोडगङ्गकेन शिवपूजाविधानैकहृद[येन]...
5. भगवत:(ते)[6] श्रीकीर्त्तिवास[7]भट्टारकाय विन(नि)म्मि(र्म्मि)तसद(ने)...
6. सपाटके[8] तैलचतुविन्सति[9]करङ्का[नक्षता]न् परिपाल्य...
7. भगवते श्रीकीर्तिवासा(य)[10] सहजसुकृतिवु(बु)द्धदेवधर्म(र्म्मी)श्रीराम...
8. तां शतवन्ति(र्त्ति)मखण्डामकरोदाचन्द्रार्कताराय गौत[म]...

ABSTRACT

The inscription begins with a symbol for *siddham.* The first line inscription mentions the date of the record in the regnal reckoning 37 of the king whose name is mentioned later in line 4. The same line also gives the date in the Śaka era in chronogram which would be same as Śaka year 1036 (AD 1114-15). Lines 2-5 contain words of eulogy in favour of Coḍagaṅga, the Gaṅga monarch and apparently indicate a structure constructed by him, who is described with the epithet of *Śiva-pūjā-Vidhān-aika-hṛdaya,* in the temple compound, for placing the perpetual lamp in favour of *Śrī-Kṛttivāsa-bhaṭṭāraka*. Lines 6-8 record the grant of a perpetual lamp containing one hundred wicks and fed by 24 *Karaṅkas* of oil in favour of the deity Kṛttivāsa-bhaṭṭāraka. The name of the *devakarmīn* or the servitor of the temple beginning with Śrī-Rāma occurs in line 7. The name of Gautama occurs in the damaged passage in the last line, probably indicating the *gotra* of the said *devakarmin.*

No. 2. **Inscription of Anantavarman Coḍagaṅga, Regnal Year 62.**

Provenance	:	The record is engraved on the south wall inside the same entrance.
Reference	:	1. D.C. Sircar, *EI,* Vol. XXX (1953-54), pp. 29-32 and plate.
		2. K.N. Mahāpātra, *Bhubaneśvara Abhilekha* (Oriya), (1998), p. 14.
Language	:	Sanskrit, in prose.
Script	:	Same as No. 1.
Date	:	Regnal year 62, on Wednesday, the first day of the dark fortnight of the month of Vaiśākha.

5. It seems to be the last letter of the expression महाराज continued from the previous line.
6. The first letter of the word भ written in the previous line is now lost.
7. The intended reading is कृत्तिवास.
8. The name of the *Pāṭaka* intended to be कृत्तिवासपाटक.
9. Read चतुर्विंशति.
10. Read श्रीकृत्तिवाससे.

TEXT[11]

1. सिद्धम्[12] स्वस्ति [।*] श्रीमदनन्तवर्म्मदेवस्य प्रवर्द्धमानविजयराज्ये
2. द्वास(ष)ष्टिसम्व(संव)त्सरे वैशाखकृष्णप्रतिपदि वु(बु)धवारे
3. विशु(षु)वति कलिङ्गविस(ष)[य] आळतडाग्रामे स्थित माङ्गा–
4. ण्डिपुत्रविराण्डिनाम्ना श्रीकीर्त्तिवाससे[13] देवाय आच–
5. न्द्रार्क्कस्थायि अखण्डदीपार्थे कलोम्बरविषये
6. तोरन्निराकुरे ब्राह्मणखण्डे सामुकविराज एवं
7. काक्व एवं मण्डलिक एवं देवधर केशव पियामि आ–
8. दित्य सुलभकर(रा) एतेषां गोचरे सुवर्ण्णमाढा(ढ)पंचकं
9. द[त्तं]। दीपदाता सव(र्व)लोके महीयत[14] इति [।।*]

ABSTRACT

The inscription begins with the symbol for *siddham* and then records that during the 62nd regnal year of Śrī-Anantavarman, a perpetual lamp in favour of the god Kīrttivāsa (Kṛttivāsa) was granted by a person named Vīraṇḍi, the son of Māṅgāṇḍi, who was originally a resident of Āllataḍā-*grāma* in the Kaliṅga-*viṣaya* and later, apparently resided in the locality of Torannirākura within Kalambora-*viṣaya.* He granted for making provision for the said perpetual lamp, five *māḍhas* of gold with the cognizance of Sāmu Kavirāja, Kākva, Maṇḍalika, Devadhara, Keśava, Piṇvāmi, Āditya and Sulabhakara.

No. 3. **Inscription of the Time of Coḍagaṅga, Śaka Year 1053.**

Provenance : The record is engraved on the wall of the *Jagamohana* of the Liṅgarāja temple.

Reference : 1. S.N. Das, *Jhaṅkāra* (Oriya), 5th year, No. 4, p. 355.
2. K.N. Mahāpātra, *Bhubaneśvara Abhilekha* (Oriya), 1998, p. 12.

Language : Sanskrit, in mixed prose and verses.

Script : Nāgarī of about 12th century AD.

Date : Śaka year 1053 (AD 1131).

---

11. From the facsimile in *EI,* Vol. XXX.
12. Expressed by a symbol.
13. The intended reading is कृत्तिवाससे.
14. Originally हि was engraved and later ही was incised below it.

TEXT[15]

1. शाकाव्दा(ब्दा)नां प्रमाणे अग्नेशु(षु)वियश्चन्द्र[16]संख्या वियाते[17] राज्ये श्रीचोडगङ्गदेव...
2. स्यो(स्य) चण्डिकासं भगवतो दीपमखण्डकं श्रीकीर्त्तिवासाय[18] वै नाम्ना प्रिय...
3. त: सकलगुणगणै: संयुत: सत्ययुक्त:।। कलेम्वोर[19] विषय समान–
4. चान्तराङ्गि[20] निवासी प्रधानी कुमरदेव सांम[न्त*]राय विजय नार(रा)यण प्रभृतिभि: गृहीत
5. सौवर्ण्णक पञ्चमाढानां मासा(ष)पादक[21] कलन्तर सुवर्ण्णपदिका: पञ्चके–
6. न तैलतिसत्क[22] कचकुन्त[23] देयमाभिवच्छिन्न एदे(वे)ति[24][II*]

ABSTRACT

The inscription records that during the Śaka year 1053, in the reign of Coḍagaṅgdeva, a perpetual lamp was dedicated in favour of the god Kṛttivāsa with the cognizance of Kumaradeva, Sāmararāya, Vijaya, Nārāyaṇa of the village Raṅgi attached to the *viṣaya* Kalambora. Five *māḍhas* of gold were accepted by the maintenance of the said lamp. The interest out of the amount at the rate of one-fourth of *māṣa*, i.e., five *māṣa-padikās* of gold were meant for providing 30 *Kuñcās* of oil for burning of the said lamp.

No. 4. **Inscription of Coḍagaṅgadeva, Śaka Year 1056.**

Provenance : The record is engraved at the entrance of the *Jagamohana* of the Liṅgarāja temple.
Reference : 1. S.N. Das, *Jhaṅkāra,* (Oriya), 5th year, No. 4, p. 355.
2. S.N. Rajaguru, *Inscriptions of Orissa,* Vol. III, Part-I, p. 169.
3. K.N. Mahapatra, *Bhubaneśvara Abhilekha,* 1998, No. 3, p. 13.
Language : Sanskrit, partly in verse and partly in prose.
Script : Nāgarī of about 12th century AD.
Date : Śaka year 1056.

15. The text, as given by K.N. Mahapatra, in *Bhubaneśvara Abhilekha,* p. 12. He has not given the facsimile of the inscription.
16. The intended reading may be वियच्चन्द्र.
17. The intended reading is वियाते. The line is metrically defective.
18. The intended reading is श्रीकृत्तिवासाय.
19. Read कलम्बोर.
20. The intended reading seems to be विषयस्यान्तपाति रङ्गि [ग्राम*].
21. K.N. Mahāpātra corrects it as मासपदिका. The expression denotes one-fourth of a *māḍha* or 40 *ratis* of gold.
22. Read तैलत्रिंशत्.
23. Read कुञ्चकं, a measure of capacity.
24. The intended reading seems to be देयमविच्छिन्नमेवेति.

TEXT[25]

1. सिद्धम्[26] [।*] शाकाव्दा(ब्दा)नां प्रमाणे रसशरवियच्चन्द्र–
संख्या प्रयाते दानैकसीम्नस्समरविजयिनश्चोडगङ्गा–
2. धिपस्य [।] प्रेयेनो(ना)म्ना सत्यनो(ना): सन्ति...
विविधगुणगणैर्मण्डितो दीपं प्रादादखंड–
3. कं त्रिभुवनविभवे कीर्त्तिवासेश्वराय[।।]...कोटिव
विषयसं...श्रीकीर्त्तिवासभटा(ट्टा)–
4. रकाय। गन्धवणग्रामनिवासिभि[:*] गृहीत
सौवर्ण्णक पञ्चमाढानां कालान्तरे तैलत्रिंशत्कुंचकं[27] देयम्।

ABSTRACT

The inscription, beginning with a symbol for *siddham*, records that in the reign of Coḍagaṅgadeva during the Śaka year 1056, a perpetual lamp was dedicated in favour of the god Kṛttivāsa-bhaṭṭāraka. For this purpose, five *māḍhas* of gold were granted which were received by the residents of the village named Gandhavaṇa. The interest earned from the said grant of gold was to be spent for providing 30 *Kuñcās* of oil for burning of the said perpetual lamp.

No. 5. **Inscription of Coḍagaṅga, Regnal Year 67.**

Provenance : The record is engraved at the entrance of the *Jagamohana* of the Liṅgarāja temple.
Reference : 1. S.N. Rajaguru, *Inscriptions of Orissa,* Vol. III, part-I, p. 210.
2. K.N. Mahāpātra, *Bhubaneśvara Abhilekha* (Oriya), p. 15.
Language : Sanskrit, in prose.
Script : Nāgarī.
Date : Regnal year 67.

TEXT[28]

1. स्वस्ति [।।*] श्रीचोडगङ्गदेवस्य प्रवर्द्ध–
2. मानु(न) विजयराज्ये सम्वत्सरे ६७[29]...

25. The text is given by S.N. Rajaguru. He has not given the facsimile of the record.
26. It seems to have been expressed by a symbol, though Rajaguru has not mentioned it.
27. According to Rajaguru, there were three or four lines of writing in Telugu script after the end of this line which are now damaged. It appears to be a bilingual inscription written in Sanskrit and Telugu.
28. The text is given by S.N. Rajaguru. He has not furnished any facsimile of the inscription.
29. There is an auspicious symbol at the end of the line as stated by Rajaguru.

3. आदत्ता द्विग्रामाय अगु...[30]
4. एकाम्ब्रे(म्रे) विनयदेवि...अखण्ड...र्धकस्य
5. .... न।।

ABSTRACT

This fragmentary record states that during the 67th regnal year of Coḍagaṅgadeva, Vinayadevī (one of the queens of Coḍagaṅgadeva) dedicated a perpetual lamp, apparently in the temple of Kṛttivāsa of Ekāmra.

No. 6. **Inscription of Vīracoḍa.**

Provenance : The inscription is incised on the wall of the *Jagamohana* of the Liṅgarāja temple.
Reference : 1. S.N. Rajaguru, *Inscriptions of Orissa,* Vol. III, Part-I, p. 67.
2. K.N. Mahāpātra, *Bhubaneśvara Abhilekha* (Oriya), p. 15.
Language : Sanskrit, in prose (mutilated verse?).
Script : Nāgarī of about 12th century AD.
Date : Not dated.

TEXT[31]

1. .... प्रयातिमधिपो नैक–
2. .... पुत्रः श्रीवीरचोड
3. .... अखण्ड त्रिभुवनाधि–
4. .... त व(ब)लाकरवासिनः[।।*].

ABSTRACT

The inscription records apparently the donation of a perpetual lamp by Śrī-Vīracoḍa, in favour of Tribhuvanādhīśvara (god Kṛttivāsa).

30. D.C. Sircar, in *EI*, Vol. XXX, p. 30 and note 1, gives the following reading of the text though he has also not given any facsimile of the inscription and read only three lines.
1. स्वस्ति श्रीच्यो(चो)डगङ्गदेवस्य प्रवर्द्ध–
2. मान विजयराज्ये सम्व ६७ श्राहि
3. मिल्वार्द्धिग्राम...

31. The reading of the text is as given by S.N. Rajaguru in *Inscription of Orissa*, Vol. III, Part-I, p. 67. He has not given the facsimile of the record. The beginning of each line is damaged, as stated by Rajaguru.

No. 7.. **Inscription of Rāghavadeva.**

Provenance : The record is engraved on the east wall inside the third entrance of the Liṅgarāja temple.

Reference : 1. M.M. Chakravarti, *JASB,* (1903), pp. 113ff.
2. S.N. Rajaguru, *OHRJ,* Vol. V, No. 4, pp. 179ff and plate.
3. Idem, *Inscriptions of Orissa,* Vol. III, Part-II, p. 294.
4. D.C. Sircar, *EI,* Vol. XXX, pp. 158ff and plate.
5. K.N. Mahāpātra, *Bhuvaneśvara Abhilekha* (Oriya), pp. 16ff.

Language : Sanskrit, in prose.

Script : Nāgarī of about 12th century AD.

Date : Wednesday, the 10th day of a particular month.[32]

TEXT[33]

1. स्वस्ति [।*] श्रीराघवदेवस्य प्रवर्द्धमान [विजयरा]...[34]
2. सु(शु)दि १० वारे वु(बु)द्ध(धे) श्रीकीर्त्तिवासेश्वरस्य[35] प्रि(प्री)तये मेडमदे[वी]...[36]
3. पदाध्वावखण्डस्थवर्ति च तस्या मातापितस्यै[37] कोमिनायक नुक...[38]
4. कीर्त्तिवासेश्वरस्य[39] प्रीतये दीपं दद्यात्[40]।। कूर्मपाटकप्रतिच...[41]
5. रसाधुप्रधानजयदेवसमवाय[42] देवधरग्राम दसपुरस्रेठि...[43]
6. हस्तात् क्रीत्वा वाहिडाखण्डक्षेत्र (त्रं) कीर्त्तिवासेश्वराय[44] धा...[45]

---

32. D.C. Sircar suggests the regnal year of the reigning king to be 13 whereas Rajaguru takes it to be the 9th.
33. From the facsimile in *EI,* Vol. XXX.
34. According to Sircar, the lost letters were probably intended to read –ज्यसंवत् १३ धनुः.
35. The intended reading may be श्रीकृत्तिवासेश्वरस्य.
36. The lost letters, as suggest by Sircar may have been –म्वाभ्याम् पुण्यार्थ श्रीकी.
37. Read मातापितरौ or मातापित्रो.
38. The intended reading of the lost letters may have been म्वाभ्याम् पुण्यार्थ श्रीकी–.
39. Read कृत्तिवासेश्वरस्य.
40. Read ददाति.
41. The lost letter is द्ध which is followed by the name of a locality ending with पुर.
42. The intended reading seems to be समवायेन.
43. Read श्रेष्ठि. Sircar suggests the word is followed in the compound by the personal name of the person in the sixth case-ending.
44. Read कृत्तिवासेश्वराय.
45. Sircar suggests the lost letters to be धापूर्व्वकं दत्तम्.

ABSTRACT

The inscription records the grant of a perpetual lamp in favour of Kṛttivāsa, by a lady named Meḍamadevī, daughter of Komināyaka, apparently for the merit of herself and her parents, during the victorious reign of Rāghavadeva. She and her parents were the residents of Padādhvāva-Khaṇḍa. The lady apparently, to cover the expenses of the perpetual lamp, purchased, jointly, a plot of land with a leading merchant named Jayadeva who was a resident of a locality attached to Kūrmapāṭaka, from the hands of a *Śreṣṭhin* of Dasapura, a piece of land called Vāhiḍā situated at Devadhara-*grāma* and granted it in favour of the god.

No. 8. **Inscription of the Time of Rāghavadeva.**

Provenance : The record is engraved on the east wall inside the third entrance of the same temple, incised immediately below No. 7.

Reference : 1. D.C. Sircar, *EI,* Vol. XXX, pp. 159ff and plate.
2. S.N. Rajagura, *OHRJ,* Vol. V, No. 4, pp. 179ff and plate.
3. Idem, *Inscriptions of Orissa,* Vol. III, Part-II, p. 295.
4. K.N. Mahāpātra, *Bhubaneśvara Abhilekha* (Oriya), pp. 16ff.

Language : Corrupt Sanskrit, in prose.

Script : Nāgarī of about 12th century AD.

Date : Regnal year 9(?), the full-moon day of the month of Kumbha, on Thursday.

TEXT[46]

1. स्वस्ती(स्ति) सकवरीस[47] नवइ[48] स्रा(श्रा)हि[49] कुम्भपु(पू)र्ण्णिम(मा) गुरू.....[50]
2. स्य दी(दि)वाकरपुतो[51] आचत्नप्रधानी[52] श्रीकी...[53]
3. खण्डदीपं(प:) दत्तं(त्त:)।। कलम्वो(म्बो)रवी(वि)स(ष)ए(ये) उत(त्त)र...
4. खण्डीदोग्रामे चन्दनसभाइ[54] आदीतक[55]...

46. From the facsimile in *EI,* Vol. XXX.
47. Read शकवर्ष.
48. Sircar suggests नवत्यां, Rajaguru suggests नवमे.
49. Sircar suggests शरदि, but it seems to indicate the regnal year of the reigning king.
50. The intended reading is गुरूवारे.
51. Read पुत्रेण.
52. Read –प्रधानेन...दीप:दत्त:
53. The lost letters may be restored as र्त्तिवासेश्वराय अ–.
54. The intended reading is समये.
55. The intended reading may be आदित्यक.

5. वरा[हि]लगोचरे भूमी(मि) वा[56] ७...[57]
6. न्दा(न्द्रा)र्कथिती[58]।।

ABSTRACT

The inscription records the grant of a perpetual lamp by Ācana Pradhāni, son of Divākara and a resident of a locality, the name of which is lost, during the 9th regnal year of the king whose name is not mentioned. To cover the expenses of the said lamp, the donor granted 7 *Vāṭis* of land in a village called Aṇḍido-*grāma* which was situated in the northern division (*Uttara-khaṇḍa*) within the Kalambora *viṣaya.* The said grant was made apparently during the time of *candana-yātrā,* with the cognizance of the persons named Ādityaka and Varāhila.

No. 9. **Inscription of the Time of Coḍagaṅga, Śaka Year 1089.**

Provenance : The inscription is engraved on the east wall inside the entrance of the temple.
Reference : 1. S.N. Rajaguru, *Inscriptions of Orissa,* Vol. III, Part-II, p. 302.
2. K.N. Mahāpātra, *Bhubaneśvara Abhilekha*, p. 19.
Language : Telugu, in prose.
Script : Telugu of about 12th-13th century AD.
Date : Śaka year 1089, on Thursday, the 8th day of the bright fortnight of the month of pauṣa.

TEXT[59]

1. सिद्धम्[60] [।*] शकवर्षमुलु १०[८९] पुस्यं(ष्य)यु
2. सु(शु)क्ल ९ यु गुरूवारमुन
3. श्रीकीर्त्तिवासदेवरकु...
4. ग(आ)त्रेयगोत्र कलिंगाधिपति[श्री]–
5. चोडगंङ्गदेवर अंत्र[61] व(ब)–

56. This letter is a contraction for the word वाटि, a land measure.
57. The lost letters may be conjecturally restored as भवतु आच–.
58. The intended reading in Sanskrit seems to be स्थिति.
59. The text as furnished by S.N. Rajaguru in *Inscriptions of Orissa,* Vol. III, Part-II, p. 302. He has not given a facsimile of the inscription.
60. Expressed by a symbol.
61. Rajaguru corrects it as अन्तर and interprets "a son in the kṣatriya race born of a concubine becomes progenitor of an *antara* branch of kṣatriyas of a parental stock".

6. विलि[62] वरीश्वरुण्डु...
7. पमु सपक(कु)लंवु(बु)...
8. सर्पणपुर लोग...
9. देवपुर...

ABSTRACT

The inscription appears to record the grant of a perpetual lamp in favour of the god Kṛttivāsa, apparently by the ruler of Bobbili (who seemed to be), the *antara* of Coḍagaṅgadeva of Ātreya *gotra,* the lord of Kaliṅga.

No. 10. **Inscription of Bhīmadeva, Śaka Year 1087.**

Provenance : The record is engraved on the east wall of the *Jagamohana* of the Liṅgarāja temple.
Reference : 1. S.N. Rajaguru, *Inscriptions of Orissa,* Vol. III, Part-II, p. 298.
2. K.N. Mahāpātra, *Bhubaneśvara Abhilekha*, p. 18.
Language : Sanskrit, in prose(?).
Script : Nāgarī of about 12th century AD.
Date : Śaka year 1087.

TEXT[63]

1. ....शाका–
2. [ब्दे] नगनागखेन्दुगणी(णि)ते
3. हयुखिने(?) सोमस्य प्रा...
4. स सुभगः श्रीभीमदेवो
5. ....ता स्वस्य पुरत पुन्य(ण्य)फल–
6. ....कीर्त्ती(र्त्ति)वासाय वै तव भक्ती–
7. ....क सुमनाः प्रादा–
8. ....।। ततः प्रदायं[।।*]

62. According to Rajaguru, the royal family of Bobbili happened to be one of the *antara* lines started by the Gaṅga king Anantavarman Coḍagaṅga.
63. The text as deciphered by S.N. Rajaguru. He has not given the facsimile of the record. It is a fragmentary inscription which he assigns to Cālukya Bhīmadeva.

ABSTRACT

The inscription records the grant apparently of a perpetual lamp in favour of the god Kṛttivāsa, by one Śrī-Bhīmadeva for accruing religious merit.

No. 11. **Inscription of Rājarājadeva, Śaka Year 1094.**

Provenance	:	The record is engraved on the wall of the *Jagamohana* of the Liṅgarāja temple.
Reference	:	1. S.N. Rajaguru, *OHRJ,* Vol. IX, Nos. 1-2, pp. 7-9 and plate.
		2. Idem, *Inscriptions of Orissa,* Vol. III, Part-II, p. 309.
		3. D.C. Sircar, *EI,* Vol. XXXV, pp. 117-20 and plate.
		4. K.N. Mahāpātra, *Bhubaneśvara Abhilekha* (Oriya), p. 20.
Language	:	Sanskrit, mixed with Oriya, in prose.
Script	:	Nāgarī of about 12th-13th century AD.
Date	:	Śaka year 1094; Regnal year 4, on Monday, the 4th day of the dark fortnight of the month of *Dhanu* (Pauṣa).

TEXT[64]

1. सिद्धम्[65] [।*] शक[व्द][66] १०९४ श्रीमद्राजराजदेवर[67] प्रवर्द्धमानविजयरा[ज्ये]–
2. सम्वत(त्) ४ धनु कृष्ण ९ [68] सोमवारे श्रीउत्तरेश्वरदेवर[69] [स्था]–
3. नपति[70] तपोधन सामवेदी[71]पादानां सोमसर [सोमेश्वर?]...
4. त तपोधनशैवाचार्याराधनतत्पर(बा)लकंच्छटि[का]...[72]
5. केन आरोपड़ा[73]ग्रामीय साधुप्रजानां(नाम्) एकच्छा–
6. [या]... दी(दि)ला। समस्त...[74]

---

64. From the facsimile in *EI*, Vol. XXXV.
65. Expressed by a symbol.
66. Read शकाब्दा.
67. It should be देवस्य in Sanskrit.
68. Sircar suggests 4.
69. Should be देवस्य in Sanskrit.
70. Sircar reads परायति and corrects it as पुरायति and in Sanskrit पुरोहिन.
71. Sircar reads साणाहारो(रि).
72. Sircar suggests to read नाम in the lost portion of the line.
73. Sircar reads the village name as आचोपडा.
74. The letters are broken away (चन्द्र or सूर्य is possible).

7. ग्रहणे सुवर्न्न(र्ण्ण) पञ्चमाढा श्रीकीर्त्तिवास[75]...[76]
8. आचन्द्रार्क्क पर्यंत[म्*] अखडदीपमेकं द[77]...
9. ....[78]

ABSTRACT

The inscription records the grant of a perpetual lamp held by an image *(Chāyā-dīpa)* by a devotee named Bālakañchāṭīka, who seems to have been a disciple of the Śaivācārya Someśvara, the head priest of Uttareśvara (Śiva) temple, during the 4th regnal year of Rājarājadeva. For making provision and maintenance of the said perpetual lamp, five *māḍhas* of gold were deposited with the chief merchant of the village called Āropaḍā-*grāma*.

No. 12. **Inscription of Aniyankabhīma III, Śaka Year 1140.**

Provenance : The record is engraved on the north wall (right) outside the third entrance of the Liṅgarāja temple.

Reference : 1. M.M. Chakravarti, *JASB*, (1903), pp. 118ff.
2. D.C. Sircar, *EI*, Vol. XXX, pp. 233-34ff and plate.
3. S.N. Rajaguru, *Inscriptions of Orissa*, Vol. V, Part-I, p. 77.
4. K.N. Mahāpātra, *Bhubaneśvara Abhilekha* (Oriya), pp. 21-22.

Language : Sanskrit, in prose.

Script : Nāgarī of about 13th century AD.

Date : Śaka 1140, regnal year 10(?); on Tuesday, the first day of the dark fortnight of the month of *Dhanu* (Pauṣa).

TEXT[79]

1. सिद्धम्[80] श्रीशाकाब्दैकाभ(द)शस(श)ते चू(च)त्वारे(रिं)शता(धि)के परमवै–
2. ष्णवानङ्कभीमदेवस्य प्रवहति सम्वत्सरे दशाङ्कताडिते[81] सू(सु)–

75. Read श्रीकृत्तिवास.
76. The lost letters were probably देवस्य or देवाय.
77. The intended reading seems to be ददाति.
78. There were probably four or five letters in this line which are now completely damaged.
79. The text as given by D.C. Sircar in *EI*, XXX, pp. 233-34 and note. He has also not given the facsimile of the record.
80. Expressed by a symbol.
81. The intended reading seems to be दशाङ्कगणिते.

3. बर्ण्णधनु(नुः)कृष्णप्रतिपदि भौमवारे स(श)[म्भो*]श्चरणारवि–
4. न्द[भ]क्तेन शाण्डिल्यसगोत्रसम(मु)द्भूतेन वैद्यदण्डपाणिदत्ते–
5. न यावद्देवोपभोगपरिस्थ(स्था)पना यावदात्मोपभोगीय–
6. द्रव्यं श्रीकीर्त्ति(कृत्ति)वासदेवस्य पुरन्तः(तः) स(श)श्वाद्दाहवते(वर्त्ति) प्रकाशरा(ना)–
7. य घृताखण्डदीपद्वयं दत्तना(मा)चन्द्रार्कप्रवर्त्तनाय[।*] ये अन्ये अ–
8. [धिकारिणो...वि]लुम्पकास्त(स्ते) देवस्य चाज्ञ[या*] बन्धनंगत ...।

ABSTRACT

The inscription records the grant of two perpetual lamps in favour of the god Kṛttivāsa, by a *vaidya* (physician) named Daṇḍapāṇidatta belonging to *Śāṇḍilya gotra*, during the reign of Aniyaṅkabhīmadeva.

No. 13. **Inscription of Aniyaṅkabhīma III, Regnal Year 19.**

Provenance : The inscription is incised on the north wall (right) outside the third entrance of the Liṅgarāja temple.

Reference : 1. M.M. Chakravarti, *JASB*, (1903), pp. 118ff.
2. D.C. Sircar, *EI*, Vol. XXX, pp. 235ff and plate.
3. S.N. Rajaguru, *Inscriptions of Orissa*, Vol. V, Part-I, p. 78.
4. K.N. Mahāpātra, *Bhubaneśvara Abhilekha*, pp. 22ff.

Language : Corrupt Sanskrit, in prose.

Script : Nāgarī of about 13th century AD.

Date : Aṅka year 23 (Regnal year 19), on Thursday, the third day of the dark fortnight of the month of *Makara* (the lunar month of Māgha).

TEXT[82]

1. सिद्धम्[83] स्वस्तिइति [।*] भगवत्पुरुषोत(त्त)मपुत्र
2. चतुःसागरपर्यन्ताधिपतिसकल–
3. विद्व[84]जनालंकृतराउ[त्त*]श्रीभीमदेवाव्दे(ब्दे)
4. त्रयो[विशन्ति][85] संवत्सरे मकरकृष्णतृ–
5. [ती]यायां गुरुवारे मघ(घा)नक्षत्रे काश्व्य(श्य)प[स*]गोत्रस्य

82. From the facsimile in *EI*, Vol. XXX.
83. Expressed by a symbol.
84. Read विद्वज्जना–.
85. Read विंशति.

6. [च]ण्डेश्वरनाम्नः पौत्रस्य कास्य(श्य)पसगोत्रस्य
7. सुराण्डिनाम्नः पुत्रस्य कास्य(श्य)पसगोत्रस्य सेना–
8. पते(:) ईर[86]नाम्नः उचि(भरिचि?)समग्रामे दक्षिणभागे वा–
9. ङ्किलाण्डा भूमि पादाधिवाटिवा(का)द्वय श्रीकीर्त्तिवा–
10. सदे[व]स्याग्रेते[87] अखण्डदीपकं (कम्) अहं ददामि
11. ।। ०।। व(ब)लभद्रपुरीये(य)भूमिमाणषट् पुण्यार्थे[।।*]

ABSTRACT

The inscription beginning with the symbol for *siddham* and the words *svasti iti,* record that during the 23rd *Aṅka* year of Śrī-Bhīmadeva (or Śrī Aniyaṅkabhīmadeva), endowed with the epithet of *Puruṣottama-putra,* a perpetual lamp in favour of the god Kṛttivāsa was granted by the general *(senāpati)* named Ira (or possibly Īśvara), the son of Surāṇḍi and the grandson of Caṇḍeśvara of Kāśyapa *gotra.* For making provision for the said perpetual lamp, a piece of land called Vāṅkilāṇḍa, measuring two and a quarter *vāṭis,* which was situated in the southern part of the village called Ucisama-*grāma*, was granted. The grant of another piece of land measuring six *māṇas* situated in a locality called Balabhadrapura is mentioned at the end of the record.

No. 14. **Inscription of Aniyankabhīma III.**

Provenance : Same as No. 13.

Reference : 1. D.C. Sircar, *EI*, Vol. XXX, pp. 236ff and plate.
2. S.N. Rajaguru, *Inscriptions of Orissa,* Vol. V, Part-I, p. 97.
3. K.N. Mahāpātra, *Bhubaneśvara Abhilekha,* pp. 24-25.

Language : Sanskrit, in prose.

Script : Nāgarī of about 13th century AD.

Date : On the full-moon day of the bright fortnight of the month of Caitra, when there was Citrā-*nakṣatra.*[88]

86. The intended reading of the name may have been ईश्वर. The rule of *sandhi* has not been observed here.
87. Read श्रीकृत्तिवासदेवस्याग्रतः.
88. The Aṅka year of the king given presumably at the beginning of line 4 is lost, due to the damaged condition of the record.

TEXT[89]

1. ....[90] [ग]वत्पुरुषोत्तमपुत्र–
2. ....[91] [र्य]न्ताधिपतिसकलवि–
3. ....[92] उत्तश्रीभीमदेवाव्दे(ब्दे)
4. ....[93] [रेचै]त्रशुक्लपौ–
5. ....[94] चित्रानक्षत्रे स–
6. .... स्य कोण्ठराङ्गविष–
7. ....[95] ग्रामे भूमिवाटिकात्र–
8. ....[96] वासदेवाय नैवेद्यं पु–
9. ....[97] वाटिकैकं पानीयपात्रीं(त्रीम्) अहं द–
10. ....[98] पानीयम्पाठिमा(म)हादेवपण्डितपुरु–
11. षोत्तमगोविन्दकरणशिउनात(शिवनाथ)करणे[99]–
12. ष्वधिकारे दातव्यो[100] मया किम्व(म्ब)हुने–
13. [ति ॥ ०॥]

ABSTRACT

The inscription records the grant of 3 *vāṭis* of land in a village situated in Koṇṭharāṅga *viṣaya* in favour of the god Kṛttivāsa apparently for making provision for *naivedya* or daily offerings to the deity. Another piece of land measuring one *vāṭi* was granted for the provision of *pānīyapātrī (dhārā-pātra* or the water-jar). The donor seems to have arranged for the proper supply of water through

---

89. From the facsimile in *EI,* Vol. XXX.
90. Sircar suggests the missing letters as सिद्धम् खस्ति इति भ– as found in the inscription No. 13.
91. The missing letters may be चन्तु:सागरप– as in No. 13.
92. The missing letters may be द्वज्जनालंकृतरा–.
93. The last expression may have been सम्वत्सरे.
94. The missing letters may apparently be –र्ण्णमास्यां.
95. The name of the village cannot be determined.
96. The missing letter may be restored as यं श्रीकीर्त्ति(कृत्ति)–.
97. The lost letters may be retored as पुनरपि–.
98. The lacuna has to be filled up with the letters दामि as is found in No. 13.
99. Read शिवनाथकरणानामधि–.
100. Read दातव्यम्.

the persons named Pāthin Mahādeva, Paṇḍita Puruṣottama, Govinda Karaṇa and Siunātā (Śivanātha) Karaṇa.

No. 15. **Inscription of Aniyankabhīma III, Regnal Year 34.**

Provenance : The record is engraved on the wall of the *Jagamohana* of the Liṅgarāja temple.

Reference : 1. M.M. Chakravarti, *JASB*, Vol. LXXII (1903), Part-I, pp. 115ff.
2. D.C. Sircar, *Indian Culture*, Vol. VI, pp. 73ff.
3. S.N. Rajaguru, *Inscriptions of Orissa*, Vol. V, Part-I, p. 117.
4. K.N. Mahāpātra, *Bhubaneśvara Abhilekha*, p. 27.

Language : Sanskrit, in prose.

Script : Nāgarī of about 13th century AD.

Date : Regnal year 34 (Aṅka year).

TEXT[101]

1. स्वस्ति [।।*] श्रीमदनीयङ्कभीमदेव –
2. स्य प्रवर्द्धमान पुरूषोत्तमस(सा)–
3. म्ब्रा(म्रा)ज्यें चतुस्तिम(चतुस्त्रिंशत्)तमे अ–
4. ङ्के श्रीभगवते कृत्तिवाससे
5. एकान्तरीय श्रीपादाचु(च)रणे अ–
6. नुदिने प्रस्तपरिमितौदन प (घ?)–
7. टिका प्रदत्ता [।*] एतत् प्रवाहार्थं
8. पाठिभ्यामञ्चाङ्गलिकाभ्यां
9. षट्चिह्नक कलन्तरीय द्र–
10. व्येण(न) देयमिति[102] स्वीकृ[तम्।।*]
11. .... श्रीरामयस(रक्ष) [।।*]

ABSTRACT

The inscription records the grant of one *prastha* consisting of 10 *paṭikās* (*ghaṭikās?*) of food (rice) every day in favour of the god Kṛttivāsa. For making provision of this offering, 6 *cinhukas* (gold coins) as the interest of the deposit was granted for purchase of the items needed for the said offering to the deity.

101. From the facsimile in *Indian Culture*, Vol. VI.

102. Read दातव्यमिति.

No. 16. **Inscription of Aniyankabhīma III, Aṅka Year 34.**

Provenance : The record is engraved on the south jamb of the porch.

Reference : 1. M.M. Chakravarti, *JASB,* Vol. LXXII (1903), pp. 115ff.
2. S.N. Das, *OHRJ,* Vol. II, Nos. 3-4, pp. 53-55.
1. D.C. Sircar, *Indian Culture,* Vol. III, pp. 122-25; Vol. VI, pp. 71-73, 75-76.
4. Idem, *EI,* Vol. XXX, pp. 17ff and plate.
5. K.N. Mahāpātra, *Bhubaneśvara Abhilekha*, pp. 24ff.

Language : Sanskrit, in prose.

Script : Nāgarī of about 13th century AD.

Date : Aṅka year 34, on Thursday, the 5th day of the bright fortnight of the month of *Makara* (Māgha).

TEXT[103]

1. सिद्धम्[104] स्वस्ति [।।*] प्रद्योतद्योत (द्युति / ज्योति–)वाहि ध्वान्तधन्सि[105]द्युतिजलधी(धि)–
2. निमग्नदि(दी)नानाथशरणैकतरणेर्भगवत: श्रीमदनि[य*]ङ्कभीम
3. देवस्य प्रवर्द्धमानसाम्राज्ये चतुसिन्सत्तमे[106] अङ्कें मकर–
4. शुक्लपञ्चमि(मी)गुरुवारे श्रीमदकलङ्कस(सु)धाधवलकलानि–
5. धिकलाका(क)लितमौलेर्भभ(ग)वतो जगदीस्व(श्व)रस्य कीर्त्तिवा–
6. ससो[107]देवस्य पर्व्वोत्सवमहोत्सवविवाहाद्युत्सवोपयु–
7. क्तप्रतिनियतमण्डपस्य प्रतिद्वादशाव्दी(ब्दी)याच्छादनाथं(र्थं)
8. कुम्भकाराय द्वे वाटिके, प्रत्यव्दी(ब्दी)यर्चूर्ण्णाविलेपनाथं(र्थं)–
9. चूर्ण्णकाराय द्वे, अनुदिनं वारत्रयम्माजं(र्ज)नार्थ मे[108]–
10. केतर(°केत्थं)लक्ष्मीसागरपटिआ[109]ग्रामीथं(य)पञ्चवाट्य:
11. परेआ सेनाअध्यक्षस(स्य) प(पु)त्र(त्रे)ण जीर्ण्णोद्धारकत्रा(र्त्रा) गो–

103. From the facsimile in *EI,* Vol. XXX.
104. Expressed by a symbol.
105. Read ध्वंसि.
106. Read चतुस्त्रिंशत्तमे.
107. Read कृत्तिवाससो°.
108. Read –र्थमेका.
109. The last letter has been read by Sircar as मा. He reads तरल्लक्ष्मी and though takes the expressions as the name of two villages, he could not identify them. The two present localities of Lakṣmisāgar and Paṭiā, retaining their old names are now included within the city of Bhubaneswar.

12. विन्दस(से)नापतिना प्रदता(त्ता) अत आसामपहरणं यः करो–
13. ति भंगाधिक(का)री न(नू)नं स भवतात(त्), दाता सुखी भवतु।।

ABSTRACT

The inscription records the grant of five *vāṭis* of land situated in the villages of Lakṣmīsāgara and Paṭiā by Govinda Senāpati, son of Pareā Senādhyakṣa. Govinda Senāpati is stated to have conducted repairs of the *maṇḍapa* of the god Kṛttivāsa. The deity is described as *jagadīśvara,* "the lord of the world". Another two *vāṭīs* of land was granted for making provision for white-washing its walls with lime once a year and further one *vāṭī* for sweeping the *maṇḍapa* thrice everyday. Thus, of the five *vāṭis* of land, two were allotted to the *kumbhakāra* (potter) for repairing the roof; two to *cūrṇakāra* (the lime-washer) for white-washing and one *vāṭi* to the sweeper. The said *maṇḍapa* is stated to have been used for performing *parva-utsava* (festivals on auspicious days), *mahotsava* (the great festival) and ceremonies such as marriage of the deities, etc.

No. 17. **Inscription of Vīranarakeśarī, Regnal Year 4.**

Provenance : The record is incised on the wall to the left of the entrance to the *Jagamohana* of the Liṅgarāja temple.

Reference : 1. M.M. Chakravarti, *JASB* (1903), pp. 118ff.
2. S.N. Das, *OHRJ,* Vol. I, No. 4, pp. 302ff.
3. D.C. Sircar and J.C. Ghosh, *Indian Culture,* Vol. III, pp. 124-25 and plate.
4. S.N. Rajaguru, *Inscriptions* of Orissa, Vol. V, Part-I, pp. 124-25.
5. K.N. Mahāpātra, *Bhubaneśvara Abhilekha,* pp. 28ff.

Language : Sanskrit, in prose.

Script : Nāgarī of about 13th century AD.

Date : Regnal year 4.

TEXT[110]

1. सिद्धम्[111] स्वस्ति [।।*] स्वकरकरवालकम्पितगणपतिभूसेनापतिगजवाजिसमाजराजराजतनुजात्मज–
2. स्य मरीचिपरास(श)राचारविचारचतुरवीरनरकेशरी[112] धराधिपस्य न्यायनम्रपरिपन्थिपृथ्वीपति किरि(री)–
3. टकोटिमणिघृणिश्रेणीभिररुणितपदसरोजस्य साम्राज्याभिषेकचतुर्थसम्वत्सरे शशिक–
4. लाशेखरशिरःस्रोतस्विनीनीरसादरनिर्मलरेतस संसारसागरोत्तारतरणिप्रतिमव्योमकेश–
5. पदकुशेशयसेवामुखरीकृतमानसेन कायभृकुटिमौलिकमलवन्दनाद् देवद्विजेन्द्रचरणाम्वु(म्बु)–

110. From the impression in *Indian Culture*, Vol. III.
111. Expressed by a symbol.
112. Sircar and Ghosh read वीरवरकेशरी.

6. जकाननैकहंसवता श्रुतस्तेन कालसो(शो)कमानसेन श्रीभगवतः सानन्दवृन्दारकवृन्दवन्दितपादार–
7. विन्दस्य कीर्त्तिवा[स]स्य[113] सिद्धलम्वो(म्बो)दरस्य चत्वारमधिकम् पञ्चदश सुरभिकुसुमकेषु त्रिशतमयद्यमानयुक्तदधि–
8. घृतव्यञ्जनसहितं आत्महिताय प्रतिशरदं पुष्पराजनीलोत्पलनित्याय ताम्वु(म्बू)लाय च कलम्वो(म्बो)रविषयमध्य–
9. पातिचिताग्रामे महिषगोपग्रामे च पञ्चदशाधिकसार्द्धवाटिका पञ्चा(प्रा)दापयत इति।

ABSTRACT

The inscription records the grant of fifteen-and-a-half *vāṭikas* of land situated in the villages named Citā-grāma and Mahiṣagopa-grāma within the *viṣaya* of Kalambora by the king Vīra-Narakeśarī, the grandson of Rājarājadeva, during his fourth regnal year, in favour of the god Kṛttivāsa and Siddha-Lambodara (Gaṇeśa). The grant is stated to have been made for the personal benefit of the donor. The said land is stated to have been granted for making provision for offering cooked rice with curry, curd and clarified butter to the said deities. Provision was also made for offering to the deities, blue lotuses every year during autumn and betel (*tāmbula*) every day.

No. 18. **Inscription of Vīra-Narasiṁha, Śaka Year 1165.**

Provenance : The record is engraved on the wall to the left of the entrance of the *Jagamohana* of the Liṅgarāja temple.

Reference : 1. D.C. Sircar and J.C. Ghosh, *Indian Culture*, Vol. III, pp. 121ff and plate.
2. S.N. Rajaguru, *Inscriptions of Orissa,* Vol. V, Part-I, p. 128.
3. K.N. Mahāpātra, *Bhubaneśvara Abhilekha* (Oriya), pp. 30ff.

Language : Sanskrit, mostly in verse and partly in prose.

Script : Nāgarī of about 13th century AD.

Date : Śaka year 1165, Aṅka year 5.

TEXT[114]

1. सिद्धम्[115] [।*] शाकाव्दे(ब्दे)शतरुद्रषष्ठि(ष्टि)विशिखे पञ्चाङ्कराज्योदये, वीरःश्रीनरसि(सिं)हदेवनृपतेय्य(र्य)स्य प्रतापाश्रयः [।*]
2. प्रत्यर्थिक्षितिभृद्धनात्यय सदा वासः स्व सञ्चारिणो[विष्व-]ग्विश्वतले जयन्ति स(द्भू)पस्य कान्तचण्डाश्य[116][।।] क(का)–
3. म्याव्य(श्र)य कुलदेवतास्ति रचिता यस्यानुमत्याश्रियः। [।*9] प्रागदिशन(?)धनसदन(?)धर्म्मेपि यो व्रती स......

113. Read कृत्तिवासस्य.
114. From the facsimile in *Indian Culture,* Vol. III.
115. Expressed by a symbol.
116. The reading of this line is doubtful.

4. सोयं कीर्त्तिपवित्रमूर्त्तिरनघज्योति:प्ररोह: श्रिया – मर्च्चामन्दिरे प्रदीपमयच्छच्छ्रीकीर्तिवासाय[117]
5. अष्टानां खलु माढानाङ्कलन्तरसैरयं वंशा..... मतोऽखण्डदीपदातास्यै कम्वलि:।।

ABSTRACT

The inscription records the grant of some (apparently eight) *māḍhas* of gold in favour of the temple of the god Kṛttivāsa by the reigning king Vīra-Narasiṁhadeva. The interest from the said deposit was meant for making provision of a perpetual lamp for burning before the god Kṛttivāsa.

No. 19. **Inscription of Vīra-Narasiṁha, Aṅka Year 24.**

Provenance : The inscription is engraved on the wall to the left of the entrance to the *Jagamohana* of the Liṅgarāja temple.

Reference : 1. D.C. Sircar and J.C. Ghosh, *Indian Culture*, Vol. III, pp. 126ff and plate.
2. S.N. Rajaguru, *Inscriptions of Orissa*, Vol. V, Part-I, p. 157.
3. K.N. Mahāpātra, *Bhubaneśvara Abhilekha*, pp. 31ff.

Language : Sanskrit, in prose.

Script : Nāgarī of about 13th century AD.

Date : Aṅka year 24, on Tuesday, the 3rd day of the bright fortnight of the month of Vaiśākha.

TEXT[118]

1. सिद्धम् स्वस्ति[।।*] श्रीमद्वीरनरसिंहदेवस्य प्रवर्द्धमान वि[जय]राज्ये चतुर्विङ्श(र्विंश)त्यङ्के वत्य(र्त्त)माने वैशाख
2. सु(शु)क्ल तृति(ती)आ(या)यां भूमिवारे[120] गौरीगुरुचरण(णा)न्त:करण(° णेन)सारासारसंसारनिरास–
3. निदानतपसा भावसदासि(शि)वगुरुणा भि[क्षोपा]जि(र्जि)तद्रव्येण पञ्चास्य(श)त मा(म)हाजनी–
4. मध्यपाति भूभागमेकं क्रीत्वा व्याकर[णपा]ठाया(य) प्रत्त: इति[121]।।

ABSTRACT

The inscription records the grant of a piece of land by a Śaivite preceptor named Bhāvasadāśiva-guru during the 24th regnal year of Vīra-Narasiṁhadeva for making provision for the study of grammar (*vyākaraṇa*). The said piece of land was apparently purchased, out of a bigger plot, from the *pañcāśat-mahājanī*(?) by means of the cash and kind earned through alms.

117. Read कृत्तिवासाय.
118. From the facsimile in *Indian Culture*, Vol. III.
119. Expressed by a symbol.
120. The intended reading is भौमवारे.
121. Read प्रदत्तमिति.

No. 20. **Inscription of Bhāvasadāśiva-Guru.**

Provenance	:	This fragmentary record is engraved on the wall of the *Jagamohana* of the Liṅgarāja temple.
Reference	:	K.N. Mahāpātra, *Bhubaneśvara Abhilekha* (Oriya), p. 32.
Language	:	Sanskrit, in prose.
Script	:	Nāgarī of about 13th century AD.
Date	:	Lost.

TEXT[122]

1. भावसदाशिवगुरुणा निर्माल्य दशमाणतण्डुलान्नेन..... अल्लारमठ(?) कृत्या ।। ० ।।
2. भावसदास(शि)वगुरुणा देवदण्डनामाङ्कित दशप्रवर्त्त दक्षिणा: दत्ता यज्ञ:..[123]
3. ....

ABSTRACT

The inscription seems to record the grant of rice weighing 10 *māṇas,* apparently to a *maṭha* attached to the temple. The second line of the inscription records the grant of 10 *pravarttas* of (paddy?), probably as *dakṣiṇā* for performing a *yajña.*

No. 21. **Inscription of Kapileśvaradeva, Aṅka Year 4.**

Provenance	:	The inscription is engraved on the right side of the doorway in the Liṅgarāja temple.
Reference	:	1. M.M. Chakravarti, *JASB,* Vol. LXII (1893), p. 108.
		2. S.C. De, *Jhaṅkāra* (Oriya), No. 4, year 4, pp. 391-95.
		3. K.B. Tripathi, *The Evolution of Oriya Language and Script* (Utkal University Pub., 1962), pp. 251-53.
		4. K.N. Mahāpātra, *Bhubaneśvara Abhilekha* (Oriya), p. 33.
Language	:	Oriya, in prose.
Script	:	Oriya of the first-half of the 15th century AD.
Date	:	Aṅka year 4, on Tuesday; on the *Saṁkrānti* day of the dark fortnight of the month of *Mithuna* (the lunar month of Āṣāḍha).

122. As furnished by K.N. Mahāpātra in *Bhubaneśvara Abhilekha*, p. 32. He has not given the facsimile of the inscription.

123. Rest of the letters are lost.

TEXT[124]

1. श्रीवि(वी)रकपिलेस(श्व)रदेवमा(म)हाराजाङ्कर विजे राज्ये समस्त ४ अङ्क श्राही
2. मिथुनसंक्रान्ति क्रीष्ट[125] मङ्गलवारे क्रितिवास[126]कटके भितरपु(पू)जा अवकासे(शे)
3. राएगुरु वासुमा(म)हापात्र भुवनेस(श्व)रमा(म)हापात्र ए दुइहे आसि लिहाइले ए
4. दुइंकरि[127] गोचरे आग्यां(आज्ञा)वोलिण होइले आम्भर ओडिशा राज्ये जे(ये)ते राजा
5. सु(शु)ण सवुहें राजाङ्कर ही(हि)ते व्रति(ती) [।*] ए(ये) आपणार सदाचारे थिबे [।*] असद मार्गे
6. न रहिबें [।*] राजाङ्क अणहिते व्रतिले राजा बाहार करि ताहार सर्वस(स्व) हरि [।।*]

ABSTRACT

The inscription records the royal order relating to the warning to vassal kings against misconduct. The said order is stated to have been incised by Rāeguru (Rājaguru) Vāsu Mahāpātra and Bhuvaneśvara Mahāpātra during the 4th Aṅka year of *mahārāja* Śrī-Kapileśvaradeva on the occasion of worship inside the temple referred to as Kṛttivāsa-*kaṭaka*. It is further stated that all the (vassal) kings should work for the good of the paramount king and should not continue on the path of evil conduct. If any of them engage in what is not beneficial to the overlord, he is to be banished from the kingdom and all his property be confiscated.

No. 22. **Inscription of Puruṣottamadeva, Aṅka Year 4.**

Provenance : The inscription is engraved on the wall of a small temple near the southern gateway of the Liṅgarāja temple.

Reference : 1. S. Tripathy, *Navajivana* (Oriya), January 1970, No. 9, pp. 563ff.
2. P.K. Ray, *OHRJ*, Vol. XV, Nos. 1-2, pp. 113ff.
3. K.N. Mahāpātra, *Bhuvaneśvara Abhilekha* (Oriya), p. 36.

Language : Oriya, in prose.

Script : Oriya of mid-15th century AD.

Date : Aṅka year 4.

124. The text is as given by K.B. Tripathi in *The Evolution of Oriya Language and Script*, pp. 251ff.
125. Read कृष्ण.
126. Read कृत्तिवास.
127. Read दुइङ्करि.

TEXT[128]

1. शुभ श्रीगजप्ती[129] गउडेसर[130] प्रताप प्रुसोत्म[131]–
2. देव मा(म)हाराजाङ्कर वी(वि)जे राइजे समस्त
3. अ४ङ्क श्राही श्रीभुवनेस(श्व)र देउले जलसर[132]–
4. मा(म)हान्ती जे वन्दी पडी(डि)थी(थि)ला ताहाकु ए–
5. ही(हि) भुवनेस्व(श्व)र लींग[133] पार कला ।। ०।।

ABSTRACT

The inscription records that during the victorious 4th Aṅka year of the Gajapati Puruṣottamadeva, a certain Jaleśvara Mahānti, who remained prostrate before the god in the temple of Bhuvaneśvara (Śiva), attained salvation by the *Bhuvaneśvara-Liṅga* (god Śiva).

No. 23. **Inscription of Puruṣottamadeva, Aṅka Year 19.**

Provenance : The inscription is engraved on the right side of the doorway in the Liṅgarāja temple.
Reference : 1. M.M. Chakravarti, *JASB,* Vol. LXII (1893), p. 103.
2. K.B. Tripathi, *The Evolution of Oriya Language and Script,* pp. 293-94.
3. K.N. Mahāpātra, *Bhuvaneśvara Abhilekha* (Oriya), pp. 35ff.
Language : Oriya, in prose.
Script : Oriya of 15th cnetury AD.
Date : Aṅka year 19, on Sunday, the second day of the dark fortnight of the month of *Tulā* (the lunar month of Kārttika).

TEXT[134]

1. वि(वी)रश्रीगजपति गउ(गौ)डेस्व(श्व)र नवकोटी(टि)कर्ण्णा[ट*] [कलवरके(गे)श्वर प्रताप पुरुषोत्तमदेव]
2. मा(म)हाराजाङ्कर विजे राइजे समस्त अ १९ ङ्क स्रा(श्रा)हि तुल कृ २ रइ(वि)वारे कृति(त्ति)वासक–
3. टके पु(पू)जा अवकासे(शे) आग्यां(ज्ञा) होइला ए ये विसि वेहारा उपरे चन्द्रवाण ये

128. From the original.
129. This is a contraction for गजपति.
130. Read गौडेश्वर.
131. This is a contraction for पुरुषोत्तम.
132. The intended reading may be जलेश्वर.
133. Read लिङ्ग.
134. As given by K.B. Tripathi in *The Evolution of Oriya Language and Script,* pp. 293ff.

4. जक (जेबे) करइ[135] सेहि ताहाकु न लागइ एते तारि ये तार कर्ता निजर प्रति भुवने–
5. स(श्व)रदेवङ्कु होइ से राजद्रोह (करइ) आइग्यां(आगा) होइला विसि वेहारा लिहाइला
6. [भुवने]स(श्व)रदेव [।।*]

ABSTRACT

The inscription records a royal order prohibiting the use of black magic against a person named Visi Vehārā. The said order states that, he who casts magic arrows at Visi Vehārā, cannot affect him. He who uses magic, rebels against himself and against god Bhuvaneśvara, and he is declared to be guilty of treason.

No. 24. **Inscription in the Inner Sanctum of the Main Shrine of the Liṅgarāja Temple.**

Reference : *Annual Report on Epigraphy* for 1977-78, p. 85.
Language : Sanskrit
Script : Nāgarī of about 11th century AD.
Abstract[136] :

No. 25. **Inscription in the Inner Sanctum of the Main Shrine of the Liṅgarāja Temple.**

Reference : *Annual Report of Epigraphy* for 1977-78, p. 85.
Languages : Sanskrit and Telugu (bilingual).
Script : Nāgarī and Telugu of about 11th century AD.
Date : Solar eclipse.
Abstract : The purport is not clear as stated in the above *Annual Report.*

No. 26. **Inscription in the Inner Side of the Liṅgarāja Temple.**

Reference : *Annual Report of Epigraphy* for 1977-78, p. 86.
Language : Telugu.
Script : Telugu of about 11th century AD (as stated in the above *Annual Report*).

---

135. This is read by M.M. Chakravarti and seems to be correct. K.B. Tripthi reads कोणरइ(?) and Mahapatra मारइ.

136. The text of the record is not available. It is stated in the above *Annual Report*, "The impressions of the inscription were received from the Superintendent of the Museum, Orissa, Bhubaneswar". But no copy of such impressions is now available in the Museum at Bhubaneswar. The abstract of the text given in the said *Annual Report* is that it is a fragmentary inscription and mentions Kokhi-*viṣaya* and Śrī-Kīrttivāsa. It seems to record some gift (apparent of oil) measuring 30 *Karaṅkas*.

Date : Viṣu[va*] saṁkrānti.
Abstract : It is a fragmentary record as stated in the above *Report*. It apparently records the gift of a perpetual lamp to the god Kṛttivāsa.

No. 27. **Inscription in the Inner Side of the Liṅgarāja Temple.**

Reference : *Annual Report of Epigraphy* for 1997-78, p. 86.
Language : Sanskrit, Telugu (bilingual).
Script : Nāgarī and Telugu of about 12th century AD.
Abstract : The purport is not clear as stated in the above *Report*.

No. 28. **Inscription in the Inner Side of the Liṅgarāja Temple.**

Reference : *Annual Report of Epigraphy* for 1977-78, p. 86.
Language : Sanskrit.
Script : Nāgarī of about 12th century AD.
Abstract : The text of the record is damaged as stated in the above *Report*. It apparently mentions Śrī Kṛttivāsa and Kalambora *viṣaya*.

No. 29. **Inscription in the Inner Side of the Liṅgarāja Temple.**

Reference : *Annual Report of Epigraphy* for 1977-78, p. 86.
Language : Telugu.
Script : Telugu of about 12th century AD.
Date : Śaka year 1053.
Abstract : It is a fragmentary record and only the date is visible as stated in the above *Report*.

No. 30. **Inscription in the Inner Side of the Liṅgarāja Temple.**

Reference : *Annual Report of Epigraphy* for 1977-78, p. 86.
Language : Sanskrit.
Script : Nāgarī of about 12th century AD.
Abstract : It is worn out and apparently mentions a king (*nṛpa*) in line 8 and records the obeisance of a person (details lost).

Appendix C

Chronology of Important Temples at Bhubaneswar

Temple	Date
Śatrughneśvara, Bharateśvara, Lakṣmaneśvara Paraśurāmeśvara	later half of 6th century
Svarṇajāleśvara	7th century
Bhavānī-Śaṅkara	7th century
Vaitāla	7th century
Śiśireśvara	8th century
Mārkaṅḍeśvara	8th century
Tāleśvara	8th century
Mohinī	8th century
Uttareśvara	9th century
Mukteśvara	8th century
Gaurī	10th century
Sureśvara	10th century
Rājarānī	10th century
Brahmeśvara	11th century
Liṅgarāja	11th century
Dākrā-Bhimeśvara	11th century
Manibhadreśvara	11th century
Ekāmbareśvara, in the Liṅgarāja compound	11th century
Vālukeśvara	11th century
Siddheśvara	12th century
Kedāreśvara	12th century
Rāmeśvara	12th century
Bhāskareśvara	12th century
Megheśvara	12th century
Pārvatī, in the Liṅgarāja compound	13th century
Ananta Vāsudeva	13th century
Yameśvara	13th century

Śārī Deula	13th century
Citrakāriṇī	13th century
Two Viṣṇu temples in the Liṅgarāja compound	13th century
Vijayeśvara	13th century
Varuṇeśvara	14th century
Mitreśvara	14th century
Makareśvara	14th century
Bakeśvara	14th century
Pāpanāśinī	15th century
Kapileśvara	15th century

Appendix D

List of Protected and Unprotected Monuments in Bhubaneswar*

ARCHAEOLOGICAL SURVEY OF INDIA PROTECTED MONUMENTS AT BHUBANESWAR

Bhāskareśvara Temple
Brahmeśvara Temple with its minor shrines in the compound
Nabakeśvara Temple
Rāmeśvara Temple
Megheśvara Temple with its minor shrines
Ananta-Vāsudeva Temple
Bakeśvara Temple
Vaitāla (Boital) Temple
Citrakāriṇī Temple
Jameśvara Temple with its minor shrines
Lord Liṅgarāja Temple with all the minor temples in the compound namely:

i. Amaṇiā Well
ii. Aṣṭamūrtti
iii. Caṇḍeśvara Temple
iv. Gopāluṇī Temple
v. Laḍukeśvara Temple
vi. Sāvitrī Devī Temple
vii. Śakreśvara Temple
viii. Ṣaṣṭhī Temple

Maitreśvara Temple with all the minor shrines in the compound
Makareśvara Temple with its minor shrines
Mārkaṇḍeśvara Temple

* Dr. B.K. Rath, Superintendent, Orissa State Archaeology, Bhubaneswar has listed 161 monuments in Bhubaneswar. The above list is based on his survey.

Mukteśvara Temple with its minor shrines excluding Marīcakuṇḍa
Paraśurāmeśvara Temple
Rājarānī Temple
Sahasraliṅga Tank
Śārī Deula
Siddheśvara Temple
Rock inscriptions of the edicts of Aśoka and elephant sculpture
Small rock-cut cell with a niche and an inscription of Śāntikara

All ancient caves, structures and other monuments or remains situated on the Udayagiri and the Khaṇḍagiri hills except the temple of Pārśvanatha on the top of the Khaṇḍagiri hill and also the temple in front of Bārābhujī and the Triśūla caves.
Ancient remains inside and outside the rampart, Śiśupālagarh
Śiśireśvara Temple
Pāpanāśinī Tank

STATE PROTECTED MONUMENTS AT BHUBANESWAR

Swarṇajāleśvara Temple
Bahiraṅgeśvara Temple
Dhabaleśvara Temple
Pañcapāṇḍava Cave
Rājā Nahara, Bhubaneswar
Lakṣmaṇeśvara group of Temples [Śatrughneśvara, Bharateśvara & Lakṣmaneśvara]
Siddha Gaṇeśa Temple, Dhauli
Mohinī Temple
Dwāravāsinī Temple
Bhavānī Śaṅkara Temple
Bibhīṣaneśvara Temple
Yakṣa Image
Sūkhameśvara Temple
Aiśaneśvara Temple

UNPROTECTED MONUMENTS AT BHUBANESWAR
(TEMPLES, SACRED TANKS, MATHAS, ETC.)

(A) TEMPLES:

Yogeśvara Temple, Kapileśvara
Śiva Temple, to the north-east corner of O.R.T. Garage, Old Town
Śiva Temples, near Kharākhiā Vaidyanātha, Old Town

Ekāmreśvara-Śiva Temple, Śyameśvara Complex, Old Town
Śyāmeśvara-Śiva Temple, near Kharākhiā Vaidyanātha, Old Town
Maṇḍapa, inside Kedāra-Gaurī Temple Complex, Old Town
Paradāreśvara Maṇḍapa, inside Paradāreśvara Complex, Old Town
Hazārī Maṇḍapa, inside Kapileśvara Complex, Old Town
Somabāra Maṇḍapa, inside Kapileśvara Complex, Old Town
Dakṣina-Kālī Maṇḍapa, inside Kapileśvara Complex, Old Town
Temple, behind the Bhavānī Śaṅkar Temple, Old Town
Viśvanātha Temple, northern wall of the Liṅgarāja Temple, Old Town
A group of Śiva Temples, on the eastern bank of Bindusāgara, Old Town
Minor Temples, Kapileśvara Complex, Old Town
Kapileśvara Temple, Kapileśvara Complex, Old Town
Bhīmeśvara Temple, Bhīmaṭāngī, Old Town
Śiva Temples, Bhīmaṭāngī, Old Town
Kukuṭeśvara Temple, Old Town
Vaideśvara Temple, Old Town
Śiva Temples, south-west of Śārī Deula, Old Town
Śiva Temples, west of Śārī Deula, Old Town
An unknown Temple, south of Pāpanāśinī Pond, Old Town
Śiva Temple, Bhimeśvara Complex to the north-east of Bindusāgara, Old Town
Viṣṇu Temple, at the eastern bank of Bindusāgara, Old Town
Hanumāna Deula, to the east of Bindusāgara, Old Town
Śiva Temple, to the east of New Market Building, Old Town
Śuka Śārī Deula, to the south of Bindusāgara, Old Town
Sarveśvara Temple, eastern side of the Old Town
Market Complex Gaṅgeśvara Temple, eastern side of the Old Town Market Complex
Jamunā Temple, eastern side of the Old Town Market Complex
Sureśvara Temple, south-east of Liṅgarāja Temple in Old Town
Suvarṇeśvara Temple, north-east of Ananta Vāsudeva Temple, Old Town
Kuśeśvara Temple, Māusīmā Square, Old Town
Laveśvara Temple, Māusīmā Square, Old Town
Tāleśvara Temple, Haramandir Square, Old Town
Pātāleśvara Temple, south-east to Haramandir Square, Old Town
Gaurīdevī Temple, Kedāra-Gaurī Complex, Old Town
Kedāreśvara Temple, Kedāra-Gaurī Complex, Old Town
Sākhi Śaṅkara Śiva Temple, Kedāra-Gaurī Complex, Old Town

Mukhaliṅga Temple, inside Kedāra-Gaurī Complex, Old Town
Śiva Temple, inside Kedāra-Gaurī Complex, Old Town
Mahāvīra Temple, Kedāra-Gaurī Temple Complex, Old Town
Gosāgareśvara Temple, north-west corner of Bindusāgara, Old Town
Paradāreśvara Temple, north-west comer of Bindusāgara, Old Town
A group of Śiva Temples, inside Paradāreśvara Temple Complex, Old Town
Śiva Temple, south-west of Liṅgarāja Temple, Old Town
Devī Temple, south-west of Liṅgarāja Temple, Old Town
Diśiśvarī Temple, near Kedāra-Gaurī Sub-Post Office, Old Town
Veleśvara Temple, to the south-east of Bindusāgara, Old Town
Śiva Temple, to the south-east of Bindusāgara, Old Town
Śiva Temple, to the south of Bhavānī Śaṅkara Temple, Old Town
Niḷakaṇṭheśvara Temple, west of Bindusāgara, Old Town
Maṇibhadreśvara Temple, near Vaitala Temple, Old Town
Uttareśvara Temple, Old Town
Śiva Temples, Uttareśvara Complex, Old Town
Śiva Temple, on the eastern bank road of Bindusāgara, Old Town
Śiva Temple, south of Śārī Deula, Old Town
Kaiñci Temple, Dasiji Sahi, Old Town
Śiva Temple, south-east of Śārī Deula, Old Town
Kaśī Viśvanātha Temple [close to the north boundary wall of Liṅgarāja Temple, (outside) Old Town]
Daiteśvara Temple, to the east of Paraśurāmeśvara Temple, Old Town
Pūrveśvara Temple, near O.R.T. Garage, Old Town
Śiva Temple, north of Mohinī Temple, Old Town
Śiva Temple, Mahatab Road, Old Town
A group of Śiva Temples, Bhāratī Maṭha Complex, Old Town
Temple with Gaṇeśa, Bhāratī Maṭha Complex, Old Town
Devī Temple, Bhāratī Maṭha Complex, Old Town
Ḍākarā Bhīmeśvara Temple, east of Liṅgarāja Temple, Old Town
Śiva Temple, to the east of Liṅgarāja and to the south of Ḍākarā Bhīmeśvara.
Śiva Temple (Ekāmreśvara) south-east of Liṅgarāja Temple (Behind Temple Office), Old Town
Koṭitīrtheśvara Temple, near Ananta Vāsudeva Temple, Old Town
Śiva Temples, Koṭitīrtheśvara Complex, Old Town
Cakreśvara Temple, Rājarānī Colony, Old Town
A Devī Temple, near Kedāra-Gaurī Sub-Post Office, Old Town

Cintāmaṇīśvara Temple, near Railway Station, Bhubaneswar
Gokarnéśvara Temple, near Śiśupālagarh, Bhubaneswar
Gourī-Śaṅkara Temple, in front of Market Building, Old Town

(B) SACRED TANKS

Cintāmaṇīśvara Pond, near Cintāmaṇīśvara Temple
Gourī Kuṇḍa, Kedāra-Gaurī Complex, Old Town
Koṭitīrtheśvara Pond, south-east of Ananta Vāsudeva Temple, Old Town
Bindu Sarovara Tank, Old Town
Cakreśvara Pond, Rājarānī Colony, Old Town
Kedāra Kuṇḍa, Kedāra-Gaurī Complex, Old Town
Yameśvara Pond, east of Yameśvara Temple, Old Town
Maṇikarṇikā Pond, south of Kapileśvara Temple, Old Town
Kapila Kuṇḍa, Kapileśvara Complex, Old Town
Paradāreśvara Pond, Paradāreśvara Complex, Old Town
Kukuṭeśvara Pond, near Kukuṭeśvara Temple, Old Town
Bhīma Kuṇḍa, Old Town
Godāvarī Kuṇḍa, north-east side of Bindusāgara Pond, Old Town
Gaṅgā Yamunā Pond, near Old Town Market Complex
Ancient Tank, Mahābhoi Sasana, Bhubaneswar

(C) MAṬHAS

Gopāla Tīrtha Maṭha, north side of Liṅgarāja Temple compound wall, Old Town
Pāpanāśinī Maṭha, north-west corner of Pāpanāśinī Temple, Old Town
Bhāratī Maṭha, Bhubaneswar.

Appendix E

Genealogy of the Somavaṁśī Dynasty*

1. Śivagupta (AD 855-880)
2. Mahābhavagupta I Janamejaya (AD 880-920)

├── 3. Mahāśivagupta I Yayāti (AD 920-955)
│ 4. Mahābhavagupta II Bhīmaratha (AD 955-975)
│ ├── 5. Mahāśivagupta II Dharmaratha (AD 975-995)
│ ├── 6. Mahābhavagupta III Naghusa (AD 995-1010)
│ └── 7. Indraratha Saṅkaratha Vaṅkaratha (AD 1010-1022)
│
└── Vicitravīrya
 └── Abhimanyu
  └── 8. Mahāśivagupta III Yayāti Caṇḍīhara (AD 1022-1040)
   ├── 9. Mahābhavagupta IV Uddyotakeśarī (AD 1040-1065)
   │ 10. Mahāśivagupta IV Janamejaya (AD 1065-1080)
   │ ├── 11. Mahābhavagupta V Puranjaya (AD 1080-1100)
   │ └── 12. Mahāśivagupta V Kama (AD 1100-1113)
   └── Abhimanyu Someśvara

---

* After Ajay Mitra Shastri.

Appendix F

Agreement between the Trustees of the Liṅgarāja Temple and Superintendent of Archaeology, Archaeological Survey of India, Eastern Circle, Calcutta, on February 10, 1958

This indenture made this day of 10th February 1958 between the Trustees of the Temple through Madanmohan Harichandan Mahāpātra, aged 63, President. Trustee Board of Lord Liṅgarāja Mahāprabhu, Bhubaneswar, S/o Late Dibyasingha Harichandan Mahāpātra of Balianta, P.S. Kothadesh, Dist. Puri, Khetriya, exproprietor (herein referred to on their own behalf and when the contexts so requires on behalf also of the successors, executors, administrators, representatives and assigns as the trustees) of the one part and the President of the Indian Union (hereinafter referred to on behalf of himself, his successor in office and assigns as the President) acting in these presents through the Superintendent of Archaeology for the Eastern Circle, Calcutta (hereinafter called the said Superintendent) of other part.

Whereas the monuments described in the scheduled hereto (hereinafter referred to as the said monuments) have been duly declared to be protected monuments under provisions of Section 3 of the Ancient Monuments Preservation Act VII of 1904 (hereinafter referred to as the said Act) by the Notification No. 578 E dated 8th April 1913 confirmed by notification No. 2488 E, dated the 1st November 1913, read with Notification No. 1730 E, dated 10th October 1918 of the Government of Bihar and Orissa in respect of the Rājārānī Temple, by Notification No. D 469/AR 46, dated 28th June 1946 of the Government of India, Department of Education, Health and Lands, in respect of the Markandeśvara temple and by Notification No. 4-1(2)/45 F and L dated 18th June 1945 of the Government of India, Department of Education, Health and Lands, confirmed by Notification No. D 569/AR/46, dated 30th May 1946 of the Department of Education, Government of India (hereinafter referred to as the Central Government), in respect of the other monuments mentioned in the scheduled hereto.

NOW THESE PRESENTS WITNESS that in consideration of the mutual benefits and covenants hereinafter contained the Trustees and the President do hereby mutually covenant and agree each with the other that is to say:

1. That the said monuments shall be maintained in repair by President through the Department of Archaeology of the Central Government PROVIDED ALWAYS that the said Department shall determine what repairs, if any, shall, from time to time, be carried out.

2. That the said Superintendent shall be the custodian of the said monuments.
3. That the Trustees shall not undertake any repairs to the said monuments without obtaining the previous sanction in writings, of the said Superintendent.
4. That the Trustees shall not destroy, remove, alter, deface or imperil the said monuments.
5. That the Trustees shall not build on or near the sites of the said monuments or cultivate the sites or any part thereof without obtaining the previous permission in writing of the said Superintendent PROVIDED that the Trustees shall have power to permit temporary sheds to be put up in the space between the compound walls and the adjoining road only during festivals with permission of the Commissioner of Hindu Religious Endownments of Orissa State Government (hereinafter referred to as the said Commissioner) with prior intimation to the said Superintendent.

   (But such of the said monuments as are used for religious worship shall continue to be used as heretofore for religious worship and such observances shall not in any way be affected by this agreement.)
6. That the public shall have free access to the said monuments subject to the following restrictions:
   a) That no non-Hindu shall be allowed to enter inside any of the said monuments, which is used for religious worship.
   b) That no shoes and leather articles shall be taken inside the compound walls of any of the said monuments which is used for religious worship.
7. That the said Superintendent or such other person or persons as he may depute for the purpose shall be permitted to inspect the said monuments at all reasonable times.
8. That the Trustees with the written approval of the said Commissioner may terminate this agreement on giving six months previous notice to the said Superintendent and the President may terminate with one month's previous notice to the Trustees and also to the said Commissioner if the Trustees failed to comply with any conditions of this agreement PROVIDED ALWAYS that the Trustees shall in such cases be liable to pay to the President on demand (should the President so claim) all the expenses incurred by him in the repairing, restoring or maintaining the said monuments during the five years previous to the termination of this agreement or during such part thereof as the agreement may have been in force.
9. That the President may terminate this agreement on giving six month's notice in which case the Trustees shall not (except as aforesaid) be held responsible for any sums previously extended by the President on the repair of the said monuments.
10. That the Trustees with the written approval of the said Commissioner shall give the Director General of Archaeology on behalf of the President six months previous notice in writing if the said monuments or any portions thereof are to be offered to sale.
11. That the right shall be reserved and is hereby given to the President to purchase at their market value, the said monuments or any portions thereof in the event of their being offered for sale by the Trustees.
12. That while this agreement is in force the Trustees shall not alienate or hypothecate or charge or burden the monuments or any portions thereof of the land on which they stand

or remove any movable property appertaining to the said monuments PROVIDED ALWAYS that this shall not apply to the jewellery and articles of use of the deities if any.

13. That the Trustees shall remove within six month's all structures between the compound wall of the Liṅgarāja Temple and the adjacent roads with the exception of the masonary platform to the right of the northern gate and the six roomed building on the eastern side which in no case shall be subject to any further additions.

14. That the Trustees shall not lease out any land or erect or have erected any permanent or temporary constructions on any land belonging to Liṅgarāja Mahāprabhu between its compound walls and the adjacent roads. In case of the rest of the monuments mentioned in the schedule the Trustees shall not lease out or erected or have erected any permanent or temporary constructions on any land belonging to Liṅgarāja Mahāprabhu within a distance of five hundred feet from the outer boundary of the said monuments.

15. That in the case of such of the said monuments as are used for religious worship the leaves, flowers, etc. offered by worshippers and thrown inside such monuments leaving of the Bhoga sold to and partaken of by worshippers and kitchen refuse such as ashes, peels of vegetables, etc., thrown inside the compound, shall be arranged to be removed by the Trustees, who shall also be responsible for keeping the premises of such monuments clean and tidy.

16. That if any of the said monuments is fitted with electrical installations the Trustees shall be responsible for the recurring and nonrecurring expenditure on the maintenance and repairs to the said electric installations and for the electric charges.

17. That except as herein expressly provided each of the parties hereto shall in relation to the said monuments have all the rights and be subject to all the duties and liabilities conferred or imposed by said Act.

18. That any dispute arising out of this agreement shall be referred to the Collector of Puri and his decision shall be final.

19. It is hereby agreed that the stamp duty chargeable on this agreement shall be payable by the President of India.

IN WITNESS WHEREOF THE parties hereto have put their hands and seals the day and year first above written.

Sd/D. Mitra,
Superintendent
Department of Archaeology
Eastern Circle
32 Chittaranjan Avenue
Calcutta - 12

Sd/Madanmohan Harichandan Mahāpātra
President of the Board of Trustees,
Lord Liṅgarāja Mahāprabhu
Bhubaneswar.

Signed in my presence
Sd/illegible

Glossary

Abhiṣeka - royal ceremony of investiture.

Agni - the god of fire; intermediary between gods and men; the guardian of the south-east corner.

Akṣamālā - rosary of bead.

Alasa-kanyā - indolent or playful maiden.

Ālati - ceremonial waving of light in honour of a deity.

Āmlaka or Āmlā - fluted disk resembling an *āmlaka* fruit *(Phylanthus Emblica)* set above the *bekī* in a *rekhā* temple.

Amāvasyā - the new moon day in the lunar calendar.

Aṅga-śikhara - miniature representation of a *rekhā* temple on the *gaṇḍi.*

Annapūrṇā - consort of Śiva.

Aṅkuśa - the elephant goad.

Anurāhā - projection adjacent to the middle segment of *sapta-ratha* and *nava-ratha* temples.

Antaratha - projection next to *kanik-pāgā* in *pañca-ratha* and *sapta-ratha* temples.

Antarala - vestibule, chamber in front of the *sanctum.*

Apsarā - nymph-like female divinities of the sky.

Ardhanārīśvara - 'lord who is half female'; the composite image of Śiva and his consort, right as male and left as female.

Āsana - a seat; a pedestal; a seated posture.

Aśokāṣṭamī - one of the fourteen major festivals in the Liṅgarāja temple celebrated in the eigth day of the bright fortnight of Chaitra. On this ocassion Liṅgarāja is taken in a chariot from his temple to Rameśvara temple in Bhubaneswar.

Asura - demon.

Āvaraṅa-devatās - secondary deities surrounding the main image of the temple, forming a protective ring.

Avatāra - an incarnation.

Āyudha - a symbolical weapon or attribute in the hand of a divinity.

Bāḍa - 'wall'; vertical part of a temple between *pīṭha* and *gaṇḍi.*

Bāḍa deula - 'big temple'; it denotes the main temple.

Bāḍa Singhāra - 'the great decoration'; dressing of the deity during the last food offering.

Baḍu - non-brāhmaṇa temple priest of the Liṅgarāja temple.

Bandhanā - set of mouldings joining the two *jaṅghās.*

Basanta - name of the topmost moulding in the *pābhāga, bandhanā* and *varaṇḍa.*

Beheraṇa - raised platform.

Bekī - 'neck'; cylindrical member above *gaṇḍi* and below *āmlā* of a *rekhā* temple; same above *gaṇḍi* and below *ghaṇṭā* of a *pīḍha* temple.

Bekī-bhairava - crouching figure in the *bekī* of the temple placed on each *rāhā.*

Bekī-siṁha - lion placed on the *bekī* as a support of the *āmlā.*

Bhāga - division, specification.

Bhairava - one of the fierce forms of Śiva.

Bhaṅgī - flexion of the body.

Bheṭi - presentation.

Bho - an ornamental motif of a *caitya*-window crowned by a *kīrtimukha* with flanking *gaṇa* figures.

Bhoga-maṇḍapa - 'hall of offering'; the refectory hall of a temple; the structure is usually found in front of the *nāṭa-mandira.*

Bhūmi - plane, horizontal division of the spire.

Bhūmi-āmlā - *āmlā* demarcating one *bhūmi* of the *gaṇḍi* from another.

Bisama - topmost course or courses of the spire immediately below the *bekī.*

Caitya - ornamental motif in the form of a stylised window moveable image.

Calanti-pratimā - moveable image.

Chajjā - projecting member over doors, windows or niches and just below the roof level.

Chatra - umbrella.

Dahi - curd, *Skt. dadhi.*

Dahi-pakhāl - rice mixed with curd.

Dakṣinā - fee paid to a priest for his ritual service.

Damaru - kettle-drum; one of the symbols of Śiva.

Dāna - a ritual gift; often a charitable donation.

Daṇḍa - stick, staff.

Darpaṇa - mirror.

Darśaṇa - visual glimpse of the deity.

Deula - a general name for the temple, also denotes the sanctuary as distinguished from the audience chamber *(jagamohana).*

Devī - goddess.

Dhvajā - flag.

Dhvaja-staṁbha - flag staff; pillar crowned with the mount of the divinity; guardians of the eight quarters such as Indra (east), Agni (south-east), Yama (north), Nirṛiti (south-west), Varuṇa (west), Vāyu (north-west), Kubera (north), and Iśāṇa (north-east).

Dīpa - lamp.

Dopiccha-siṁha - figures of lion with one forepart and two hind parts right angles to each other placed on the *bekī* of the temple.

Dvārapāla - guardian of the door; door-keeper.

Farakā - a class of *Baḍu Sevaka* of the Liṅgarāja temple.

Gadā - mace, emblem of Viṣṇu.

Gaja-Lakṣmī - auspicious motif of Lakṣmī being bathed by elephants.

Gaja-vidāḷa - (Sanskrit *gaja-vyāḷa),* a rampant lion springing on a crouching elephant.

Gaṇas - a group of demi-gods attending on Śiva.

Gandharvas - a class of celestial musicians.

Gaṇḍi - trunk, curvilinear spire or pyramidal roof between the *bāḍa* and *mastaka* of a temple.

Garbhagṛha - innermost chamber of the temple containing the image or symbol.

Garbhamuda - lowermost ceiling of the *sanctum.*

Gaurī - a name of the consort of Śiva.

Gavākṣa - window of thc *jagamohana.*

Ghaṇṭā - 'bell', bell-shaped member set in the finial of a *pīḍha* temple, also called *Śrī.*

Grahas - planets; they are depicted in a line on the architrave above the lintel of the main doorway.

Guṇas - attributes; qualities.

Hari-Hara - composite form of Viṣṇu and Śiva in which Viṣṇu is on the left and Śiva on the right.

Jagamohana - audience chamber or hall in front of the *sanctum.*

Jaṅghā - 'thigh'; the broad part of a temple, vertical wall of the *bāḍa* above the *pābhāga;* the lower one between the *pābhāga* and *bandhanā* is called lower *jaṅghā,* the upper one between the *bandhanā* and *varaṇḍa* is called upper *jaṅghā.*

Japamāḷā - rosary.

Jaṭāmukuṭa - matted hair forming a conical crown.

Jyotirliṅga - 'the *liṅga* of light'; a manifestation of Śiva as a brilliant column of light.

Kalaśa - water jar; the structure in the shape of a pitcher placed as crowning element of the temple.

Kaṇi - 'pointed edge', fillet having a sharp edge.

Kaṇikā-pāgā - corner segment, outermost pilaster of a temple.

Kānti or Kāṇṭhi - 'throat'; vertical recess between *pīḍhas.*

Kanyā - damsel; decorative female figures on the body of a temple.

Kārttikeya - the son of Śiva, also known as Skanda.

Khai - puffed rice with sugar coating used as offering to the Liṅgarāja.

Khākharā-deula - a temple with a semi-cylindrical crowning member.

Khākharā-muṇḍi - miniature representation of *khākharā* temple used as an ornamental motif.

Khaṇḍi - recess between *pāgās.*

Khapurī - 'skull'; structure resembling a flattened bell-shaped member above the *āmlā,* forming a part of the finial of the temple.

Khei - remuneration of the temple priests in kind.

Khura - 'hoof'; lowermost moulding with an S-shaped profile used in the *piṣṭa* or *pābhāga* of a temple.

Kirīṭa-Mukuṭa - conical type of crown studded with jewels worn by Viṣṇu and Sūrya.

Kīrtimukha - 'face of glory'; decorative motif with a face of a lion from the mouth of which festoon of pearls hang down.

Kṛṣṇa Pakṣa - the waning fortnight of the lunar month.

Kṣetra - sacred place or land.

Kṣetrapāḷa - guardian of the field or land.

Korā - sugar candy.

Kubera - chief of yakṣas, a dikpāla.

Kukuṭa - a cock; one of the attributes of Kārttikeya.

Kuṁbha - water pot; pitcher-shaped moulding of the *pābhāga,* a class of base moulding.

Kuṇḍa - a sacred water reservoir for bathing.

Kuṭhāra - axe, one of the attributes of Gaṇeśa.

Liṅga - the phallic emblem or sign of Śiva.

Liṅga pūjā - worship of the phallic emblem of Śiva.

Maheśvara - 'the great lord'; a name of Śiva.

Mahādīpa - great lamp taken to the temple spire on the fourteenth day of each fortnight.

Mahāsuāra - 'great cook', surname of the temple cooks.

Makara-toraṇa - *toraṇa* or arch with *makara* motif at the base.

Maṇḍapa - porch; hall of a temple.

Mandira - temple.

Mastaka - 'head'; crowning elements above the *gaṇḍi* of a temple.

Mātṛkās - divine mothers.

Mekāpa - store-keeper of the temple.

Mithuna - amorous couple.

Modaka pātra - bowl of sweets, usually held by Gaṇeśa.

Mokṣa - liberation; freedom from the cycle of birth and death.

Muhānti - vertical portion at the base of *khura, khākharā* or *khapurī.*

Mukhaśāḷā - 'front hall'; *pīḍha* temple in front of the sancturary; also known as *jagamohana.*

Mukti - liberation; *mokṣa.*

Nāga - 'serpent'; figure with a human bust and serpent tail carved on the walls.

Nāga-staṁbha - pillar encircled by Nāga figures.

Nandī - Śiva's bull.

Nāṭa-mandira - dancing hall of a temple.

Naṭarāja - Śiva as the lord of cosmic dance.

Navagrahas - nine planets; the *navagrahas* are usually depicted on the lintel or architrave of the front doorway of a temple. They are Ravi, Soma, Maṅgala, Buddha, Bṛhaspati, Sukra, Sani, Rahu and Ketu.

Nava-ratha - a temple having the nine projecting *pāgās* on its facade.

Nāyikā - female figures carved in various poses on the walls of a temple.

Niyoga - caste council of the leading temple functionaries.

Niśā-deula - small shrine erected in front of the *rāhā* niche of the *deula.*

Pābhāga - 'foot part'; division of the wall corresponding to the foot of the *bāḍa;* a set of mouldings forming the lowest part of the *bāḍa* of a temple.

pāda - foot; the lowest division of the *bāḍa* of a temple.

Padma - lotus.

Pāgā - segment, also known as *ratha.*

Pāḷi - service assignment among the temple functionaries for worship.

Palinki Āpaṭa - carriers of palanquin.

Pañcāṅga - *bāḍa* with five divisions, also called *pañcakarma.*

Pañca-ratha - temple having five *rathas* on its facade.

Parichā - superintendent of the temple.

Pārśva-devatās - accessory deities placed in the outer niches of the central projections of the sanctuary. In a Śiva temple Gaṇeśa on the south, Kārttikeya on the west and Pārvatī on the north are usually the *pārśva-devatās.*

Pāśa - noose.

Paṭa - moulding with a square edge.

Pīḍha - flat wooden seat; projecting elements with which the roof of the *pīḍha-deula* is composed.

Pīḍha-deula - temple of which the pyramidal roof is made of *pīḍhas;* a structural motif; miniature representation of a *pīḍha* temple used as an ornamental motif.

Piṣṭa or pīṭha - pedestal; stylobate; platform.

Poṭala - chapter, group of *pīḍhas.*

Pradakṣiṇa - circumambulation; walking in clockwise direction keeping the deity on the right.

Pradakṣiṇa-patha - processional passage or ambulatory.

Pūjā - ritual worship of the deity.

Pūrṇimā - the full moon day of the Hindu lunar calendar.

Rāhā - projected central segment of a temple; the *pārśvadevatās* are housed in its niche.

Rathayātrā - the chariot festival of a divinity.

Rekhā-deula - order of temple characterised by a curvilinear tower; this type of structure is usually limited to the main temple.

Śākhā - literally a branch; jamb of a door frame.

Śālabhanjikā - woman and tree motif.

Sandhi-sthaḷa - wall portion connecting the *deula* with the *jagamohana.*

Śaṅkha - conch-shell.

Sapta-ratha - temple with seven segments or *pāgās* on its facade.

Sevaka - temple functionary; service renderer.

Śikhaṇḍaka - mode of coiffure with three locks.

Śikhara - spire; tower of a temple.

Śilpa Śāstra - ancient Indian treatises on building construction and allied arts.

Siṁha - lion.

Siṁhāsana - lion throne; pedestal of the presiding deity.

Śivarātrī - 'the night of Śiva'; the greatest Śaiva festival held in the fourteenth day of the dark fortnight of *Phalguna.*

Śrī - bell-shaped member above *bekī* in *pīḍha* temple.

Staṁbha - column, pillar.

Sṭhapati - master craftsman.

Śukla pakṣa - the waxing fortnight of the lunar month.

Surasundarī - heavenly damsel; celestial beauty; a motif in temple art.

Svayaṁbhu - self-manifested; uncreated; the images or the *liṅgas* which appeared of their own accord.

Tanku - projection in the form of a triangle, semi-circle or quadrant of a circle at the edge of mouldings or *pīḍhas.*

Tīrtha - holy place of pilgrimage.

Toraṇa - arch, gateway in the form of arch rising from two pillars.

Tripurāntaka - form of Śiva as destroyer of the three fortresses of demons.

Tri-ratha - temple with three *pāgās* on each side.

Triśākhā - trident-shaped light carried during the procession of the deity.

Triśūla - trident; attribute of Śiva.

Uḍā-siṁha - flying lion.

Vāhana - 'vehicle'; especially the divine animal or bird on which a god habitually rides according to Hindu mythology.

Vajra-mastaka - ornamental motif on the *gaṇḍi* of the temple consisting of a *caitya*-window motif with *kīrtimukha* at the apex.

Vajra-muṇḍi - ornamental motif with a highly intricate *caitya* window design on the facade of the roof.

Varaṇḍa - crowning set of mouldings of the *bāḍa* separating the cube of *sanctum* from the *śikhara.*

Bīlva - the wood apple tree whose leaf is used in the worship of Śiva.

Vidyādhara - mythical being who flies in the sky, usually carrying a garland.

Vimāna - towered sanctuary, main temple in which the deity is enshrined.

Virāḷa or Viḍāla - (Sanskrit *vyāla)* mythical monster used as a sculptural and architectural motif; the representation of *viḍāla* is of various types, e.g. *gaja-viḍāla, nara-viḍāla,* etc.

Yajña - a sacrificial rite.

Yantra - geometric diagram; abstract symbol of divinity used as a tool for meditation.

Yātrā - procession in religious festivals; pilgrimage.

BIBLIOGRAPHY

INSCRIPTIONS

Annual Report on Indian Epigraphy for 1977-78, Archaeological Survey of India, New Delhi, 1986.

Chakravarti, M.M., "Uriya Inscriptions of the Fifteenth and Sixteenth Centuries", *JASB,* Vol. LXII, 1893.

Das, S.N., "The Votive Inscriptions in the Liṅgarāja Temple of Bhubaneswar" [Inscription of Vīra Narasimha Deva of the Aṅka year 4], *OHRJ,* Vol. I, No. 4, 1953, pp. 301-305.

——, "The Votive Inscriptions in the Liṅgarāja Temple" [Stone Inscription Govinda Senapati], *OHRJ,* Vol. II, Nos. 3-4 Sept. 1953 and Jan. 1954, pp. 53-54.

Kielhorn, F., "Two Bhubaneswar Inscriptions", *Epigraphic Indica,* Vol. VI, 1900-1901, pp. 198-203.

Nath, B.V., "The Pārvatī Temple Inscription at Bhubaneswar", *OHRJ*, Vol. III, No. 3, 1954, pp. 146-149.

Panigrahi, K.C., "Three Temple Inscriptions from Bhubaneswar", *OHRJ,* Vol. I, No. 2, 1952, pp. 97-106.

Rajguru, S.N., "Puri Inscription of Purushottama Deva in the Bhubaneswar Temple (Oriya)", *JASB,* Vol. LXII, p. 103.

——, *Inscriptions of Orissa,* 5 vols., Orissa State Museum, Bhubaneswar, 1958-1976.

——, "Two Liṅgarāja Temple Inscriptions of the Time of Śrī Raghava Deva", *OHRJ,* Vol. V, Nos. 3-4, 1956-1957, pp. 179-182.

——, "The Liṅgarāja Temple Inscription of the Time of Rajaraja Deva", *OHRJ,* Vol. IX, Nos. 1-2, 1960, pp. 7-9.

——, *Inscriptions of Orissa,* Vol. IV, Bhubaneswar, 1966 [Somavaṁśī Inscriptions].

Ray, P.K., "The Oriya Inscription of the Liṅgarāja Temple", *OHRJ,* Vol. XV, Nos. 1-2, 1967, pp. 113-114.

Shastri, A.M., *Inscriptions of the Sarbhapuriyas, Panduvamsi and the Somavaṁśī,* 2 Parts, Delhi, 1995.

Subramanyam, R., *Inscriptions of the Suryavamsi Gajapatis of Orissa,* Delhi, 1986.

Tripathy, S., *Inscriptions of Orissa,* Vol. VI, Orissa State Museum, Bhubaneswar, 1974.

TEXTS AND TRANSLATIONS

Agni Purāṇa, ed. by Baladeva Upadhyaya, Kashi Sanskrit Series, Chaukhamba Publications, Varanasi, 1966; Eng. tr. in 4 Parts by N. Gangadharan, Motilal Banarasidass Publishers, Delhi, 1987.

Aparājitā Pṛccha by Bhvanadeva, ed. with Introduction by P.A. Mankad, GOS No. CXV, Baroda, 1950.

Architecture in the Ajitāgama and the Rauravāgama, ed. by Bruno Dagens, New Delhi, 1984.

Brahma Purāṇa, ed. by J.L. Shastri and Eng. tr. by a Board of Scholars, 5 Parts, Ancient Indian Tradition and Mythology Series, Vols. 22-26. Delhi, 1985-1986. Text with Hindi tr. by T. Jha, Hindi Sahitya Sammelan Prayag, Allahabad, 1993.

Brahmāṇḍa Purāṇa, ed. by J.L. Shastri and Eng. tr. by a Board of Scholars, Ancient Indian Tradition and Mythology Series, Motilal Banarasidass Publishers, Delhi, 1971.

Bhakti Bhāgavata of Jivadevacarya, vide *JAS,* Vol. IV, No. 1, 1962, pp. 23-27.

Bhuvana-Pradīpa (See *Canons of Orissan Architecture),* by N.K. Bose, Calcutta, 1932.

Devī Bhāgavata, Pandit Pustakalaya, Kasi, 1969.

Ekāmra Candrīkā, Oriya Translation, Kedarnath Gaveshana Pratisthan, Bhubaneswar, 1995.

Ekāmra Purāṇa (Text in Oriya character), ed. by Ratnakar Gagrabatu, Cuttack, N.D.

Ekāmra Purāṇaṁ, ed. by U.N. Dhal, Nag Publishers, Delhi, 1986.

Hayaśīrṣa Pañcarātra, ed. by B.M. Sankhyatirtha, Vol. I, Ādi Kāṇḍa, I.14, Varendra Research Society, Rajasahi, 1952.

Īśānasivagurudeva-Paddhati, ed. by T. Ganapati Sastri, Trivandrum, 1920; with Intro. by N.P. Unni, 4 vols., Bharatiya Vidya Prakashan, Varanasi, 1988.

Kālasāra of Gadādhara, ed. by Sadasiva Mishra, Vol. I, *Bibliotheca Indica,* Calcutta, 1904.

Kapiḷa Purānaṁ (A Critical Edition), ed. in Sanskrit by S. Tripathi, the Chaukhamba Surbharati Granthamala, No. 57, Varanasi, 1981.

Kapiḷa Saṁhitā (Text in Oriya character), Cuttack, 1928.

Kaṭaka Rājavaṁśāvalī: A Traditional History of Orissa, Text and tr. by G.C. Tripathi and H. Kulke, Allahabad, 1987.

Liṅga Purāṇa, ed. by J.L. Shastri, Eng. tr. by a Board of Scholars, 2 Parts, Ancient Indian Tradition and Mythology Series, Vols. 5-6, Motilal Banarasidass Publishers, Delhi, 1990.

Mādalā Pāñji, ed. by A. Mohanty in Oriya, Utkal University, Bhubaneswar, 1940.

Matsya Purāṇa, Anandasrama Edition, Poona, 1907; Eng. tr. Oriental Publishers, Delhi, 1972.

Nityācāra-Pradīpa of Narasimha Vajapeyi, ed. by V.V. Bhattacharya *et al.*, Vol. I and II, *Bibliotheca Indica*, Calcutta, 1907-1928.

Pañcarātra Prāsāda-Prasādhanaṁ: A Pañcarātra Text on Temple Building, ed. and annotated by H. Daniel Smith, Madras, 1963.

Pratitha Lakshanasāra Samuchhaya, 2 vols., National Archives of Nepal, Kathmandu, 1966.

Samarāṅgaṇa Sūtradhāra of King Bhoja, ed. by V.S. Agrawala, GOS No. 25, Baroda, 1966.

Sāralā Mahābhārata (Vana Parva), ed. by A.B. Mohanty in Oriya, Part-II, Dept. of Culture, Govt. of Orissa, 1966.

Śilpa Prakāśa, Medieval Orissan Sanskrit Text on Temple Architecture, Ramachandra Kaulacara, tr. and annotated by Alice Boner and S. Ratha Sarma, Leiden, 1966.

Śilparatna of Śrī Kumāra, ed. by K. Sambasiva Sastri, Trivandrum, 1929.

Śilpa Ratnākara, ed. by B. Mohanty in English, Orissa Lalitakala Akademi, Bhubaneswar, 1995.

Śilparatnakoṣa: A Glossary of Orissan Temple Architecture, ed. by B. Baumer and R.P. Das, Text with Eng. tr. with Illus., Motilal Banarasidass Publishers, Delhi, 1994.

Śivalilāmṛtamahākāvyaṁ, ed. and tr. into English by Bhagaban Paṇḍā, Bhubaneswar, 1978.

Śiva Purāṇa (Uttara khaṇḍa), Eng. tr. and Introduction by U.N. Dhal, Delhi, 2000.

Śiva Purāṇa, ed. by J.L. Shastri and Eng. tr. by a Board of Scholars, 4 Parts, Ancient Indian Tradition and Mythology Series, Vols. 1-4, Motilal Banarasidass Publishers, Delhi, Reprint-1992-96.

Svarṇādri Mahodaya, ed. by R. Gargabatu, 1st edition, Calcutta, Śaka 1834 (1912).

Tīrthacintāmaṇi by Vachaspati Misra, ed. by Kamalakrishna Smrititirtha, *Bibliotheca Indica,* No. 1256, Asiatic Society of Bengal, Calcutta, 1912.

Tīrtha Sāra, ed. by Gopinath Kaviraj, Allahabad, 1936.

Vāstusūtra Upaniṣad: The Essence of Form in Sacred Art, ed. and tr. by Alice Boner, S.R. Sarma and B. Baumer, Delhi, 1982.

Vīramitrodaya Tīrtha Prakāśa, ed. by Pt. Mitra Mishra, Varanasi, 1917.

BOOKS AND ARTICLES

Acharya, Chintamani, *Bhubaneswar* (Oriya), Cuttack, 1949.

Acharya, P., *Studies in Orissan History, Archaeology and Archives,* Baripada, 1969.

——, "Studies in the Temple Architecture in Orissa", *OHRJ,* Vol. XII, No. 1, 1964, pp. 9-21.

——, "Varities of Stones used in Building Temples and Making Images in Orissa" (Quarries and Method of Transport), *OHRJ,* Vol. XIII, No. 2, 1965, pp. 9-20.

——, "Date of the Liṅgarāja Temple at Bhubaneswar and the Jagannath Temple at Puri", *Studies in Orissan History, Archaeology and Archives,* Baripada, 1969, pp. 292-296.

Agrawala, V.S., *Śiva Mahadeva: The Great God,* Varanasi, 1996.

Arnott, M.H., *Report with Photographs of the Repairs Executed to Some of the Principal Temples of Bhubaneswar between 1989 and 1903*, London, Waterlow and Sans Ltd., 1903.

Arya, B.V., "Chronology of the Temples of the Soma Dynasty", *OHRJ,* Vol. XI, No. 1, Bhubaneswar, 1962, pp. 41-49.

Asher, F.M., *The Art of Eastern India,* Minnea Polis, 1980.

——, "Pancayatana Śiva Liṅgas: Sources and Meaning", *Kaladarsana,* American Studies in the Art of India, ed. by J.G. Williams, New Delhi, 1981.

Banerjea, J.N., *The Development of Hindu Iconography,* Calcutta, 1956 (Second Edition).

——, *Puranic and Tantric Religion (Early Phase),* Calcutta, 1966.

——, *Religion in Art and Archaeology,* Lucknow, 1968.

Banerjee, R.D., *History of Orissa,* 2 vols., Calcutta, 1930-31.

Bäumer, Bettina, "Unmanifest and Manifest Forms according to the Śaivagamas", *STIA,* 1989.

—— (ed.), *Kalatattvakosa,* Vol. II, Indira Gandhi National Centre for the Arts, New Delhi, 1990.

——, "The Rājrānī Temple Re-identified", *India International Centre Quarterly,* Vol. XXI, No. 1, New Delhi, 1994.

Behera, K.S., "The Evolution of Sakti Cult at Jajpur, Bhubaneswar and Puri", in *The Sakti Cult and Tara,* ed. by D.C. Sircar, Calcutta, 1967, pp. 74-86.

——, "Three Images of Mahisamardini from Orissa", *Proc. Ind. History Congress,* Vol. XXVII, 1967, pp. 34-37.

——, "Odisara Mandira Sthapatyara Krama Vikasa" (Oriya), *Nabarabi,* Vol. I, No. 4, 1970, pp. 61-72. [The gradual development of the temple architecture of Orissa.]

——, "Laksmi in Orissan Literature and Art", in *Foreigners in Ancient India and Laksmi and Sarasvati in Art and Literature,* ed. by D.C. Sircar, Calcutta, 1970, pp. 91-105.

——, "Brahmanical Temples of Orissa", *Orissa Review* (Monument Special), P. & I.R. Department, Govt. of Orissa, Bhubaneswar, 1976.

——, "An Outline of the Art and Architecture of Orissa", in *Utkal Historical Research Journal,* ed. by K.M. Patra, Vol. III, Utkal University, Bhubaneswar, 1992, pp. 130-134.

——, *Temples of Orissa,* Orissa Sahitya Akademi, Bhubaneswar, 1993.

——, *Konarka: The Heritage of Mankind,* New Delhi, 1996.

Behera, K.S. and T.E. Donaldson, *Sculpture Masterpieces of Orissa: Style and Iconography,* New Delhi, 1998.

Behera, K.S. *et al.* (eds.), *Charles Grome's Report on the Jagannatha Temple, 1805,* Bhubaneswar, 2002.

Behuria, N.C., *Orissa State Gazetteer, Orissa State,* 2 vols., Govt. of Orissa, Cuttack, 1990-91.

Bhandarkar, R.G., *Vaisnavism, Saivism and Minor Religious System,* Varanasi, 1928.

Bhattacharya, T., "Some Notes on Mithuna in Indian Art", *Rupam*, 1973.

Boner, Alice, "Extracts from the Silpasarini", in *Studies in Indian Temple Architecture*, ed. by Pramod Chandra, Varanasi, 1975, pp. 57-79.

Boner, Alice, S.R. Sarma and R.P. Das, *New Light on the Sun Temple of Konarka*, Varanasi, 1972.

Bose, N.K., "Some Ancient Remains from Bhubaneswar", *JBORS*, Vol. XV, No. 1-2, 1929, pp. 259-262.

——, *Canons of Orissan Architecture*, Calcutta, 1932.

Bose, N.K. *et al.*, "Organization of Services in the Temple of Liṅgarāja in Bhubaneswara", *Journal of the Asiatic Society Letters*, Vol. XXIV, No. 2, 1958, pp. 85-129.

Brown, Percy, *Indian Architecture (Buddhist and Hindu Period)*, Mumbai, 1997 (Reprinted).

Brown, W.B., *A Guide to Principal Places of Interest in Orissa*, 1900.

Chakravarti, M.M., "Notes on the Geography of Orissa in the Sixteenth Century", *JPASB*, Vol. XII, 1916, pp. 29-56.

Chanda, R.P., "The Liṅgarāja or Great Temple of Bhubaneswar", *Annual Report of Archaeological Survey of India: 1923-24*, New Delhi, 1926, pp. 119-122.

——, "Exploration in Orissa", *MASI*, No. 44, 1930.

Chandra, Pramod, "The Kaula-Kapalika Cults at Khajuraho", *Lalit Kala*, No. 1-2, 1955-56.

—— (ed.), *Studies in Indian Temple Architecture*, AIIS, Varanasi, 1975.

Coburn, T.B., *Devi Mahatmya*, New Delhi, 1988.

Coomaraswamy, A.K., *History of Indian and Indonesian Art*, New York, 1965.

Craven, Roy C., *Indian Art*, London, Reprinted 1987.

Das, R.K., *Bhubaneswar and its Environs*, Bhadrak, 1982.

Dash, M.P., "Inter Relation between Vaisnavism and Saktism in Orissa", *OHRJ*, Vol. XI, No. 4, 1963, pp. 273-281.

De. S.C., "Ardhanarisvar Image of Śiva", *OHRJ*, Vol. XI, No. 2, 1962, pp. 103-105.

Deheja, V., *Early Stone Temples of Orissa*, Delhi, 1979.

Desai, Devangana, *Erotic Sculpture of India: A Socio-Cultural Study*, New Delhi, 1985.

——, *The Religious Imagery of Khajuraho*, Mumbai, 1996.

Desai, Kalpana S., *Iconography of Viṣṇu (In North India)*, New Delhi, 1973.

Deva, Krishna, *Temples of Khajuraho*, 2 vols., New Delhi, 1990.

Dhaky, M.A., *The Vyala Figures on the Medieval Temples of India*, Varanasi, 1965.

—— (ed.), *Encyclopaedia of Indian Temple Architecture, North India, Beginnings of Medieval Idiom c.* AD *900-1000*, American Institute of Indian Studies, Delhi, 1998.

Dhal, U.N., "Rathayatra in Ekāmra Ksetra", *Cultural Indica*, ed. by B. Banerjee, New Delhi, 1944, pp. 38-42.

——, *Goddess Laksmi: Origin and Development*, Delhi, 1995.

——, "A Note on the Sacred Rituals at Ekāmra Ksetra (Bhubaneswar)", presented to the *National Seminar on Pilgrimage, Tourism and Conservation of Cultural Heritage Experiences and Revelations*, January, 21-23, 1995, Allahabad (Unpublished).

Dixon, Henry, *Orissa: Its Temples and Rock-cut Caves*, Cuttack, 1860.

Donaldson, T.E., "Propitious-Apotropaic Eroticism in the Art of Orissa", *Artibus Asiae*, Vol. XXXVII, 1975, pp. 75-100.

——, "Door frames on the Earliest Orissan Temples", *Artibus Asiae*, Vol. XXXVIII, 1976, pp. 189-219.

——, "Development of the Vajra-mastaka on Orissan Temples", *East and West*, Vol. XXVI, Nos. 3-4, 1976, pp. 419-433.

——, "Decorative Programme of the Superstructure on the Orissa Rekhā-deul", in *Slide Lights on History and Culture of Orissa*, ed. by M.N. Das, Cuttack, 1977, pp. 565-613.

——, "Decorative Scroll Motifs on Orissan Temples", *East and West*, Vol. XXVIII, Nos. 1-4, 1978, pp. 225-260.

——, "Development of Nāṭa-mandira in Orissan Temple Architecture", in *Kaladarsana: American Studies in the Art of India*, ed. by J.G. Williams, American Institute of Indian Studies, Varanasi, 1981, pp. 35-46.

——, "Naga Images and the Cult of Mansa in Orissan Art", in *Rupa Pratirupa*, ed. by Bettina Baumer, New Delhi, 1982, pp. 99-108.

——, "Ekapada Śiva Images in Orissan Art", *Arts Orientalis*, Vol. XIII, 1982, pp. 153-168.

——, *Hindu Temples Art of Orissa*, 3 vols., Leiden, 1985-87.

——, "Coiffure in Orissan Sculpture: Iconographic and Stylistic Evolution", *Arts of Asia*, Vol. XV, No. 4, Hong Kong, 1985, pp. 82-96; Vol. XV, No. 5, 1985, pp. 68-79.

——, "Bhiksatanamurti Images from Orissa", *Artibus Asiae*, No.XXXXVII, No. 1, 1986, pp. 51-76.

——, "Erotic Rituals on Orissan Temples", *East and West*, Vol. XXXVI, Nos. 1-3, 1986, pp. 137-182.

——, *Kamadeva's Pleasure Garden: Orissa*, Delhi, 1987.

——, "Rsis, Kings and the Pursuit of Love: The Secularization of the Iconographic Programme of the Orissan Temple", *Bulletin*, Annual Journal of P.G. Department of History, Utkal University, ed. by Prof. K.S. Behera, Bhubaneswar, 1988, pp. 86-111.

——, "Rare Orissan Sanctum Images Associated with the Agni-Soma Symbolism of the Enshrined Śiva-Linga", *Berliner Indologische Studien*, Band, 4-5, 1989, pp. 327-337.

——, "The Sava-Vahana as Purusa in Orissan Images from Camunda to Kali", *Artibus Asiae*, Vol. XXXXXI, Nos. 1-2, 1991, pp. 107-141.

——, "The Sava-Vahana of Bhairava in Orissan Images – A Sakta Tantra Concept", in *Kṛṣṇa Pratibha: Studies in Indology* (Prof. K.C. Panigrahi Commemoration Volume), eds. H.C. Das, S. Tripathy and B.K. Rath, Delhi, 1994, pp. 105-131.

——, "Bhubaneswar (Ekāmra-Kshetra): Temple Town and Cultural Centre", *Marg*, Vol. XXXXXII, No. 3, 2001, pp. 12-27.

——, *The Iconography of Vaisnava Images in Orissa,* New Delhi, 2001.

Eschmann, A., H. Kulke and G.C. Tripathi (eds.), *The Cult of Jagannath and the Regional Traditions of Orissa,* New Delhi, 1978.

Fabri, Charles, *History of the Art of Orissa,* New Delhi, 1974.

Fergusson, J., *Picturesque Illustrations of Ancient Architecture in Hindostan,* London, 1847.

——, *History of Indian and Eastern Architecture,* 2 vols., New Delhi, 1994 (Reprint).

Ganguly, M.M., *Orissa and her Remains (Ancient and Medieval),* Calcutta, 1912.

Ganguly, O.C., "Lion on Elephant in Orissan Art", *OHRJ,* Vol. IV, Nos. 1-2, 1955, pp. 1-6.

——, *Orissan Sculpture and Architecture,* Calcutta, 1956.

Gonda, J., *Visnuism and Sivaism: A Comparison,* New Delhi, 1976.

Goswami, A., *Designs from Orissan Temples,* Calcutta, 1950.

Hardy, Adam, *Indian Temple Architecture, Form and Transformation,* New Delhi, 1995.

Harley, J.C., *The Art and Architecture of the Indian Subcontinent,* London, 1986.

Hazra, R.C., *Studies in the Puranic Records on Hindu Rites and Customs,* Dacca, 1940.

——, "The Ekāmra Purāṇa: A Work of Orissa", *Poona Orientalist,* Vol. XVI, Nos. 1-4, 1951, pp. 70-76.

——, *Studies in Upa Puranas,* 2 vols., Calcutta, 1958 & 1963.

Hunter, W.W., *Orissa,* 2 vols., London, 1872.

Huntington, S.L., *The Art of Ancient India,* New York, 1985.

Jaiswal, S., *The Origin and Development of Vaisnavism,* New Delhi, 1981.

Jayaswal, K.P., "Copper Plates in Bhubaneswar Temples", *JBORS,* Vol. V, 1919, pp. 298-299.

Jha, D.N. (ed.), *Society and Ideology in India, Essays in Honour of Prof R.S. Sharma,* New Delhi, 1996.

Kalia, Ravi, *Bhubaneswar from a Temple Town to a Capital City,* New Delhi, 1994.

Kane, P.V., *History of Dharmasastra,* 5 vols., Poona, 1932-1962.

Keith, A.B., *Catalogue of the Sanskrit and Prakrit MSS in the Library of the India Office,* Vol. II, Parts I & II, Oxford, 1935.

Kramrisch, Stella, *The Hindu Temple,* 2 vols., Calcutta, 1946.

——, "The Walls of Orissan Temples", *JISOA,* Vol. XV, 1947, pp. 178-196.

——, "Kaliṅga Temples", *JISOA,* Vol. II, No. 1, pp. 43-60.

——, "The Temple as Purusa", in *Studies in Indian Temple Architecture,* ed. by Pramod Chandra, Varanasi, 1975, pp. 40-46.

——, *The Presence of Śiva,* Princeton, 1981.

——, "The Great Cave Temple of Śiva in Elephanta: Levels of Meaning and their Form", in *Discourses on Śiva,* ed. by Michael W. Meister, 1984.

Kulke, H., "The Chronicles and the Temple Records of the Madlapanji of Puri – A Reassessment of the Evidence", *The Indian Archives,* Vol. XXXVI, No. 1, 1987, pp. 1-23.

Kulke, H. and G.C. Tripathi (eds.), *Religion and Society in Eastern India,* New Delhi, 1994.

Kuraishi, M.H., *List of Ancient Monuments Protected under Act VII of 1904 in the Province of Bihar and Orissa,* Calcutta, 1931.

Lal, Kanwar, *Temples and Sculptures of Bhubaneswar,* Delhi, 1976.

Lorenzen, D.N., *The Kapalikas and Kalamukhas: Two Lost Saivite Sects,* New Delhi, 1972.

Lourie, W.F.B., *Orissa: The Garden of Superstitution and Idolatry; Including an Account of British Connexions with the Temple of Jagannath,* London, 1850.

Mahāpātra, K.N., *Descriptive Catalogue of Sanskrit Manuscripts of Orissa,* 4 vols., Bhubaneswar, 1958-1963.

——, "Liṅgarāja Mandira Nirmana Kala" (Oriya), *Gopabandhu Death Anniversary Issue of the Samaj,* 1970, pp. 19-20.

——, "Temples of Bhubaneswar", in *Side Lights on History and Culture of Orissa,* ed. by M.N. Das, Cuttack, 1977, pp. 542-564.

——, *Bhubaneswar Abhilekha* (Oriya), Bhubaneswar, 1998 [Inscriptions of Bhubaneswar].

Mahapatra, M.M., *Traditional Structure and Change in an Orissan Temple,* Calcutta, 1981.

Mahapatra, R.P., *Archaeology in Orissa (Sites and Monuments),* 2 vols., Delhi, 1986.

Mahasupakar, N., *Bhubaneswar Aitihya* (Oriya), Bhubaneswar, 1998 [Heritage of Bhubaneswar].

Mahatab, H.K., *The History of Orissa,* 2 vols., Cuttack, 1959-1960.

Majumdar, R.C. (ed.), *The Struggle for Empire,* Vol. V, Bharatiya Vidya Bhavan, Bombay, 1964, Second Edition.

Meister, M.W. (ed.), *Discourses on Śiva,* Bombay, 1984.

Meister, M.W. and M.A. Dhaky (eds.), *Encyclopedia of Indian Temple Architecture, North India, Period of Early Maturity (c. AD 700-900),* Vol. II, Part-II: Text and Plates, American Institute of Indian Studies, Delhi, 1991.

—— (ed.), *Encyclopedia of Indian Temple Architecture, North India, Foundations of North Indian Style (c. 250 BC-AD 1100),* Vol. I, Part-I: Text and Plates, American Institute of Indian Studies, Delhi, 1988.

Michell, George, *The Hindu Temple: An Introduction to its Meanings and Forms,* London, 1977.

Mishra, K.C., *Cult of Jagannath,* Calcutta, 1971.

Mishra, K.C. and R.K. Mishra (eds.), *Studies in Saivism,* Institute of Orissan Culture, Bhubaneswar, 1993.

Mitra, Debala, *Bhubaneswar,* ASI, New Delhi, 1961.

——, *Udayagiri and Khandagiri,* ASI, Kanpur, 1960.

——, *Konarka,* ASI, New Delhi, 1992.

Mitra, R.L., *The Antiquities of Orissa,* 2 vols., Calcutta, 1961 (Reprint).

Mohanty, B. (ed.), *Ekāmra Kshetra (Oriya)* Cuttack, 1993.

Morley, G., *Indian Sculpture,* Varanasi, 1985.

O' Malley, L.S.S., *Puri: A Gazetteer,* Calcutta, 1908.

Pal, Pratapaditya (ed.), *Orissa Revisited,* Marg Publications, Mumbai, 2001.

——, *Hindu Religion and Iconography; According to the Tantrasara,* Los Angeles, 1981.

Paṇḍā, L.K., "Kṛttivāsa-Vimardini O' Devi Padahara" (Oriya), *Jhaṅkāra,* Vol. XVII, No. 10, 1973, pp. 855-864.

——, *Saivism in Orissa,* New Delhi, 1985.

Panigrahi, K.C., *Archaeological Remains at Bhubaneswar,* Cuttack, 1981.

——, *Itihasa* O' *Kimvadanti* (Oriya), Utkal University, Bhubaneswar, 1962 [History and Legends].

——, *History of Orissa (Hindu Period),* Cuttack, 1981.

Parida, A.N., *Early Temples of Orissa,* Delhi, 1999.

Pathak, V.S., "Ekāmra Bhubaneswar in Inscriptions", *OHRJ,* Vol. VII, No. 1, 1958, pp. 47-50.

Patnaik, S., *Brahmanical Religion in Ancient Orissa,* New Delhi, 1987.

Pichard, P., *Tanjavur Brhadisvara: An Architectural Study,* New Delhi, 1995.

Rajaguru, S.N., *Invocatory Verses from Inscriptions,* 2 vols., Bhubaneswar, 1973.

——, *Odisara Itihasa* (Oriya), Vol. I, Cuttack, 1985 [History of Orissa].

Rangarajan, Haripriya, *Varaha Images in Madhya Pradesh: An Iconographic Study,* Bombay, 1996.

Rao, C.V. Ramachandra, *Administration and Society in Medieval Andhra (AD 1038 1538) Under the Later Eastern Gangas and the Suryavamsa Gajapatis,* Nellore, 1976.

Rao, P.R.R., *Bhubaneswar: Kaliṅga Temple Architecture,* Hyderabad, 1980.

Rao, T.A. Gopinath, *Elements of Hindu Iconography,* 2 vols., Delhi, 1971.

Ratha, B.K., *Cultural History of Orissa,* Delhi, 1983.

—— (ed.), *The Forgotton Monuments of Orissa,* 3 vols., New Delhi, 1996.

Ratha Sarma, S., *Sthapatya re maithunakala* (Oriya), Puri, 1975 [Mithuna Art in Architecture].

Rawson, Philip, *The Art of Tantra,* London, 1978.

Ray, P.K., *Prachi Valley: Archaeological Survey Report 1974-75,* Bhubaneswar, 1975.

Sahu, N.K. *et al.* (eds.), *A History of Orissa,* 2 vols., Delhi, 1980.

Saraswati, S.K., "The Temples of Orissa", *OHRJ,* Vol. I, No. 4, 1953.

——, *A Survey of Indian Sculpture,* Calcutta, 1975.

Sarkar, U.N., "An Historical Account of the Temples in Orissa", *IHRC Proceeding,* Vol. XXXII, Part-2, Patna, 1956, pp. 87-90.

Sarma, B.K., *Somavaṁśī Rule in Orissa,* Calcutta, 1983.

Senapati, N. and D.C. Kuanar (eds.), *Orissa District Gazetteer,* Puri, Govt. of Orissa, Cuttack, 1977.

Seymour, Susan (ed.), *The Transformation of a Sacred Town: Bhubaneswar, India,* Boulder, U.S.A., 1980.

Sharma, R.S., "Material Milieu of Tantricism", in *Indian Society: Historical Probings in Memory of D.D. Kosambi,* New Delhi, 1977.

Singh, Upendra, *Kings, Brahmanas and Temples of Orissa,* New Delhi, 1994.

Sircar, D.C., *The Sakta Pithas,* Delhi, 1973.

Sivaramamurti, C., *The Art of India,* New York, 1977.

Smith, Walter, "Ceiling of the Muktesvara Temple in Bhubaneswar", *Artibus Asiae,* Vol. XLV, 1984.

——, *The Muktesvara Temple in Bhubaneswar,* Delhi, 1994.

Soundara Rajan, K.V., *Early Kaliṅga Art and Architecture,* Delhi, 1984.

Srivastav, B., *Iconography of Sakti: A Study Based on Sritattvanidhi,* Varanasi, 1978.

Stirling, A., "An Account Geographical, Statistical and Historical of Orissa Proper or Cuttack", *Asiatic Researches,* Vol. XV, 1825, pp. 326-333.

Tripathy, K.B., "The Palaeography of Early Oriya Inscriptions", *OHRJ,* Vol. IV, Nos. 12, 1955, pp. 11-27; Vol. V, Nos. 3-4, 1956, pp. 144-155.

——, *The Evolution of Oriya Language and Script,* Utkal University Publication, Bhubaneswar, 1962.

Tripathy, S., "Ekāmra-Bhubaneswara", *OHRJ,* Vol. XXXIII, Nos. 1-2, 1987, pp. 132-155.

——, *Odisara Puratattva* (Oriya), Kedarnath Gavesana Pratisthana, Bhubaneswar, 2001 [Archaeology of Orissa].

Trivedi, R.D., *Iconography of Pārvatī,* Delhi, 1981.

Vasini, A.K., *Iconography of Śiva,* Delhi, 1992.

Vatsyayan, Kapila, *Classical Indian Dance in Literature and the Arts,* New Delhi, 1977.

Vaz, J.L., "Architecture of Bhubaneswar", *Journal of the Indian Institute of Architects,* Vol. XX, No. 2, 1954.

Williams, Joanna G., *The Two-Headed Deer: Illustrations of the Ramayana in Orissa,* Berkeley, 1996.

——, *Kaladarsana: American Studies in the Art of India,* Varanasi, 1981.

Zimmer, H., *The Art of Indian Asia,* 2 vols., New York, 1955.

——, *Myths and Symbols in Indian Art and Civilization,* London, 1974 (Reprint).

Index